CARE IN EVERYDAY LIFE

An ethic of care in practice

Marian Barnes

First published in Great Britain in 2012 by

The Policy Press
University of Bristol
Fourth Floor
Beacon House
Queen's Road
Bristol BS8 1QU
UK
t: +44 (0)117 331 4054
f: +44 (0)117 331 4093
tpp-info@bristol.ac.uk
www.policypress.co.uk

North American office:
The Policy Press
c/o The University of Chicago Press
1427 East 60th Street
Chicago, IL 60637, USA
t: +1 773 702 7700
f: +1 773-702-9756
sales@press.uchicago.edu
www.press.uchicago.edu

British Library Cataloguing in Publication Data
A catalogue record for this book is available from the British Library.

Library of Congress Cataloging-in-Publication Data
A catalog record for this book has been requested.

ISBN 978 1 84742 822 6 paperback
ISBN 978 1 84742 823 3 hardcover

Cover design by Qube Design Associates, Bristol.
Front cover: image kindly supplied by www.alamy.com
Printed and bound in Great Britain by TJ International, Padstow
The Policy Press uses environmentally responsible print partners.

Contents

About the author

Marian Barnes has researched the lives and experiences of older people, disabled people, those who live with mental health problems, and those who care for them, for over 30 years. She developed a particular interest in different forms of collective action through which people both support each other and seek to shape policies and services. Her work on participative and deliberative democracy and social movements developed from this. In the way in which she researches these issues with colleagues, Marian tries to reflect the value of collaboration in the process of producing knowledge and she has made an important contribution to the development of participatory research. Her more recent work on an ethic of care has caused her to reflect on the personal and political dimensions of the issues she has researched throughout her career. It has also opened up new interests and commitments to ethical social policy and the practices through which this can be achieved which she is currently exploring with colleagues.

Acknowledgements

Thanks to the University of Brighton for the sabbatical time to write this.

My thanks to Judy and to Mark for letting me use their stories. To Lizzie Ward, Nicki Ward and Tula Brannelly for good conversations and supporting the conviction that this was worth doing. My thanks to Selma Sevenhuijsen whose work I discovered just at the right time and to Joan Tronto for articles and ideas for further directions. Thanks too to the older people who worked on the well-being project and took no convincing about the importance of an ethic of care. As always, my thanks to David Prior for love and caring in so many ways, and in particular for the reference list!

And to all those care givers and care receivers I have encountered and worked with who have shown me the importance of all this. My hope is that this might help others recognise that care is necessary not only to individual well-being, but also to social justice.

ONE

Introduction

Care is an enduring and contested issue in social policy. Empirical research and policy analysis have addressed issues concerning the political economy of care; shifting assumptions about where care responsibilities lie; the issues of 'who cares' and what are the personal, interpersonal and social impacts of care giving and receiving. Beyond the discipline of social policy, care has been the subject of sociological, psychosocial and philosophical debates as well as critiques and challenges from those who have experienced both lay and professional care as oppressive and a denial of citizenship. While political and practice debates continue, everyday discourse remains suffused with the language and images of care; literature and poetry frequently take different forms of care as their subject matter; popular TV programmes focus on the everyday joys and tragedies of family life and friendship in which issues of care giving and receiving feature prominently, and documentaries and newspaper articles reflect on the absence of care in supposedly caring institutions and agonise over what can be done about this. Care is fundamental to the human condition and necessary both to survival and flourishing. While in the UK official discourse has sought to marginalise care within social care practice, in people's everyday lives care is an essential part of how they relate to others.

This book aims to contribute to a large and growing body of literature which seeks to understand the importance of care in securing individual and collective well-being, and which considers the relationship between care and justice and what social policies and practices that are grounded in political as well as personal concepts of care might look like.

Joan Tronto and Berenice Fisher's definition of care suggests the breadth of the significance of care.

> On the most general level, we suggest that caring be viewed as a species activity that includes everything that we do to maintain, continue, and repair our 'world' so that we can live in it as well as possible. That world includes our bodies, our selves, and our environment, all of which we seek to interweave in a complex, life-sustaining web. (Quoted in Tronto, 1993, p 103)

Critics have argued that this definition cannot sustain the claims made for care, but it has nevertheless formed the basis of an expanding body of empirical research and scholarship. This, if not without its own critics, demands to be taken just as seriously as the longer established body of work on rights and social justice that has informed official policy making, and the claims of marginalised and disadvantaged groups for proper treatment to ensure respect, dignity and access to public goods. In this book I will both apply and interrogate Tronto and Fisher's definition of care by considering its relevance in diverse contexts. My aim is to develop a critical analysis of care ethics through considering both what this can offer, and what are the limits of a 'care' perspective to interpersonal relationships in different contexts; to social policies, as well as to processes through which policy decisions are made; the way work is organised in order to deliver services, and to the ways in which people interact with their environments. My approach here is deliberately broad in order to explore the contribution of a care perspective, or 'care thinking', to contexts beyond those in which it is typically addressed in a social policy context, as well as within the familiar contexts of health and social care. I have selected examples in order to illustrate how care might help us to think about different types of social relations and about how we might achieve justice and well-being in different contexts. Thus I necessarily deal briefly with a range of topics and do not claim either to be comprehensive in coverage, or to offer the depth that would be possible in selecting one area for study.

Care ethics originated from psychology and the work of Carol Gilligan (1982) who challenged gendered assumptions of moral development by proposing a 'different voice' in which moral deliberation might be conducted. It has been developed within moral and political philosophy and applied in social work, social policy, nursing, education and other applied disciplines and practices. There is now a substantial literature that explicitly engages with care not only as a form of practice, but as a set of moral principles that can guide conduct in contexts as varied as responses to violence against women in refugee camps in Darfur (Miller, 2010), how we might respond to the dilemmas of supporting people with dementia and their families (Brannelly, 2006), and as a basis from which we can evaluate public health policies (Sevenhuijsen, 1998) and schemes for assessing compensation in cases of institutional abuse (Hankivsky, 2004). In this book I deliberately consider diverse contexts for care in order to offer a reflection of the practical advantages of care ethics as a basis on which to build social and public policies that can enable nurturing, flourishing and well-being, and that support the practices of those who seek to 'do care' in their private lives and professional work.

Thus my approach in this book is rather different from that of Sevenhuijsen and others who have used an ethic of care as an evaluative basis for policy analysis. My starting point is to explore different examples of social and political contexts and relationships in order to consider the place of care within them. I then offer suggestions about the implications for policy, rather than offering a detailed critique of policy from an ethic of care perspective. This reflects much of my other work which builds from lived experience – whether of ageing, living with mental illness, caring for a close relative, or engaging in collective action with other service users and carers – to reflect on the significance of such experiences for policy and practice. My starting point is the everyday significance of care in the context of real lives. This is a position that has been reinforced by my own research with those who are identified by policy makers as 'carers' or 'care givers' (Barnes, 2006), by collaborative work that has highlighted the centrality and ambivalence of care in accounts by older people of what contributes to their well-being (Ward, Barnes and Gahagan, 2012), as well as by others' accounts made public through research and published personal reflections. I consider how lay accounts might both inform and be informed by some of the more theoretical work of care ethicists, and how we might draw useful conclusions about policy from both perspectives.

This approach can also be seen to respond to Peta Bowden's (1997, p 5) argument regarding the 'aura of invisibility' that surrounds the significance of care in everyday life. Care is so fundamental to our capacity to live together that we simply cannot see its significance and it becomes possible to ignore it. As a friend responded to another's observation about the dedication of a man taking his wife for dialysis three days a week: "why would he not do it?" What I aim to do here is lift the cloak of invisibility that makes it possible to both disregard and devalue care. At the same time I also want to question the ubiquity of the use of the word 'care' and to argue that we need to be more discriminating in what we refer to as care.

Much of the theoretical work on care has been carried out in the US by moral and political philosophers such as Daniel Engster (2007), Virginia Held (2006), Eva Feder Kittay (1999) and Joan Tronto (1993). The absence of a discipline of social policy in the US, itself in part consequent on the absence of a welfare state, perhaps accounts for a rather less developed body of work that applies this thinking to practical policy and service delivery. One objective of these

American philosophers can be seen as making the case for collective responsibility for welfare that, even in hard times, is better established in most European countries than it is in the US. Thus in arguing the need for a political theory of care, Engster articulates what are, to many European readers, familiar arguments underpinning political and academic debates within social policy. It is European scholars, such as Selma Sevenhuijsen (1998) and Fiona Williams (2001), who have done rather more to offer a sophisticated analysis of social policy from an ethic of care perspective, although Olena Hankivsky (2004) has also applied an ethic of care to Canadian social policy. One of my objectives is to make a further contribution to that literature which not only bridges the divide between political philosophy and practical social policy, but which also relates to the lived experience of people caring about and caring for each other at work, at home and in their everyday encounters in public spaces.

But first I need to say something about the way I am approaching 'care' in this book.

What is care?

I adopt a rather different way of approaching the subject of care here to that which I took in a previous book: *Caring and Social Justice* (Barnes, 2006). That book started by setting out the way in which 'care' had been analysed by researchers who were working to understand what care giving involves for family members, and sometimes friends, who were providing care to people who, by virtue of age, frailty, illness or disability needed more help than most of us do in our everyday lives. Thus I was considering what care meant in terms of the work, the emotion, the activities, the relationships and types of care involved in care giving in very particular circumstances. In that book I sought to understand care giving within the broader context offered by ethic of care analyses, but my focus was on what have come to be known as caring relationships within British social policy, which have led to the identification of 'carers' as subjects of social policy, and which have been the subject of substantial empirical research focusing on the work of care and the impact of care giving on unpaid carers. My focus in this current book is rather broader. Thus my starting point in posing and addressing the question: 'what is care?', which I also addressed in my previous book, is also a more expansive one.

Here I am thinking of care in three distinct, but related, ways. Firstly, care as a way of conceptualising personal and social relations. Such relationships certainly include the intense, intimate and personal relationships associated with giving care to those who are old, young, ill or disabled, as well as those that result from interactions in the context of 'care work'. But they also encompass other social relationships that may less usually be thought of as caring relationships. These include friendships or work relationships, relationships generated by political activity or through encounters in the process of policy making; they include the way in which we relate to our physical environment, both those environments we create for ourselves, individually and collectively in our homes and neighbourhoods, and the 'natural' environment that we both find and shape in the world around us. They also include the way we relate to ourselves: looking after our bodies and our emotional and social well-being. This reflects the Tronto and Fisher definition of care as something that permeates all aspects of our lives – or can do so. None of these relationships necessarily or inevitably embodies 'care' – although if this is absent in what are typically described as 'caring relationships' this is more problematic than it would be in some other contexts. I will develop this idea later. But we can view these diverse relationships through the lens of care to ask whether they embody the qualities associated with care and to evaluate them on this basis. I develop my discussion of those qualities in Chapter Two, but they can be summarised as being attentive to needs and taking responsibility for making sure needs are met in order to enable people to flourish.

The issue of evaluation highlights the second aspect of what I mean by care in this book. Care comprises a set of values, or 'moral principles' as Tronto elaborates, that offers a way of thinking about what is necessary for human well-being, flourishing and indeed survival. Here the argument is not solely that we can describe whether or not care is evident in different relationships and contexts, but that we can make assessments of whether personal relationships, work relationships, friendships, processes of political decision making etc are capable of enabling the conditions in which we can live well (or as well as possible) both individually and together. As Tronto (2010) has argued, one of the characteristics of care that we need to keep in mind is its purposiveness. It is thus a highly normative concept and one that is as essential to the analysis and practice of social policy as that of social justice. But the normative nature of care is not solely of relevance to the assessment of social policies (Sevenhuijsen, 2003a). As Sayer (2011) elaborates, normative questions are important in our everyday lives both because of our dependence on others and because we care about things and people. Thus: 'we are necessarily evaluative beings, continually having to monitor and evaluate how we and the things we care about are faring, and to decide what to do' (p 23). We assess others by reference (among other things) to their capacity to care; to assess someone as 'care less' is a judgement that they are deficient in an important respect.

Third, we need to think about care as a practice – we need to be able to recognise what is involved to 'do care' or, as Tronto has put it, we need not only to care about but also to care for. This reflects the significance of a focus on the work and activities of care giving that have been emphasised both by feminist researchers seeking to make visible the unpaid work done by many women, and by carers themselves through their campaigns and organisations. A key objective of such campaigning has been to secure recognition not only for the work carers do and the impact this has on them, but also for what this saves the state in terms of the unpaid labour provided (Barnes, 2001, 2011a). However, the development of care as a normative concept alerts us to the need to consider whether all such work of 'care giving' in practice does embody care. The resistance among disabled people and others to being recipients of care reflects the potential for what is called 'care work' to become something else (see Chapter Four). And a perspective that recognises the significance of care to a range of contexts and relationships also suggests we need to develop an understanding of what care looks like in practice in contexts that are very different from those that have been the subject of the substantial body of research into care giving. What does caring for colleagues and employees look like? What does 'deliberating with care' in the context of participative policy making require of public officials? Realising the potential of an ethic of care in practical social policy and in everyday life requires not only more effective theorisation, but also the development of ethical sensibilities and skills to be applied in different practices in different contexts. We need to be able to recognise care and its absence.

There are two additional issues that need to be considered in introducing the way in which I am applying care in this book. The first concerns what has been called the 'dark side' of care (eg Fine, 2007). It is important to acknowledge and address the reasons why care has come to be the subject of powerful critiques from within the disability movement (eg Wood, 1991; Beresford, 2008) and, similarly, why its usage in many social policy contexts has been relegated to a marginal position – even those that purport to be concerned with social care (Barnes, 2011b). If care as I and others have approached it embodies values and practices necessary to human survival and flourishing, why does it not receive universal acceptance as fundamental to policies and practices focused on achieving welfare, well-being and citizenship? Why are 'choice and control' identified as the key values in social care and 'care' itself has become lost from social work discourse? Tronto has suggested an important reason for the devaluing of care in terms of the 'privileged irresponsibility' felt by those in powerful positions who do not want to recognise the extent to which such positions are enabled by the care they do and have received from others: 'By not noticing how pervasive and central care is to human life, those who are in a position of power and privilege can continue to ignore and to degrade the activities of care and those who give care' (Tronto, 1993, p 111). The 'autonomy myth' (Fineman, 2004) is a powerful one and one that suits politicians and policy makers seeking to promote individual rather than collective responsibility for welfare and well-being. To be or become 'dependent' is to be identified as of lesser worth (Fraser and Gordon, 2002) and to be a recipient of care is associated with such dependency. I have suggested that the power of the autonomy/independence discourse vis-à-vis that of interdependence and relationality is one reason why those who experience themselves as powerless (in this instance many disabled people) want to shrug off any association with values or practices linked to care (Barnes, 2006, p 146). It is evident that many older people have internalised the negative connotations that link care receiving with being a burden and are reluctant to seek help as a result (Ward, Barnes and Gahagan, 2011).

But resistance to care cannot solely be accounted for by the political attractiveness of autonomy to neo-liberal politicians, or the impact of the discursive power of independence on those reluctant to be defined as recipients of care. Nor is care devalued just because those who typically do the work of care are those occupying comparatively powerless positions: women, particularly black and working class women, and migrants. What has been called 'care' has been and remains associated with practices that are anything but 'caring'. From the oppressive and demeaning way in which people with learning disabilities were often treated in long stay institutions (Ryan and Thomas, 1980) to the recent exposures of the compassionless 'care' of people towards the end of life in hospital (Health Service Ombudsman, 2011), evidence of 'poor care' from those ostensibly undertaking caring roles has underpinned and fuelled campaigns to assign care to the past. But is it helpful to respond to undoubted evidence of 'bad care' by seeking to abandon care itself? Here we need to return to the ubiquity of the term 'care' in both everyday and professional usage.

As I hinted earlier, there is much that is called care that is not care. Indeed, it could be argued that 'bad care' is an oxymoron. Care as a normative concept that can only exist through practices embodying the values and moral principles of care is, by definition, 'good'. But those engaged in care do not always get it right and there are certainly times when what is called care becomes something else. Family as well as paid care givers can be overprotective, sometimes to the point of denying the opportunity for self expression or crushing any potential for development. But protection, as Tronto (1993) has argued, is often different from care: 'Caring seems to involve taking the concerns and needs of others as the basis for action. Protection presumes the bad intentions and harm that the other is likely to bring to bear against the self or group, and to require a response to that potential harm' (p 105). A nursing assistant who shouts at an elderly person who cannot feed herself or who has soiled herself because her pleas for assistance to use the toilet have been ignored, cannot in any way be considered to be doing care, in spite of being employed as a care worker. Care for others can become self sacrifice or martyrdom without awareness of the need for self-care, while care for self can veer into narcissism and self-centredness without attentiveness to the needs of others. One of my arguments in this book is that we need to become more discriminating in our use of the term care if we are to realise its value. That requires much closer attention to the characteristics of care and how these can be realised in different types of relationship. Associated with this, the development of the ethical sensibilities necessary to practice care will require the ability for self-reflection as well as for critical analysis of policy and practice to assess whether what is called care does, in fact, demonstrate this. There may also be times when protection is more appropriate than care, but in order to make this judgement we need to understand better the differences between caring for someone and ensuring their protection.

Does this demand for greater discrimination in the use of the term care conflict with my other argument that we should apply the concept of care to a range of contexts which are not typically thought of by reference to the significance of care within them? Tronto and Fisher's definition has been subject to critique because, it is argued, it is too embracing to be useful. Others who have written on an ethic of care have argued its relevance and usefulness in diverse contexts. Held (2006, 2010) for example, has applied care ethics not only to questions of global justice, but also to violence in domestic and public contexts. One of my aims in this book is precisely to address the question of the relevance and usefulness of an ethic of care in diverse contexts relevant to social and public policy. I seek to explore what it can offer, but also to reflect on its limitations. The expansion of interest in an ethic of care can be seen as part of a broader shift within social science and in some practice contexts towards a re-emphasis on values, ethics, emotions and relationality (eg Lynch et al, 2009; Sayer, 2011). This work reflects the poverty of both politics and social science that assumes people are autonomous, rational actors and builds social policies and practices around such assumptions. The increasing profile of concepts such as social capital and well-being within academic and policy discourse and the disputed nature of these indicate a struggle to find ways of re-conceptualising social relationships and the ends of social policy in terms of achieving both individual and collective good (Barnes and Prior, 2007; Jordan, 2008; Taylor, 2011). In this book I want to demonstrate what an ethic of care, based in feminist scholarship and struggle, has to offer to such a project.

In Chapter Two I discuss key ideas about and applications of an ethic of care, drawing on international publications on the subject, and focusing in particular on those that I have found most useful and influential in my own thinking. I also relate these ideas (briefly) both to other ways of conceptualising connectedness that have been significant in a social policy context over recent years, and to other non-Western philosophical traditions in which the liberal emphasis on the autonomous individual has been less dominant. The following chapters explore the significance and potential of care as a lens through which to view social relations and practices in different contexts. I start in Chapter Three with the 'obvious' context – that of care giving and receiving in the context of intimate personal relationships within families. Chapter Four considers care work, addressing what constitutes 'care full' practice in this context as well as the critiques of care and the alternative values, in particular choice, that have been proposed as a means of empowering those who need to make use of health and social care services. I return to more personal relationships in Chapter Five where I consider care in the context of relationships with friends, neighbours and among those who share membership of a community of identity or place. Chapter Six considers the relevance of care in the context of 'stranger relationships'. There have been arguments both for and against the relevance of care ethics beyond relationships with known others. Supporters have argued that this is relevant to issues of global justice and to both attitudes and actions of policy makers in relation to issues such as international aid, and of people generally in terms of willingness to, for example, donate to disaster relief. Here I also consider more everyday interactions with unknown others that can impact on well-being and consider whether care ethics offer a useful way of conceptualising such relationships. In Chapter Seven I interrogate Tronto and Fisher's inclusion of 'the environment' within the web of care. This has potentially very broad implications, encompassing our relationships with the micro environments in which we live, as well as the collective relationship of humanity to the planet on which we live. I take three different examples of environmental relationships as the focus for my discussion here: the significance of immediate home and neighbourhood environments and older people's relationships with them to their well-being; the messages given through environmental design and maintenance about the care of public bodies for those who have to live within the areas for which they are responsible; and thirdly, the macro and micro environments of work. Chapter Eight applies the moral principles of an ethic of care to the process of making policy, in particular to participative policy making in which public officials meet in face to face dialogue with those whose lives are directly affected by the decisions that are reached. Finally, in Chapter Nine I conclude by highlighting the key ways in which I have developed an approach to an ethic of care in practice, address the contested politics of care, and affirm the necessity and value of care to social policies and the practices through which these are delivered.

TWO

Conceptual, philosophical and political perspectives on care

In this chapter I consider the re-emergence of a search for connections in response to dominant emphases on the rational, choice-making individual of the neo-liberals, and ways of conceptualising and theorising this. Work on an ethic of care has become influential in analyses of social welfare policies and practices as it has extended beyond its origins in feminist psychology (Gilligan, 1982). Political philosophers (eg Tronto, 1993; Sevenhuijsen, 1998; Kittay, 1999) have developed an analysis of care as a political as well as a personal practice and have argued the necessity of care to social justice, based on an analysis of dependency and interdependency, rather than autonomy, as fundamental to human survival and well-being.

There is now an extensive body of literature on an ethic of care that I am not attempting to summarise here. Rather I want to address three key issues and questions that are directly relevant to my aim of understanding the significance of care ethics in everyday life, and to considering what type of social policies and practices can best support caring relationships capable of ensuring not only survival, but also flourishing. The first of these is: what concept of the person is assumed by an ethic of care? The second is the moral principles of care, and the third is the relationship between care and social justice. In discussing these I also refer to ideas within other non-Western philosophies in order to reflect on the connections between care ethics as developed by Western feminist philosophers and other ways of thinking that have been influential in different times and places.

Concepts of the person

As Selma Sevenhuijsen has highlighted in her articulation of the method she developed to apply an ethic of care to the analysis of social policies, assumptions about 'human nature' – and not only how people are, but how they should be – are fundamental to the way in which social policies are constructed. Such policies are designed not only to reflect human needs, characteristics, and circumstances, but to influence human behaviour. Thus:

> ... one of the most influential notions in late modernity is that of the self-interested, calculating individual ... a related notion is that of abstract individuals: persons are frequently constructed as individuals who are expected (or even supposed) to be led by self-interested motives. As a consequence dependency appears as something that has to be overcome (citizens have to be made independent), instead as [sic] something that has to be dealt with on a daily basis. (Sevenhuijsen, 2003a, pp 8-9)

These two related notions – that individuals basically make rational decisions to act in their best interests, and that they do this from a position in which they see themselves as (and are) disconnected from others and able to act not only rationally but autonomously – have themselves been the subject of extensive analysis by social scientists, philosophers and policy analysts. Some have sought to promote this view, others to critique it, and others to find a way of challenging an inevitable association between autonomy and individualism (eg Mackenzie and Stoljar, 2000; Fineman, 2004; Le Grand, 2007). In spite of its origins in liberalism and its association with neo-liberal social policies advocating market-based solutions to welfare needs, the idea of the individual as autonomous agent, choosing to live in the way s/he wishes, has been attractive to many within disability and other welfare users' movements because it holds the promise of giving recognition to claims for self-determination. The dominance of individual choice as a basis on which to determine how needs should be met has not only been welcomed but promoted by disability activists as a means of securing control over the help they receive and reducing an unwelcome dependence on professional service providers (www.in-control.org.uk). This has, as I indicated in Chapter One, been accompanied by a rejection of care as a basis on which support or 'help' (Shakespeare, 2000) should be provided. This is a position that enables those who have experienced the negative consequences of being identified as 'dependents' to instead assert their identities as autonomous, choice-making individuals of equal worth to other adults who appear not to need care.

Associated with a concept of the subject of social policy as an autonomous choice maker is that of the active citizen. A raft of policies in different European welfare states has been aimed at creating active citizens who take responsibility not only for their own welfare and well-being, but also for that of others – both their families through direct care and support and members of the communities in which they live through their active participation in community life as volunteers and participants in local governance (Barnes and Prior, 2000; Newman and Tonkens, 2011). Care has been and remains a key focus for exhortation and encouragement to active citizenship (Anttonen and Häikiö, 2011; Barnes, 2011a). However the way in which care giving is constructed within social policy tends to emphasise this as an activity undertaken by individuals, rather than as something that takes place through relationships (Lloyd, 2000).

In contrast to this emphasis on the autonomous individual, care ethics, or care theory as Engster (2007) describes it, has a fundamentally relational view of human beings. This starts from the recognition that basic survival depends on care. Human babies, more than the young of any other species, depend on intensive care over an extended period of time to ensure their basic survival needs for food, warmth and shelter are met. And beyond this, for a longer period of time, human individuals need care to ensure their developmental, emotional and social needs are met and to enable them to engage successfully in social relationships in order not only to avoid serious harm, but also to flourish as effective participants within human society (Doyal and Gough, 1991). This fact alone (and it is hard to describe it as anything other than a key aspect of the reality of the human condition) means that care is necessary to all human individuals, and thus that we cannot and should not confine the need for care to a group of people who are defined and distinguished specifically by their need for care. From a policy perspective the implication of this is that a fundamental responsibility of states is to ensure that all receive the care that is necessary to survival and growth, not only for the benefit of the individuals themselves, but for that of society as a whole.

But it is also the case that the universal need for care is not restricted to babyhood and childhood. It is also a fundamental aspect of the human condition that we grow older and that during the life course, however long this lasts, we are likely to experience times of illness and physical or emotional frailty that mean we need help from others. And while Shakespeare (2000) advocates, instead of care, the term 'help' in all its guises (helpers, helping and helpful) as a means of challenging the disempowerment experienced by recipients of care as this has been demonstrated within professionalised social care services, he ultimately links his concept of helpfulness to the value-based approach to care of Tronto, Sevenhuijsen and other care ethicists. Some individuals, throughout their life course, live with physical or cognitive impairments, or with long-term illnesses (both physical and mental) that necessitate enduring care over and above what generally healthy, non-disabled adults might expect to need over their lifetime. Indeed O'Brien (2005) argues that disability should not be seen as an exceptional condition because most people face some form of disability, particularly as their bodies age. Kittay (1999) writes of the 'inevitable dependencies and asymmetries that form part of the human condition – those of children, the aging and ailing – dependencies that often mark the closest human ties' (p 14). In highlighting the danger of building either a moral philosophy or a policy system on assumptions of 'elusive equality' (p 2) Kittay prompts us to recognise that a genuinely just system of welfare requires the acknowledgement that we need to name dependency on the care of others as something that is fundamental to our lives and not, as Rawls' (1971) theory of justice would have it, something that can be left for later when we have dealt with how we achieve justice for autonomous adults who comprise the norm from which all others deviate. This issue will be discussed in more detail later.

Care offers a counterbalance to a perspective that emphasises the cognitive and rational dimension of what it is to be human. As Julia Twigg has eloquently demonstrated, we cannot adequately address care without also focusing on the significance of the body and embodiment. I quote at length from her study of the work of bathing assistants.

> It is at the front line that the true nature of care reveals itself. It is there that it is created; and only there can it be judged. We can sense this truth through imaginative engagement. We can picture a continuum of care that at one end represents the best sort of care and at the other verges on abuse. Even if not involving positive cruelty, we can imagine rough handling, denigrating language, sneering or nasty words, a silent refusal to recognise the person, the demeaning exposure of the body, cold indifference to embarrassment or anxiety. At the other end, we can imagine the very best sort of care, where the careworker brings a sense of life and fun into the house, where the older or disabled person is encouraged and sustained, where what is particular about them is endorsed and valued, where care is structured around their preferences, and where lapses of the body are smoothed over. (Twigg, 2000, pp 1-2)

Twigg's study highlights not only the way in which care requires us to consider how we handle (both literally and figuratively) the embodied nature of humanity, but also how this intersects with our emotional responses to processes of ageing and impairment and their impact on our sense of self. We are emotional beings and it is impossible to understand how we can retain a sense of well-being in the face of the inevitable bodily deterioration of old age without learning how we ourselves and others can care for us in this changed condition (Ward, Barnes and Gahagan, 2012). We respond emotionally not only to our own frailties, but to those of people close to us and those emotions say important things about what it is we value and how our lives can be made better in situations in which we or others are suffering and vulnerable (Nussbaum, 2001; Sayer, 2011). Engster (2007) demurs from a view that care inevitably involves an affective dimension, describing this as a 'sentimental' view of care. However, his description of a brusque encounter between a doctor and his patient that, he claims, is evidence of care in spite of the absence of affective quality, appears at odds with his inclusion of 'respect' as one of the moral principles of care. Twigg's comparison of the best and the worst of care implies that respect and sensitivity to both the emotional and bodily dimension of people's experiences are necessary to care. Annemarie Mol's (2008) work on diabetes care also emphasises care in relation to bodies and what happens to them when they become diseased, recognising the need to care for both body and the emotional aspect of illness in a way that responses based in a 'logic of choice' cannot comprehend.

While our interdependencies are most evident when we are very young, ill, disabled or have became frail in old age, we are relational beings throughout our lives: 'the quality of people's lives depends hugely on the quality of the social relations in which they live, and on how people treat one another' (Sayer, 2011, p 7). Most seek some sort of life partner or close friends from whom we can receive care and to whom we can give care. It matters to us how we are treated by work colleagues, by those on whom we depend for services we are unable to carry out ourselves (whether that is sorting out plumbing problems or providing financial advice), and taking part in voluntary or political action is often as much about seeking connections with others as it is about the content of the activity itself (Barnes, Harrison and Murray, 2012). Care ethics prompts us to give attention to ways in which such connections can be supported to improve the well-being of all, rather than limiting care to a marginal position of relevance only *in extremis*.

My discussion of the concept of the person and of what it means to be human, in common with similar discussions in the ethic of care literature, contrasts this conception with what has become the dominant view in Western politics and philosophy. But the similarities between an ethic of care and other systems of philosophy suggest that the dominant Western position may be aberrant – or at least questionable in its assumption about the nature of humanity. For example, African philosophy is based on a view that: *Motho ke motho ka batho* (a person is a person through other persons) (Ramose, 2003). This is reflected in a 1997 South African Government White Paper for Social Welfare which recognises *ubuntu* – humanity or humanness – as follows.

> The principle of caring for each other's well-being ... and a spirit of mutual support ... Each individual's humanity is ideally expressed through his or her relationship with others and theirs in turn through a recognition of the individual's humanity. Ubuntu means that people are people through other people. It also acknowledges both the rights and responsibilities of every citizen in promoting individual and societal well-being. (DW, 1997, p 12)

Coetzee (2003) reflects on the communitarian basis of morality in African philosophy, the social nature of the concept of a person and the highest value attached to kinship – which is itself both a biological and social category. This description of *ubuntu* as a communitarian philosophy suggests a potential for it to offer a rather exclusive view of the 'people' encompassed within the notion of humanity (to be discussed later). This is an issue directly addressed by Louw (2010) when he addresses the 'challenge' of *ubuntu* ethics in a contemporary, multicultural context. He considers the presumption of consensus and sameness within *ubuntu* but rejects this, arguing that it can 'handle plurality insofar as it inspires us to expose ourselves to others, to encounter the difference of their humanness so as to inform and enrich our own'. His analysis emphasises the importance of not treating any philosophical system as fixed within a particular temporal frame, but rather the need to rearticulate it to utilise the positive insights on offer in a critical but creative way within the contemporary context.

It is also possible to see the impact of a view of kinship as social rather than exclusively biological in the distributed mothering that takes place among African communities of the diaspora where sharing responsibilities for the care of children not only reduces individual burdens, but also strengthens the community in the face of shared oppressions (James, 1993). Similar practices are evident in Diné (Navajo) communities where 'helping' among kin and neighbours is understood as a way of expressing interconnectedness and of sustaining a positive identity (Waller and Patterson, 2002). In Maori culture the principle of *Whanaugatanga* or relationship building also refers to both kin and broader relationships. People's ability to develop their 'self' is seen as relating to their understanding of themselves as Maori through their relationships with others. Its application to a range of welfare interventions is evident in descriptions and analyses of initiatives designed to address mental health issues, violence and disenchantment among young people, and initiatives to address domestic violence and child abuse (eg Brannelly et al, 2009).

We might conclude that the everyday significance of the relational qualities of care is so well recognised as not to need justification as the basis for either a system of moral philosophy or welfare. It has certainly been my recent experience that introducing these ideas to a group of older people with whom I and colleagues have been working has prompted an immediate recognition of their relevance. On the other hand, speaking with health and social care practitioners and policy makers has prompted a more ambivalent response, in particular among younger workers schooled in the priority of choice rather than care. Older workers tend to respond positively to the permission this grants to speak of something that they think is really important, but have learnt to put aside. The discourse or 'logic' of choice (Mol, 2008; Barnes, 2011b) has become powerful in contemporary health and social care systems at the expense of a discourse of care. I agree with Mol that this is at best unhelpful and at worst highly dangerous. If we are to counteract this we need to give much closer attention to what the interdependent nature of being human means to policies and practices intended to meet human need and ensure well-being and social justice.

The moral principles of care

Most ethical systems aim for abstract universal positions and principles to guide action in pursuit of the good. An ethic of care argues that we need to focus on the particularities of day to day interactions and understand the need for care to be given and received in particular circumstances in order to enable human flourishing. The 'different voice' that Gilligan (1982) identified in relation to moral reasoning was one that took into account particular aspects of situations, rather than reaching conclusions based on abstract principles. Thus, while an ethic of care is universal in scope, it requires practical applications specific to particular contexts. To understand care we must look at the practices of care or the activities that comprise care in concrete situations, not just the principles that should guide these. It is those philosophers who have responded to the real life and often messy moral dilemmas that people can struggle to make sense of in their everyday lives who have developed an ethic of care, not those who seek to determine moral principles through a process of logical argumentation. It is not a coincidence that Selma Sevenhuijsen (1998) opens her book with an account of an 'activity supervisor' in a nursing home sitting with an elderly lady, stroking her arm and offering her a marshmallow, or that Eva Feder Kittay (1999) tells the story of establishing an effective way of sharing the care for her severely disabled daughter with another woman. These are not only reference points for their arguments, but embody the essential insights that care and care ethics are grounded in everyday interactions where moral decisions have to be made. As Annemarie Mol (2008) observes in discussing experiences of living with and receiving treatment for diabetes, conversations in the consulting room between patients and their doctors or nurses often relate to such apparently mundane issues as socks and other 'endless practical details of daily life' (p 28).

But while care cannot be encompassed in abstractions, this does not mean that it is only a matter of practical details. As Mol powerfully evokes, there is a 'logic' to care that needs to be understood through the everyday realities of what it means to need, to give and to receive, care. Care is not a soft option – the work of making moral judgements about the best thing to do in often difficult circumstances, which could result in harm being caused as well as prevented, requires considerable rigour, strength and understanding. There is not a precise set of rules to follow to determine how to establish relationships of care in circumstances as diverse as collaborative research (Ward and Gahagan, 2010); deliberative decision making (Barnes, 2008a; see also Chapter Eight) or providing services to homeless people (Reitz-Pustejovsky, 2002). But this does not mean that care ethics does not offer a principled framework within which to assess practice in diverse circumstances. The way in which an ethic of care understands the relational ontology of humanity and offers an analysis of what is necessary to be well and live well in the world can be expressed in terms of sensitising principles to guide, but not determine, practice.

But if care is, as I have suggested, an everyday necessity for survival, growth and well-being, is it necessary to think about it from an ethical perspective? Should we not simply accept it as a practical necessity and have done with it? The danger of this is, as we have also seen, that there are competing conceptions of the individual and hence of how a good life can be secured for all persons – including those who do not meet the assumptions of rational self-interest that underpin liberal and neo-liberal theory. These differences affect the decisions that are made by states concerning both the allocation of resources to welfare and the policies and strategies adopted to enable well-being. Care is, as Tronto (1993) has helpfully argued, both a moral and a political issue.

> A concept that can describe both a moral and a political version of the good life can help us to escape from the dilemmas of seeing morality and politics as separate spheres. I argue that care can serve as both a moral value and a basis for the political achievement of a good society. (p 9)

The boundary between politics and morality is one that Tronto seeks to break down. Another boundary is the one between public and private life, a focus for much feminist critique (eg Lister, 1997). This reinforces the importance of a perspective that links the way in which care is demonstrated (or not) in everyday interactions between family, friends, workers and strangers; the way in which public policies are produced and implemented; and the moral principles or ethical sensibilities that inform these. An understanding of care as practical, political and moral provides a robust and critical basis on which to build relationships in diverse contexts (eg Robinson, 1999; Brannelly, 2006; Peters et al, 2010; Ward and Gahagan, 2010) as well as to interrogate public policies in terms of their capacity to deliver well-being (eg Williams, 2001; Sevenhuijsen at al, 2003; Barnes, 2011b; Paszkiewicz, 2011).

Some have suggested that an ethic of care, because it emphasises relationality and contextuality rather than abstract principles, and requires continual dialogue and negotiation to establish needs and how they should best be met, does not share with other schools of moral philosophy an established set of principles of conduct. In fact Tronto (1993) has elaborated four moral principles of care and others have added to these. What is distinctive about these principles is that they do not define a particular set of practices or behaviours, but rather provide a guiding framework within which negotiations can take place. Engster (2007) suggests an ethic of care combines elements of a 'theoretical-juridical' model of morality which proposes general rules, aims or guidelines for what should be done, and an 'expressive-collaborative' model which argues that continual negotiation is required in order to reach understanding. So what are those guiding principles within which negotiation should take place?

Tronto identifies four principles that need to be integrated into a whole to achieve what she refers to as the 'integrity of care': attentiveness, responsibility, competence and responsiveness. Sevenhuijsen (1988) adds a fifth: trust, while Engster also suggests another: respect. Tronto's identification of these ethical elements is also contained within an analysis of the four phases of caring: caring about, taking care of, care giving and care receiving. These phases indicate that there first of all needs to be a recognition that care is necessary; that there is then some recognition that action is required to respond to the need for care, but that this will not always involve 'hands on' care; care giving is the direct process of meeting needs, while the inclusion of 'care receiving' highlights the importance of recognising and understanding the experience of those receiving care and including this in the process of care.

Without *attentiveness*, an awareness and recognition of the need for care, then care cannot be given. An assumption that we are, or should be, autonomous individuals who do not require support is likely to mean that such attentiveness is lacking. Being attentive to one's own needs, that is, recognising that our own capacity for survival and flourishing requires care from others, can sensitise us to others' needs. But we also need to be able to 'suspend one's own goals, ambitions, plans of life and concerns, in order to recognize and be attentive to others' (Tronto, 1993, p 128). Attentiveness needs to encompass not only a personal attentiveness to the particular situation of others, but also recognition of the social and cultural circumstances and factors that affect the experience and nature of need. It is this that means that care is not solely a matter of private concern for known others. Thus, for example, a failure to name the particular experiences of forced migrants, in the context of defining contexts in which eligibility for social care services is set out, amounts to inattentiveness not only to specific individuals, but to a group of people who are likely to experience suffering and to need care (Paszkiewicz, 2011). Robinson (1999) argues that attentiveness to unknown but concrete others is fundamental to a moral policy for international relations. Attentiveness can be prompted by direct encounters, whether with those who are close to us through ties of kinship or friendship, or through particular contexts in which people seek help from others who are designated as providers of care, or through our collaborations with colleagues or those with whom we work on campaigns or political projects. But attentiveness can also be prompted by media reports of suffering among people we do not know and are never likely to meet. The expansion of electronic communication that puts people in contact with others they will never meet face to face raises significant questions about the capacity for attentiveness beyond face to face encounters. Wright (2000) has suggested that older adults can experience benefits from support provided via the internet which implies that attentiveness to particular needs may be developed without face to face contact. Initiatives such as the Sunshine Bank (www.sunshinebank.co.uk) appear to aim to encourage attentiveness to others via virtual exchanges and there are any number of websites which offer support to others who share health or other problems and encourage peer support (see Chapter Six).

Without action to follow the awareness of need, care cannot be complete. Thus the second moral principle that Tronto outlines is that of *responsibility* – accepting that action is required in response to the identified need. Both she and Sevenhuijsen distinguish their use of responsibility in the context of an ethic of care from that of 'obligation'. This is important not least because of the way in which responsibility as a counterbalance to rights has been articulated in much recent policy discourse (Blunkett, 2003; Newman, 2011). This asserts that any claims that persons may make on the state for help or support should be balanced by duties owed to the state to behave in particular ways – to be an active and responsible citizen. This is one way in which the state seeks to delimit *its* responsibilities; those who do not do their bit, either because, like forced migrants, they do not contribute their labour or taxes and are not 'citizens' at all, or because their behaviour is such that they are considered to place themselves outside of the social contract between state and citizen (Dwyer, 2000; Flint, 2009), cannot make claims on the state for help.

Tronto (1993) suggests that the concept of obligation implies the existence of formal bonds, duties and agreements such as those that exist de facto or de jure within some form of contract. In contrast, she defines responsibility as more of a sociological or anthropological concept than a political one: 'a term that is embedded in a set of implicit cultural practices, rather than in a set of formal rules or a series of promises' (pp 131-2). The implications of this definition are that recognising and accepting a responsibility for care does not require a pre-determined set of responses, regardless of the particular circumstances and context. Rather, the ways in which the need for care should be met are determined through a process of flexible negotiation. For example, in many cultures there is an expectation that adult children will care for their elderly parents, a responsibility that is based in the value afforded to both kin relations and a contractual notion of reciprocity – parents cared for their children when they were young; children should care for their parents when they are old. In some moral traditions, such as Confucianism, those responsibilities are embedded in legal codes which set out quite precisely what adult children should do. Arguments that Confucianism shares core attributes with an ethic of care (Li, 2008) have been questioned not least because it is the formal status relationship (father, son etc) that defines the nature of the responsibility, rather than the particularity of needs and relationships in context (Star, 2002). In most contemporary Western cultures there would be strong resistance to any attempt to give legal force to any particular responsibility for the provision of either financial support or personal care for elderly parents. Nevertheless, complete abandonment by adult children is frowned upon. What is expected is that adult children will take some responsibility for ensuring care: either though 'taking care' of this by ensuring domestic or residential care is available if needed, or by directly giving care themselves. Which of these options is followed is determined by reference to the particular circumstances involved, and this encompasses both the practical circumstances of children and their parents: whether they live nearby, what other demands there are on children's time, energy and resources, the parents' financial circumstances etc; and by relational issues: how well they get on, the personal preferences for intimate care being provided by a daughter or son rather than a paid care giver etc.

The political implication of the inclusion of responsibility within the ethical principles of care is that states should accept the responsibility for ensuring care for their citizens. It is notable that ethic of care literature emanating from the US is in part prompted by reaction to the absence of the state health and welfare provision that is available (if under threat) in many European welfare states. However, the global movements of people and the interdependencies that exist between states that affect the capacity for survival, growth and well-being also imply that it is insufficient to understand such responsibilities solely as residing between states and those they accept as their citizens. Miller (2010), Held (2006), Engster (2007) and Robinson (1999) have argued that care theory and ethics are not only relevant, but necessary, to cosmopolitan or global ethics and justice. I discuss this further later.

But before leaving this section on responsibility it is important to consider the way in which Engster develops a 'theory of obligation' which he regards as an essential element to a theory of care. Basically what Engster seeks to do is to establish the order in which we should accept our moral responsibilities for others. He starts with our responsibilities to care for ourselves because: 'A person who does not care adequately for himself or herself may eventually be unable or unwilling to care for others' (Engster, 2007, p 56). This is followed by secondary responsibilities to care for those with whom we are in some kind of special relationship, which includes not only family or friends, but also, for example, someone we might come across in a remote area who is injured and is circumstantially dependent on us for their care or indeed survival. Thirdly, our responsibilities are to those with whom we share a close physical proximity or social relationship – that is, those who might be considered members of a community of place or identity. Finally, there are general duties to care for all others in need. A key principle underpinning this hierarchy of responsibilities is our capacity to understand and be in a position to respond to the needs of individuals in these different relationships to us. I reflect on issues raised in this hierarchy of obligations in subsequent chapters.

Tronto's third and fourth principles of care are *competence* and *responsiveness.* I am dealing with these together because they both, in different ways, refer to the need to consider the consequences of care giving as necessary aspects of the moral principles of care. Competence refers to the necessity that the work of care is performed competently for care to have been given. This reflects the point made in Chapter One that activities that are described as care should not always be understood as such: 'Intending to provide care, even accepting responsibility for it, but then failing to provide good care, means that in the end the need for care is not met' (Tronto, 1993, p 133). Tronto justifies her inclusion of a consequentialist principle within the moral principles of care quite precisely by pointing to the failures of so called 'caring institutions' to ensure the resources and supports necessary to enable good care are in place. It is not enough to argue that staff have been recruited, policies developed, procedures implemented if, in practice, older people become malnourished while in hospital because their need for help in eating is not recognised; if the parents of a severely disabled child are left to carry their daughter up and downstairs every day because of delays in installing a chairlift (Barnes, 2006, p 40); or if the unwillingness of a man with dementia to cooperate is interpreted as 'catastrophic' capacity and thus inappropriate decisions are made about a move to a residential placement (Brannelly, 2006).

The principle of responsiveness as elaborated by Tronto refers to the need to understand how receiving care is experienced and what it means to the person on the receiving end. It quite explicitly does not invite the care giver to reflect on how they would be likely to react in a similar situation, but to see and understand how the other is responding and what it means to *them*. It reflects the typical inequality between care giver and care receiver. Because the care receiver is likely to be in a position of vulnerability and because there is a real potential for abuse of power in care-giving relationships, the care giver needs to be alert to this in order to avoid domination and subordination and instead use power creatively (Tronto, 1993, p 135). Again, this principle is important in considering the critiques of care that have been advanced by those who have negative experiences of 'being cared for'. An absence of responsiveness constitutes a lack of care. Care full practices should embody an awareness and understanding of the response of the other – which once again highlights the necessity of attentiveness, drawing the circle comprising what Tronto refers to as 'the integrity of care'. I consider what such 'care full' practices that include the care receiver as an active participant in care look like in Chapters Three, Four and Five.

Sevenhuijsen's addition of 'trust' to these four moral principles emphasises the inequality and vulnerability present in many caring relationships which requires that the care receiver can trust that the care giver is acting in his or her best interests. It also requires an attitude of trust towards the moral agency of individuals to negotiate the 'conflicting responsibilities of care for "self, others, and the relationships between them"' (Sevenhuijsen, 2003b, p 11). The importance of trust is that it emphasises the capacity of care givers and receivers to engage in dialogue about needs and responses in circumstances of inequality. The story told by Eva Feder Kittay (Kittay, 1999, p 157) about Peggy, a paid care giver, and Eva's daughter Sesha, who has no speech and cannot verbally explain her needs and understanding to others, illustrates the relationship between responsiveness and trust. Peggy was tired and frustrated by her inability to teach Sesha the walking exercises that she had been assigned. As she sat down and gave up the struggle she watched Sesha moving her head from side to side to watch a leaf falling. Peggy recognised that what she was seeing was Sesha coming up with her own way of exercising and that she, Peggy, needed to learn from Sesha's responses what worked for her in terms of exercise and, more broadly, how she could support and care for her. Not only did Sesha have to learn to trust her care givers, they had to learn to trust her capacity to communicate her needs and her own way of meeting them.

Engster makes a similar point by reference to his inclusion of 'respect' as a virtue of care.

> ... the recognition that others are worthy of our attention and responsiveness, are presumed capable of understanding and expressing their needs, and are not lesser beings just because they have needs they cannot meet on their own. One respects others in this sense by treating them in ways that do not degrade them in their own eyes or the eyes of others, and makes use of the abilities they have. (2007, p 31)

He notes the importance of this virtue, once again, by reference to the consequences of a failure to demonstrate respect in some social services programmes that are less than effective because they fail to treat their users as knowledgeable and capable persons. The inclusion of responsiveness, trust and respect within the moral principles of care highlights the relational character of care in a particular way. Not only does care reflect the relational ontology of human life, and not only is it provided through relationships, it can generate dialogic processes that develop relational capacities among both care giver and care receiver. We develop our capacity to care through the practice of care with others.

Care and justice

The genealogy of care ethics lies in Gilligan's (1982) work which questioned assumptions that moral maturity resides in the capacity to make moral judgements from a position of detachment. From a 'detached' Kantian perspective, just decisions require the application of abstract rules, regardless of context, whereas Gilligan argued that women expressed moral dilemmas in a 'different moral voice' that emphasised the importance of situated judgements and which highlighted the importance of maintaining connections with others, rather than the formal application of rules of conduct. Her work prompted fierce debate about the relationship between gender and forms of moral reasoning and is the origin of continuing debate about whether the moral principles of care and justice can be reconciled; if so does care precede justice, can it be subsumed within liberal theories of justice, or should we understand care as a necessary component of justice? Since social justice is a central concept within social policy these questions are fundamental to a consideration of the place of an ethic of care in shaping policies and practices. Before I address the relationship of care to justice I need to consider (briefly) the notion of justice itself.

Social justice is also a contested concept. Within social policy much emphasis has typically been on distributive and redistributive meanings of the term, with contemporary policy debate often focusing on the difference between equality of opportunity and equality of outcome. Socioeconomic injustice derives from the unequal distribution of material wealth, the capacity to generate this and to control the fruits of one's own labour (Fraser, 1997, p 13). From this flows a series of inequalities – in particular relating to educational performance, health status and living circumstances that constrain capacities to live well and to realise aspirations. The sufficiency of this largely materialist concept of justice has been challenged in practice by social movements among those whose identities have been marginalised or stigmatised, including women, ethnic minorities, lesbian, gay, bisexual or transgendered (LGBT) people and users or survivors of mental health services. While material inequalities are certainly a significant dimension of their experiences, a redistributive response would be insufficient to address the impact of disrespect and mis-recognition that affect their lives and may undermine their sense of self. Theoretically Fraser, Honneth and Young (Young, 1990; Fraser, 1997; Fraser and Honneth, 2003; Honneth, 2005) have also emphasised the cultural and symbolic significance of disrespect, disparagement and violation of identity that constitutes injustice just as much as socioeconomic exploitation, deprivation or marginalisation. More recently Fraser (2009) has added 'representation' to her argument that justice requires not only redistribution and recognition, but also participatory parity in the process of decision making.

This expanded conceptualisation of social justice is highly relevant to a consideration of the relationship between care and justice. There are important arguments about both access to care and care giving as distributive rights. For example Lynch et al (2009) discuss the importance of 'affective equality', encompassing both the degree to which needs for love and care are satisfied and the unequal distribution of work that goes in to meeting them. It has been widely recognised that paid care work is poorly rewarded financially, undervalued and unequally undertaken by women, migrants, people from minority ethnic groups and others who have little economic power (Ehrenreich and Hochschild, 2003; Cangiano et al, 2009). The distribution of unpaid care work is similarly unequal. This has prompted arguments for policies and attitudinal shifts to encourage men to take on more substantial roles as carers (eg Coltrane and Galt, 2000). Michel (2000) argues for the right to be a mother in the face of expectations that all women should work outside the home, regardless of whether they are also mothers. She considers the different political, religious and cultural positions of organisations in the US that campaign for women's rights to be 'stay at home' mothers. It is interesting that the English carer movement has not explicitly campaigned for the 'right to care' and it could be argued that aspects of its campaigning have been co-opted to encourage carers of older and disabled people (like mothers) to undertake paid work as well as their caring responsibilities (Barnes, 2011a). But they do campaign for support for carers to undertake this role: 'care for the carers' has been a campaigning slogan from the early days of this movement and individual carers' stories frequently narrate the experiences and impact of an absence of care for themselves (Barnes, 2006). Kittay argues for support for care givers through adopting a form a reciprocity she refers to as *doulia* (this derives from the allocation of a 'doula' – a woman who helps mothers immediately after birth, to care for the mother as she cares for her child): 'these nested dependencies link those who need help to those who help, and link the helpers to a set of supports. The equality concept inherent in the idea that we are all some mother's child utilizes such a notion of nested dependencies' (1999, p 132). Engster (2007) says that the corollary of his argument about obligations to care is that we all have a right to care when we need it and that those who advocate an ethic of care should not be shy of also adopting the language of rights to argue for this.

Thus a consideration of the relationship between care and justice can, in part, be addressed by reference to issues of distribution: who cares – both as paid and unpaid carers – and how is this work rewarded in terms of income, security and protection of employment (Daly, 2001); how can it be supported in order to enable care givers to continue to care without disadvantage to themselves (Kittay, 1999, 2001); and are all types of need for care adequately met in terms of the availability of sufficient, appropriate resources?

However, in conceptual and philosophical terms the care versus justice debate is usually couched in terms of competing principles. If we include the principle of recognition as well as redistribution within our understanding of the concept of justice, then, I argue, the apparent lack of consistency is much less evident.

Honneth grounds his analysis of justice and recognition in the work of Hegel and Mead. Writing of 'Love, Rights, Solidarity' he could almost be writing from the perspective of an ethic of care.

> ... for Hegel, love represents the first stage of reciprocal recognition, because in it subjects mutually confirm each other with regard to the concrete nature of their needs and thereby recognize each other as needy creatures. In the reciprocal experience of loving care, both subjects know themselves united in their neediness, in their dependence on each other. (2005, p 95)

For Honneth, recognition is akin to the principle of attentiveness. Fraser's (1997) more political approach to proposing policy responses to the recognition/redistribution duality of social justice also suggests the importance of attentiveness to the particularity of needs associated with membership of marginalised or disadvantaged groups, without thereby essentialising them. Elsewhere I wrote of this:

> The application of an ethic of care perspective which unsettles the notion of care-givers and care-receivers as

> distinct, and of care as something relevant only in situations where one person can be defined as needy and the other has responsibility for meeting that need, reinforces Fraser's advocacy of an approach to justice which is not focused on action directed solely at ameliorating the situation of an already disadvantaged and stigmatised group, but of transforming the way in which such disadvantage and stigmatisation is produced. (Barnes, 2006, p 152. See also Barnes et al, 2010)

I have referred to Kittay's (1999) argument about 'nested dependencies': in order to provide care to those who need this, care givers also need to be cared for to ensure their own needs do not go unmet. This is clearly reflected in the political claims that motivated the UK carer movement and which continue to be pursued at local and national level (Barnes, 2011a). Underpinning Kittay's argument is the understanding that we are interdependent beings, that care is a universal need (although it is acknowledged that there are times when that need is greater than others) and that any adequate theory of justice cannot start from an assumption of equality and autonomy. Such a position is precisely that from which liberal theories of justice, most notably and influentially that of John Rawls (1971), do start; and it is this that care theorists and others (Nussbaum, 2006) dispute. Rawls' work comes from what is known as a 'contractual' basis for justice. The social contract that forms the basis for just treatment among persons living together in whatever form of social organisation assumes parties to that contract who are 'free, equal and independent'. Each of these conditions is seen as necessary to the pursuit of justice: people cannot enter unforced into a contract if they are in the power of another – that is, as a slave to another; for a contract to be freely entered into also requires not only moral equality but an equivalence in terms of power and resources; and finally parties to a social contract should not be asymmetrically dependent on others. Since it is quite obviously the case that these conditions do not apply to everyone, theories of justice based in such principles are exclusionary. Nor is it enough to argue that the *objective* of such an approach to justice is to create the conditions in which all individuals can achieve such conditions as this is blatantly impossible. Babies and children will usually grow into adults who may attain these conditions, but how can they expect justice before they reach this position? Do we assume that there are some who, towards the end of life, experience progressive dementia that renders them unequally dependent on the care of others and thus who should no longer expect to be included within a system of justice? And what about those who are born with severe cognitive disabilities that endure throughout their lives? Extreme positions deriving from an assumption of the necessity of the ability to reason as fundamental to the definition of what it is to be human have led to suggestions that some non-human animals have a greater claim to just treatment than people with such disabilities (Kittay and Carlson, 2010).

The implication is that liberal theories of justice that start from an assumption of 'elusive equality' (Kittay, 1999, p 2) cannot be adequate. Human interdependency means that care is necessary to justice. But how, precisely should we understand the relationship between care and justice? Tronto (1993) seeks to break down the 'moral boundaries' that assign care and justice to falsely dichotomous ethical starting points. Engster (2007) describes care as 'the heart of justice'. Held (2006) not only considers the consequences of adopting feminist ethic of care perspectives for specific issues of justice – for example, 'why do laws against rape protect men from false accusations better than they protect minority women from forced sex?' (p 65) – but looks more broadly at the implications for issues of social valuing of different activities and the resources and rewards that flow from this. Held regards the need to integrate issues of care and rights as central to feminist moral inquiry and she, like others (eg Fraser and Bedford, 2008), is not interested in banishing rights in order to promote care.

This example from Held highlights an issue that has not been made explicit in the writings of those who approach an ethic of care from a position within moral or political philosophy. The concept of 'justice' applied in these contexts is not qualified. In contrast, from a social policy perspective, my primary interest is in 'social justice'. The first example from Held that I cited earlier refers to what those in UK contexts would understand as criminal, rather than social, justice. While there have been recent arguments that the separation in both disciplinary and policy terms between social and criminal justice is unhelpful and hard to sustain (Hughes et al, 2007), in practice they do tend to be dealt with separately. In contrast, the key question from within philosophy is that of how 'just decisions' can be reached – regardless of whether those decisions concern the distribution of access to welfare (social justice) or the proper treatment of someone who has committed an offence (criminal justice). Thus, the origin of the care versus justice distinction in Gilligan's work refers to the different processes of moral reasoning she identified (initially distinguishing these according to gender) in response to examples of what might be considered 'wrong doing', rather than issues of responses to need or the distribution of welfare resources. It is in this context that the question arose of whether it is right to apply abstract moral principles in all circumstances, or whether just decisions require attention to and consideration of the particular circumstances.

Nevertheless, this question of the application of abstract, universal rules in comparison with the assessment of particular circumstances, and determining the 'right thing to do' on the basis of contextualised judgements, is also relevant to issues of social justice. In different areas of social policy at different times the broad approach adopted is closer to the one rather than the other position. Thus, in the English benefits system, entitlement to a specific monetary benefit has typically been based in eligibility according to fixed criteria (albeit with scope for contested assessment of whether or not those criteria are met), whereas in a social care context access to support services has been based more on an assessment of needs in the context of particular circumstances (the level of disability, availability of a family carer, preferences regarding daily activities etc), with the precise response to this being increasingly a matter of discussion between the worker undertaking the assessment and the service user (see Chapter Four). In daily practice a key task of front-line workers is to determine whether a need exists and how it should be met. A care perspective is necessary for determining the particular responses that will enable justice in diverse circumstances.

Engster's (2007) hierarchy of responsibilities for care that encompasses all those in need, regardless of their spatial location, indicates that what Fraser (2009) has termed the expansion of the 'frame' of justice beyond that of a 'Westphalian' political imaginary should also encompass the way in which we think about the frame in which we consider the relationship between care and justice. Others have also argued the global relevance of a care perspective. For example, Robinson (1999, 2010) has extended the ontology of interdependence and the unsettling of the notion that people can be divided into distinct groups of care givers or care receivers, or in her terms as 'victims' or 'guardians', to the context of an international political theory. Miller (2010) includes a care perspective within notions of cosmopolitan justice and Held (2006) expands the political implications of an ethic of care to the global level. Thus: 'The ethics of care has resources to understand group and cultural ties, and relations between groups sharing histories or colonial domination or interests in nonmarket development' (p 157). I develop the implications of these perspectives when I consider the relevance of care to stranger relationships in Chapter Six.

The development of a critical, political ethic of care means that neither a theoretical nor a policy separation between care and justice can be sustained. The relational ontology of care calls attention not only to the particular, personal needs of individuals, but also to the sociopolitical context in which those needs are produced and experienced, and to the processes by which difference and consequent exclusions are constructed. This will become clearer as I explore the significance of care in different contexts. But before moving on to explore these it is necessary to consider other ways in which relational concepts of the individual have been promoted as a basis for policy.

Communitarians and social capitalists

I have already noted that, in the context of African philosophy, the idea that 'we are people through other people' is understood as an example of a communitarian philosophy. Communitarianism became influential in the US and UK from the 1980s to the 1990s as a means of counteracting a perceived dominance in practice of individualism, rather than as a critique of the dominant ideological stance of neo-liberalism. As the term implies, it gave priority to 'community' as a focus for the exercise of responsibilities and proper behaviour. It was influential in the UK in promoting programmes of 'civil renewal' (Blunkett, 2003) that emphasised responsibilities both to avoid and to take action in response to social problems such as drug misuse, anti-social behaviour and truancy. In that context its use was closely linked to the promotion of the role of civil society in solving social problems, and to the self-government of communities. The programmes this gave rise to were focused on neighbourhoods or 'communities' characterised by deprivation and disadvantage, and raised questions about the preparedness of government to accept its responsibility for the structural inequalities within which such disadvantage was experienced. Friedman (1993) and Kittay (2001) have acknowledged the superficial similarity between feminist critiques of individualism and those pursued within communitarian arguments, but have also highlighted the political differences between a feminist public ethic of care and family policies based in communitarian assumptions of traditional gender relationships. Robinson (1999) has undertaken a similar critical analysis in the context of communitarian arguments in international relations. The 'community' of communitarians is a convenient shorthand for maintaining and promoting conservative social relations, rather than calling to attention the way in which social relations structure forms of domination and oppression. It privileges relationships between those in direct proximity that conform to dominant norms, the 'communities' it invokes are those of 'family, neighbourhood and nation' (Friedman,

1993, p 237), and can be a source of intolerance of difference and exclusion of others. It therefore needs to be distinguished from a critical ethic of care that: 'recognize[s] the potential of relational thinking not only in understanding moral relations but in problematizing the norms and structures that underwrite and sustain exclusionary structures' (Robinson, 1999, p 132).

Social capital is another concept that has enjoyed social and public policy influence as a way of understanding and promoting the importance of social networks to collective benefit. Wilkinson and Bittman (2003, p 2) have advanced what they call 'the civic model of care' based in social capital theory and contrasted this with care as derived from an ethic of care. Their claim is that:

> What flows from the particularistic notion of care is the idea that care is fundamentally a private concern. However, the concept of social capital allows us to view care as a public concern and an aspect of the public relations of citizens, rather than of our personal ones, and thus enables the makings of a civic model of care. (p 6)

Their assumption of the public–private dichotomy is perhaps based on the fact that their source of writing on an ethic of care is limited to Noddings' early (1984) book on this topic. Empirically, their argument is based on survey data that shows that 'co-residential carers' are less likely than those who help someone outside the household to engage in civic associations. There is no indication that the levels of demand that co-residential care usually makes might be understood as a reason for this association. Wilkinson and Bittman conclude that 'co-residential care is isolating and privatising in nature, and therefore is unable to provide the impetus for making more generalised social connections with others' (p 21). This draws a flawed theoretical conclusion – that social capital theory is necessary to advance the notion of public care, from an empirical reality – that care giving within households can result in carers becoming isolated.

Jordan (2008) notes the breadth of the individual and collective benefits that social capital theorists have argued flow from enhancing relations with others. He bases his discussion on three ways in which social capital is understood to generate benefit:

- Entering into relationships constitutes a better way of achieving certain purposes. (Although Doyal and Gough (1991) suggest that

it is not an option but a necessity to enter into relationships in order to achieve diverse purposes.)
- Social interactions create resources which are of value.
- Individuals benefit directly from interactions – that is, they are intrinsically valuable.

But the moral quality of those relationships is not developed in social capital theory and it has nothing to say about experiences of abuse, hurt, disrespect or invisibility that a care perspective can offer. Rather the focus is on the economic and social benefits to be derived from its promotion and Jordan concludes that the link between social capital and well-being is so tenuous as to be unconvincing. Social capital, as the language within which the theory is expressed captures, comes down to another way of proposing an economic model of welfare (p 88).

Conclusion

The body of literature on care ethics has developed exponentially since the early work prompted by Gilligan's naming of different forms of moral reasoning in the early 1980s. It has offered a critique of individualist and masculinist assumptions of the stages of moral development, and of the allocation of care to the private spaces in which women carry out reproductive rather than productive activity. In so doing it has shifted into a political gear and has started to influence the way in which policy and practice can be both constructed and analysed. The scope of this work goes well beyond a concern to theorise intimate relationships, to promote what have been understood as private, feminised virtues and to advance an ethical understanding of how to meet the individual needs of vulnerable and dependent people. It has expanded in this way at the same time as critiques of an over-professionalised and oppressive system of welfare in many Western states, and the claims of user movements in opposition to this, have reinforced dominant neo-liberal assumptions of the benefits of choice-based, individualised models of support, rather than the collective responsibilities and responses to needs for care. In the process, care as a value has been lost sight of and attempts have been made to banish care from the vocabulary of social care policy and practice. There has thus been a real tension between the apparently progressive campaigns of social movements of service users and the arguments of care ethicists (Watson et al, 2004). The promotion of the human and civil rights of disabled people has emphasised an unhelpful contrast between rights and care. This has served to reinforce the moral boundaries between care and justice that Tronto and other care ethicists have sought to dismantle.

At the same time the development of a political ethic of care has brought care in to places in which it has not previously been seen. The relational ontology on which care ethics is based refers not only to personal relationships between known individuals, but to the interdependencies that exist between peoples in different parts of the globe. The importance of care, as well as rights to cosmopolitan conceptions and practices of justice, offers a different way of thinking about our responsibilities to unknown as well as known others. It challenges not only the individualism that dominates conceptions of the person within Western social policy, but also the notion that we can reach moral decisions about policies within the boundaries of nation states.

As I develop my discussion of the place of care in everyday life and the implications of this for social policies that can deliver justice and well-being, I will continue to reflect on the nature of and reasons for resistance to care, as well as to argue the necessity of care to justice – not only for disabled people, for older people and for others who are the subjects of social policies, but for all of us.

THREE

Care in families

The archetypal image of care is that of a mother and child. The universal and enduring nature of that relationship of care is one that is repeated time and again in discussions of the significance of care. For Nel Noddings, one of the 'first wave' care ethicists, it is the mother–child relationship that serves as the model from which to describe and assess other caring relationships (Noddings, 1984). This position has been critiqued by others both because of its tendency to essentialise gender and because of its individualised approach to care (eg Sevenhuijsen, 1998), but no-one has suggested that an understanding of mother–child relationships is irrelevant to care ethics. Kittay (1999) argues that because we are all 'a mother's child' we all have an entitlement to claim care and we have all experienced care. Peta Bowden (1997) identifies mothering as 'a privileged example of the possibilities of human connectedness' (p 21) and highlights the way in which the complexity of the processes of first biological and second social individuation of child from mother, while also maintaining their relatedness, challenges set ideas of dependency and interdependency. From a rather different disciplinary perspective, psychologist Wendy Hollway (2006) has considered the development of a 'capacity to care' within the context of family dynamics, particularly the infant–mother relationship. In her work key questions include: whether developing a capacity to care matters; how this relates to parenting and gender relations; and how understanding of the capacity to care relates to ethic of care debates about autonomy and relationality. Parenting and family relations are central to her analysis.

By identifying the shared experience of being 'a mother's child', Kittay names the universal experience of receiving care. The inclusion of care receiving as the fourth moral moment of care (Tronto, 1993) is an important reminder of the need to address care as a relational practice. Most of the empirical work on care within a social policy perspective has focused on carers and the work and experience of care giving – the study by Forbat (2005) of 'two sides to the story' is an exception by including the perspectives of care receivers. This focus on care giving has contributed to a recognition of the importance of carers to individual and collective well-being, for example the 2008 Carers Strategy in England was called Carers at the Heart of 21st Century

Families and Communities (HM Government, 2008), but has also focused the disputes between disability activists and those promoting the recognition and rights of carers. There is empirical work that offers a balance to this emphasis on care giving rather than care receiving, such as Jenny Morris's (1995) study of disabled women's experiences of receiving assistance with daily living, and work on older people's well-being that includes consideration of their responses to their needs for care (Ward, Barnes and Gahagan, 2012). From a theoretical position Noddings (1996) argues that the perspective 'I am cared for' is necessary for caring to be achieved and offers an expanded conceptualisation of the role of the care receiver, including a discussion of the ethical responsibilities of those in this position. In this chapter I will seek to consider care giving and receiving in the context of intimate personal relationships focused within families.

Giving and receiving care

Care giving and receiving are probably most immediately understood in the context of close personal relationships where one person has greater needs for support than the other and it is 'naturally' expected that they are in a relationship that will be the source of care. It is usually kin relationships that are seen as the source of care, and usually women who are the key care providers. However, as we have already seen and as I will go on to discuss (Chapter Five), we should not only think of 'family' when considering 'who cares' and how caring relationships might be developed and supported. In recognising the unequal distribution of caring labour we should not assume that caring is 'naturally' the role of women rather than men. And fixed ideas about who are 'the carers' and who are those who receive care are not helpful – care giver and care receiver do not define two distinct groups of individuals. For example, as Nicki Ward (2011) has demonstrated, the increase in longevity of people with learning disabilities means that many of those formerly identified as in need of care are taking on vital caring roles in relation to ageing parents. While the naming of carers as a distinct social group has been important in gaining recognition and support (Barnes, 2011a), some have argued that the term 'carer' should be discarded, in part because it polarises two individuals, allocating them discrete roles, rather than focusing on the relationship between them (Molyneaux et al, 2011). In my previous work (Barnes, 2006) I have argued the impossibility of understanding caring relationships without considering the individual and shared biographies of those involved.

The circumstances in which the need for care is most obvious usually occur at the start and end of life, but intimate caring relationships are experienced throughout the life course. Caring relationships are frequently neither visible nor obvious. One of the surprises I experienced when embarking on life history interviews with family carers for a previous book was the number of different caring relationships they spoke about (Barnes, 2006). I had approached people to interview because they had been identified as 'carers' in the context of a service system that needed to allocate such an identity in order to determine eligibility for forms of assessment and support. Those identifications referred to a specific dyad. Nell cared for her disabled son James; Emily had cared for her husband Edward who had developed dementia; Bridget had cared for her mother Anne. What such identification did not recognise was what we might call the 'care history' of these people, both as care givers and care receivers; nor did it recognise the care history of those they currently cared for as givers as well as receivers of care. Such histories included the experiences of a mother of an autistic son whom I discovered was herself disabled. She spoke of the care she had received as a child from her mother, and also identified herself as a care giver from the time she had looked after other children at the special school she attended, through looking after both her parents when they became ill, and through her work in residential child care. It also included the wife of a man (who had died before I spoke to her) who had developed dementia, who not only talked about her husband's caring responsibilities for his aunt and younger sister, and her care for her mother who had lived with them, but also told the story of their son who had developed severe mental health problems and who had disappeared out of their lives many years before. In my naivety I had not expected nor been prepared for the complexities of the caring relationships I learned about through these interviews. There is similar evidence of multiple caring relationships throughout the life course in Forbat's (2005) study of care givers and care receivers.

What these stories and the accounts generated by others who have explored caring relationships within families have uncovered are the ways in which families negotiate an ethic of care in their everyday lives (Finch and Mason, 1993; Brechin et al, 2003; Williams, 2004a; Morris, 2007; Breheny and Stephens, 2009). To these research-based accounts we need to add the reflections and understandings, often hard won, that come from academics and others who write about care in their professional lives and who have personal experience of intimate caring relationships. These include Eva Feder Kittay, a philosopher who draws on her experiences of being a mother to her disabled daughter Sesha in developing her sophisticated ideas about care ethics, and in reflecting more broadly on the academic discipline of moral philosophy in which she has spent her working life (Kittay, 1999; Kittay and Carlson, 2010); Barbara Hillyer (1993) who explores what it means as a feminist to try to enable her disabled daughter Jenny to become the woman she wants to be; Judith Okely (1999), an anthropologist who had studied ageing in Europe and who found herself undertaking personal ethnography as she sought to understand what was happening to her mother, who was subsequently found to have died from Creutzfeldt-Jakob disease (CJD); and Linda Grant (1999) a journalist who tells the story of her mother as she develops dementia and how she, as her daughter, struggles to relate both to the woman her mother was and who she has become.

None of the women cared for by Kittay, Hillyer, Okely or Grant are in a position to write their own accounts of what it means to them to be cared for, or of the ethical or personal dilemmas they face as they seek to become an adult disabled woman, or to retain their personhood in the face of dementia or CJD. Jenny Morris (1991, 1995), a disabled feminist, has researched the subjective experiences of disabled women and what 'being cared for' means to them in the context of parent–daughter and partner relationships. For some, receiving care was experienced as one aspect of the expression of love, while for others, particularly those receiving help from parents, being looked after contributed to a feeling of unwelcome dependence. Morris's perspective as a feminist also led her to focus on experiences of powerlessness and abuse within relationships between disabled women, parents and partners.

What all these accounts remind us of is that we cannot read off from any 'type' of personal relationship within which care is given and received an assumption about whether it is 'good' or 'bad'. They reflect the personal and interpersonal struggles and conflicts involved in care, but they do not suggest that abandoning care for a less emotionally or ethically charged concept such as 'help' or 'support' will be helpful in understanding how such struggles can be supported to enable the well-being of both care givers and care receivers.

What is significant about an ethic of care perspective in the way that it has been developed by Tronto, Sevenhuijsen and others, in relation to the political as well as the personal significance of care, is that we can no longer understand the relationships within which care is given and received as solely 'personal' or 'private'. Care cannot be separated from other aspects of interpersonal relationships that embody gendered expectations, power relationships and the potential for abuse as well as nurturing. People's capacity to do care well within families is affected by the extent to which care is valued and supported socially and practically.

The expansion of activism within the disabled people's movement, the mental health service user/survivor movement and the carer movement has led to personal accounts from diverse perspectives that offer insights relevant to understanding the experiences of care giving and care receiving (Parker, 1993; Swain et al, 1993). Many of these accounts reflect the personal and political dimensions of care giving and receiving, from the perspective of care givers whose experiences have sometimes led them to campaign both on behalf of carers and of disabled people (Hillyer, 1993; Barnes, 2006), and activists within the disability and survivor movements whose campaigning has included opposition to the perceived oppression of both lay and paid care givers (Beresford, 2008). The feminist slogan 'the personal is the political' has been adopted within the disability movement (Campbell and Oliver, 1996) and an obvious success of the carer movement has been to make public the significance of personal care giving (Barnes, 2011a). Care within families has been brought into the public domain and an ethic of care offers a perspective within which to understand both its challenges and significance.

The personal, interpersonal and ethical negotiations that arise from living with a loved one who is or becomes disabled, mentally ill or physically frail are neither easy nor straightforward, nor are they often explicit. They take place within particular personal, social and cultural contexts, and they demonstrate the way in which difficult decisions over the 'right' or the 'best' thing to do intersect both with personal histories and individual subjectivities. They also reflect the way in which care, dependency, autonomy and relationality are constructed within dominant discourses. Care giving and receiving are part of family life in most situations, but there are particular contexts in which such negotiations take on especial significance in terms of personal survival, well-being and people's capacity to develop or sustain a social presence beyond the family. These contexts also highlight the broader social and political significance of care as a value in promoting the worth of people whose need or dependency is greatest, and also provide a focus for contestations over 'rights not care'. These include what happens when parents separate or divorce and decisions need to be made over care of and contact with children; when families are living in a situation of material disadvantage and in physical environments that make everyday survival a struggle; and when migration and spatial separation mean that sustaining contact is hard work and that cultural differences and marginalisation also need to be negotiated in working out how best to care (eg Mason, 2004; Baldassar, 2007). Such situations also include the experience of giving birth to a disabled child and all that flows from this; of mental health difficulties and the impact of this on either or both one's capacities to care for others and on existing close relationships; and of ageing and the physical, emotional, health and relational changes that often accompany this.

A key argument of an ethic of care is that care as practice and as moral and political value cannot be understood in the abstract. We need to consider the lived experiences of giving and receiving care, and how context, conflicts and power impact the difficult moral decisions as well as the practical tasks of care. It is not possible to do justice to all these different contexts within this chapter and so I have selected three examples in order to offer some insights into the different dynamics involved. These are care among families at times of change and in difficulty; relationships between mothers, fathers and disabled children, and the impact of ageing on older people themselves and care relations within families.

Families in change and difficulty

Anxiety over the consequences of changing family norms and structures has been a feature of both official and populist discourse for decades. One perspective on this has been to identify a 'loss of commitment, a self-seeking individualism, a parenting deficit and a moral decline' (Williams, 2004a, p 6). In part in response to this Fiona Williams and her colleagues carried out a programme of research – Care Values and the Future of Welfare or CAVA – to explore people's practices in their relationships with those close to them and what this suggested about their commitments and the way they negotiated 'the right thing to do' in times of change. The overall conclusion of this programme, which considered how people negotiated parenting following divorce, and whether it was better to be a 'full-time' parent or to go out to work in order to provide as well as possible for their children, was that: 'Far from the dystopian vision of self-seeking individualism and moral decline which fills public debate, we found people who are seeking to create new moral frameworks in which "fairness" to and "respect" for others are key aspirations' (p 41). One way of understanding family life that emerges from these studies is that a key task for families is to develop practical, everyday ethics to ensure good enough care for children, but also for partners. And in the context of separation and divorce, as in others where, for example, a parent is disabled or becomes ill, children need to be understood not only as recipients but as givers of care and as moral agents actively engaged in processes of care within families (Haugen, 2007). Haugen's analysis of the story of Nora, a teenage girl whose parents have divorced, demonstrates not only the extra responsibilities that Nora takes on following her parents' divorce and the worsened financial situation that results from this, but also the emotional labour involved in 'shielding' her mother from information about her father and his new family that might hurt her. A key task for social policy is to create the context within which people of all ages can negotiate their caring commitments, and this requires valuing care as both ethic and practice.

The families in the CAVA studies were often facing difficult financial circumstances and relationship issues, but they had not been identified as 'problematic' or 'needy' and thus a focus for professional intervention. In the UK when families were considered unable to or incapable of continuing to look after one or more of their children the intervention of social services authorities used to be referred to as 'taking the children into care' – that is, the local authority took over parental responsibility. This terminology is no longer used. Following the passage of the 1989 Children Act, children became 'looked after and accommodated' – another reflection of ambivalence about the concept of 'care' and the wish to remove this from both official and professional discourse. However, it is still the case that a key task for social workers is the assessment of parents' abilities to care for their children at times of difficulty. These contexts include circumstances where one or both parents have significant drug or alcohol problems, or are experiencing mental health problems; in cases where there is domestic violence or child abuse within the family; or where the child's behaviour is considered out of control and there is concern that the child is demonstrating violent or abusive behaviour and/or drug and alcohol problems. It is less often the case that poverty or material disadvantage is a cause for intervention, though such experiences may well be part of a complex set of circumstances that such families have to negotiate. Anne Power (2007) has explored the experiences of families living in disadvantaged inner city neighbourhoods. Many live in poverty, and this clearly constrains their capacity to enable their children to experience the range of activities they would wish. But it is often factors such as fear of the behaviour of others on the streets, and in particular the level of crime in the areas in which they live, that constrain their sense of being able to care as they would want. Fear can lead parents to prioritise tight controls over their children in the knowledge that this may also restrict chances for development.

Intervention in cases where parenting has been judged to be inadequate can result in a number of outcomes, including the child being removed from the family and accommodated elsewhere; formal care being transferred from parents to grandparents or other family members; or supervision and support being provided to the parents to enable the child to continue living safely with them. High-profile cases where children have been 'removed' in circumstances that have subsequently been demonstrated not to be dangerous, or not removed and subsequently abused and killed by parents or other family members, emphasise the emotionally charged, ethically and professionally complex nature of such cases.

At the core of professional intervention with families in these situations is a question about whether all parents can care for their children and whether normative conceptions of what care looks like are adequate to encompass what can be chaotic relationships and apparently 'care less' practices. However, recent work has looked at what happens when such families are given the opportunity to develop their own ideas about how to address acknowledged problems regarding the care and nurturing available to their children. It suggests a care ethic can operate within contexts that do not immediately appear conducive to care. Family group conferences are designed to bring together all those within the family network who are considered to have a role to play in resolving difficulties (Marsh and Crow, 1997). The aim is to provide a space within which family members can propose how the situation can be improved and what help is needed from formal services to enable this. In a study of the operation of such conferences in one local authority in England, Kate Morris (2007) demonstrated not only that the outcomes from this process (at least in the short term) were more likely to avoid the use of formal care arrangements and alternative accommodation for children, but also that families used the conferences as safe spaces in which they could articulate their ethic of care. Here is one of the examples cited by Morris.

Child C was placed with the local authority because of her mother's chaotic lifestyle and imprisonment for prostitution. She needed a long-term stable placement, something her grandmother wanted to offer. The family plan says (written by the grandmother):

> I want to care for C full time, give her love and support she needs ... she is my flesh and blood and I will do everything to help her. I will take her to nursery or playgroups I will go with her to see places. I will teach her all the things she needs to know. We all as a family want what is best for C,

> we want her to read, write, interact with other kids ... I want her to be herself as C. (pp 18-19)

This statement is an important expression of what care means in enabling the nurturing and growth of children to become relational beings, who are able to develop their own identities within a family and wider social network. It not only expresses a commitment to care for this child, but to do so in a way that enables her to develop other relationships in and through which she may give and receive care. It reflects an understanding of care as practical, moral and relational and reminds us that many of the assumptions of 'good' parenting that are based in middle class values and practices adopt an exclusive view of care.

But it is obviously also the case that some families are not able to care for their children and when birth families are no longer considered able to continue to care safely, one option is that children may be fostered within another family setting. Pithouse and Rees (2011) have considered foster care from an ethic of care perspective noting that care for fostered children may be 'complicated, contrary and contingent' (p 198), but reflects similar open ended and emotional processes that are at play in biological families. Care is refracted though everyday processes such as sharing meals, the enabling of bodily care and the nurturing that takes place through this, and through the touch that is necessary to children's emotional and physical development. However in this context, perhaps in a way that is related to parenting of disabled children, 'caring as an applied art of everyday living' (p 207), is, of necessity, a more self-conscious process and one in which the contested ethical and relational dimensions call forth greater sensitivities and sensibilities than is the case in most families.

I suggested in Chapter One that we need to be discriminating in our use of the term 'care'. We cannot assume that the way in which parents treat their children, or children treat their parents, necessarily embodies care. But an ethic of care perspective with its emphasis on the particular and the contextual helps us recognise care that might be given and received in different ways in families that are having to negotiate difficult circumstances.

Mothers, fathers and disabled children

The relationship between parents (particularly mothers) and their disabled children has been one of the key points of contention between the aspirations and campaigning of disabled people for recognition of their rights as autonomous adults, and recognition of the importance of care as a source of well-being and social justice. Barbara Hillyer (1993), writing of the situation in the US, is scathing of the mother-blaming stance of parts of the disability movement there, while in the UK attempts to find an accommodation between what have been seen as opposing camps have not been entirely successful. Sara Ryan and Katherine Runswick-Cole (2008), both non-disabled mothers of disabled children, have written of occupying a position of liminality, both because of being non-disabled researchers of disability, and because of the distance between being a mother, and being the mother of a disabled child. My purpose here is not to 'take sides' but to consider how an ethic of care can help understand the processes of negotiation that are part of the everyday life of parents and their disabled children as they learn to live and grow together. I argue that an emphasis on relationality, rather than on competing rights, offers a better way of understanding the lived experiences of carers and those who receive care.

One focus for the different perspectives of disabled people and their parents is the widespread experience of giving birth to a disabled child as embodying some aspects of loss. This contrasts with the resistance of disabled people to the notion that their lives are personal tragedies that should generate such feelings among those who are close to them. Mark Liam Brown is the father of a disabled son and has worked with me as a research student. He has written various pieces about his experiences, to be included in training materials for professionals as well as in workshop sessions with other parents. Appealing to professionals to understand what it means to parent a disabled child, he writes:

> Thinking back all I can remember is a sense of numbness. I had seen the train coming, felt the growing sense of concern; the awareness that he was somehow different somehow not what we had thought. I can't remember the words that the consultant used, I don't know if it was done delicately, if he was sensitive to our situation, although I suspect he was. All I can remember is feeling numb. Was it grief? Was it some sense of chronic loss? Had my middle class expectations of brilliance, university, marriage and grandchildren been shattered by the impact of those few words? Probably.

Mothers such as Hillyer (1993) and others she cites identify grief, sorrow and loss associated with the birth of a disabled child as chronic states that may reappear at particular milestones in the anticipated or actual stages of child and adult development. In my study of carers Nell, working class mother to James, described her experience as one of bereavement and suggested that it is not only middle class parental hopes that can be dashed.

> When you're pregnant you think your child will be prime minister or play for England, or whatever your aspirations are. And then you have to let go of all these things, like they are never going to get a job, and they are never going to have a family, they are never going to be able to give you grandchildren [pause] and they are never really going to be able to survive without people around them. (Barnes, 2006, p 56)

It is precisely the recognition that disabled children need others in order to survive for longer than most other children that is at the heart of an ethic of care in this context. And it is the challenge for mothers and fathers of learning how to support a disabled child as they grow from childhood through adolescence and into adulthood, in a way that enables them to be as close as possible to who they want to be, without burdening them with the weight of disappointed aspirations or continuing to feel that they are 'indispensible' (Shakespeare, 2000, p 47), that embodies the depth of understanding about the significance of care that comes from this experience. Parents of disabled children experience transitions in the process of parenting that are different from those experienced by parents of non-disabled children. For example, in a Norwegian study Ytterhus et al (2008) discuss the practical and existential/emotional transitions that occur when their disabled children are between 8 and 11. These are associated with changes in the supports available at this stage, changes in the way in which children start to interact with peers and the shift between providing intimate care for a 'small' and a 'big' child.

How parents respond to parenting disabled children reflects different aspects of people's lives, identities and experiences. Nell came from a background that assumed that women would get married and have children (Barnes, 2006). She had to learn not only how to enable James to access experiences that other teenagers and young adults expect – donning a leather jacket to take him to rock concerts, for example – but how to recognise her own worth as 'not only' a mother, but someone who understood disability and care giving and who could become an effective advocate and supporter of other mothers through her public role in a carers' organisation. In helping her disabled daughter to become a woman, feminist Barbara Hillyer had to learn to recognise that all women have limitations, that being a 'whole person' can include being a whole person who has disabilities, just as she herself is a whole person who has had to learn 'to live outside the illusion of self-sufficiency and to accept help' (1993, pp 247-8). Her perspective as the feminist mother of a disabled daughter is a counterpoint to Jenny Morris's perspective as a disabled feminist. In her work Morris has explored the struggles of young disabled women seeking to move into adulthood and to negotiate separation from their parents (Morris, 1995). Both she and Walmsley (1993) have identified the shift in relationships and the reciprocity that can emerge when disabled children start to care for parents as they grow older. For Eva Feder Kittay, the personal professional journey that she has undergone, in applying her experiences as the mother of a cognitively disabled daughter to her own analysis of dependency work, has also involved the development of a broader critique of moral philosophy. She has taken on those who argue that people like her daughter do not share with others the fundamental characteristics that qualify them to be recognised as 'human' (Kittay, 2010).

Men also struggle with both gendered assumptions about care and with how to negotiate power within caring relationships. Mark Brown, whose learning disabled son was 16 when he wrote the following reflections, considered what fathering meant to him both before and after he learned of his son's disability. In doing so he acknowledges that he does not conform to the traditional image of a father.

> ... the earliest thing I can remember, was feeding and singing. Feeding was fun because of the amount of time that you would spend looking into their eyes and these bright shiny orbs of colour and life would somehow seem to smile all on their own. It's an incredibly relaxing experience and I've come to the conclusion that it's almost impossible not to smile when you are looking into the eyes of a feeding child; unless of course if they've got wind. I used to sing a lot too, with my son in the rucksack on my back, I'd wash up, hoover and iron. If he got upset I'd sing to him, gently rocking him either to sleep or back to a smile. (This and subsequent quotes come from a personal communication)

As Robert grew older Mark's fathering encountered the impact of public responses to his son – strangers evidencing 'discomfort and unease as they mentally decide whether or not my son represents some form of threat to their well being' – and his own uncertainties about his use of parental power. Currently, this is focused around Robert's reluctance to go to school and Mark's reluctance to accept that it is OK for him not to do so.

> Does my son have the capacity to decide whether or not he wants to go to school? Yes he undoubtedly does, does this mean that I should respect his decision to not to want to go to school? Well up until the end of the academic year in which he turned 16, I have encouraged and verbally insisted that he goes to school. But what happens then after he has finished his year 11, do I still have the right to insist that he goes to school because I deem it to be good for him? I may disagree with his choice to want to stay at home, because I think that it is unwise and not in his long term best interests – or mine for that matter – but do I have the right to try and impose my logic and rationality on his choices.

Such experiences are particular examples of common conflicts between parents and teenage children. For example, the majority of the disabled children in a study by Connors and Stalker (2007) emphasised what they had in common with their non-disabled peers, including struggles with their parents to gain greater independence.

In each of the very different, named cases discussed earlier the parents have struggled to find ways to enable their children to grow as well as possible. They have experienced disablism with their children (Ryan and Runswick-Cole, 2008). They have also used their personal learning to share insights with others. They have shown, both personally and politically, the importance of care, and, in turn, the recognition given to care givers has supported the development of a carer movement that has had important impacts on social policies (Barnes, 2011a). Traustadottir's (2000) study of women carers identified a number who engaged in what she termed 'extended caring' and took part in a range of advocacy activities: 'The majority of the mothers, workers and friends who participated in this study had a vision of a better and more just society. They were on a mission to change things: they wanted to create a society where people with disabilities are welcomed, accepted and included' (p 260).

This approach to advocacy is often rooted in the practicalities of families' everyday lives. Mark Brown also wrote:

> ... as any family with an older disabled child will tell you, there is nothing less precious about a disabled child, they are no less likely to be good people, they are no less likely to love and no less likely to be happy; they are sometimes more likely to have to endure pain and sometimes in doing so they will be heroic. But the challenges they face will arise as much from the stupidity and ignorance of those who believe they are tragic, as they will from the nature of their impairment.

The belief that severely disabled children are unable to communicate and interact is one of the ideas that underpins the notion of the disabled child as tragic. In the intensive interaction that characterises everyday caring many parents are able to develop meaningful insights into the creativity of their children's communication. Mark uses a semiotic approach to his son's multimodal means of communication which he argues can only be interpreted through close knowledge of his interests and his idiosyncratic use of vocabulary and symbol. Thus any understanding of how Mark's son feels about his daily life and the care he receives from his father and other family members comes from the ways in which he expresses himself symbolically and the words and descriptions of others who know him well. The ability of parents to understand what their communication disabled children have to say relies on their close attentiveness to their child's emotional responses and their non-verbal communication (Barnes, 1997b) as the story of Peggy and Sesha Kittay (told in Chapter Two) also demonstrates. Rose, another of the mothers I interviewed for my study of carers, spoke with sadness and frustration about other people's assumptions about her daughter's lack of understanding because she was unable to communicate this verbally.

> We know how she feels and we know what she understands and everything. If she was there, my son was just that way and he was playing and she was – her eyes would go towards him. And she was looking at him and my dad couldn't believe it. He said that she knows her brother .... (Barnes, 2006, p 39)

This attentiveness relates to a finely tuned understanding of how their children respond to the way they are treated. Rose is well aware of the balance between Surya's enjoyment of lively action and her fear of voices raised in anger. The affective dimension of experience and communication takes on a particular significance when the cognitive dimension is less developed. When I interviewed Rose, Surya was 7 years old and Rose's main anxiety was that she should receive the care and treatment that would enable her to grow to adulthood. Both Eva Feder Kittay and Barbara Hillyer have reflected on the changes in their relationships with their daughters as they have reached adulthood, as did Nell about her son James. After a crisis that meant Nell was no longer prepared to have James living with her she realised his need to develop his own life separately from her. She helped him find and establish his own accommodation and has continued to support him alongside the paid support workers and technology that enable him to live in his own home. Nell described their current relationship as a very loving one and mother and son maintain a very close relationship. Both Sesha Kittay and Jennifer Hillyer moved into residential accommodation with other young people with cognitive disabilities. In these cases, as in many such contexts, there is a shift from 'care giving' to 'taking care of' that does not mark the 'end' of care, but a transition in the way in which this is expressed.

The processes of individuation that take place as children move into adulthood are often more drawn out for disabled children. This transition to greater independence from parents can require more conscious planning and exploration of options. As Walmsley (1993), Morris (1995) and Ward (2011) demonstrate, in some cases children do not move away and they may become carers for their parents as they grow older. One thing that parenting disabled children demonstrates is that what constitutes a 'normal' family encompasses a range of circumstances and experiences. The virtues, challenges, isolations and overprotectiveness, as well as the joys, reciprocities and simple enjoyment of each other's company, that are all a potential part of mothering and fathering non-disabled children are also part of what it means to live with disabled children. Finding ways for parents to care for themselves and each other may be both harder and more necessary than is the case with non-disabled children. Reflecting on the high divorce rate in families with disabled children Mark Brown commented:

> In a family where both the man and the woman adopt the role of carer the more repetitive aspects of care can be shared and stopped from being a grind or a burden. In a family where there is a stark division of labour according to traditionally gendered identities then the more repetitive aspects of care tend to fall on the shoulders of the '*mother*'... Once established as a system of relations and identity within

> a family with a disabled child and reinforced by a system of support that is equally gendered if not institutionally sexist, this set of relationships makes the adoption of a caring identity problematic for men.

The significance and ambivalence of care in old age

Care in old age is an issue that has broad and increasing significance as populations age. The demographic shifts that have been a focus for policy debate in Western societies for many years are now starting to become apparent in countries in Central and South America, India and other states where social policy has previously been focused primarily on issues relating to children and young families (ECLAC, 2007). Global ageing requires not only consideration of how the costs of increased longevity can be met to ensure justice for all generations, but also learning about how we can live well together in an unfamiliar situation in which the number of older people outstrips the number of children, and living to be 100 or more is increasingly common. The number of people living to the age of 100 or more in the UK more than quadrupled from 2,600 in 1981 to 11,600 in 2009. By 2033 it is estimated that there will be almost 80,000 people aged 100 or over. By 2034 it is estimated that 23% of the population will be 65 or over compared with 18% under 16 (www.statistics.gov.uk). Central to our capacity to respond well in this situation is how we can learn to give and receive care without this being seen as burdensome and an indication of moral weakness.

Older people are well schooled in what Fineman (2004) has called 'the Autonomy Myth'. English social policy constructs well-being in old age as linked to independence and active consumption.

> In developing modern public services for older people, our overarching objective is to promote well-being and independence. We want to achieve a society where older people are active consumers of public services, exercising control and choice, not passive recipients. (DWP, 2009, p 44)

Similar positions are evident in the policy discourses in other Western states (eg Breheny and Stephens, 2009; Walker, 2009). As I and colleagues have argued, contemporary conceptions of well-being place a high bar for 'being well' and assume a forward-looking, active individual that does not sit well with the reality of life for many older people, particularly those who are the 'older old' (Ward et al, 2012). We have adopted instead the notion of being 'well enough', recognising that well-being does not necessitate independence, but can co-exist with needing the support of others in their everyday lives. Taylor (2011, p 783) argues normative conceptions of well-being 'employ a unitary notion of the rational actor fully in control of a set of actions cognitively oriented toward self-fulfilment'. When older people talk about what well-being means to them and what contributes to their experience of this, they reflect their concerns about becoming a burden, their unwillingness to seek help and yet the importance of care in their everyday lives to retaining a sense of their own value. How they are treated by others within their close family interacts with the more public discourse of the worthlessness of dependency to shape their responses and experiences.

We can see this in the account of Grace, a 97-year-old widow who lives on her own and whose mobility problems mean that she is unable to get out to do her shopping without being taken by car. She has a son whom she sees regularly, but, while he does take her shopping, he offers a purely functional service with little conversation or sense that he values being with her. He does not demonstrate care as he provides this help. This leads Grace to maintain a fierce independence:

> 'I never ask the family to do anything, not a thing,' but at the same time 'My heart's breaking but I mean I've cried all the tears but then I sit down and I think "pull yourself together there's nothing you can do about it, just take it as it comes."' She contrasts the functional service offered by her son with the way in which similar help is provided by a friend's son who makes her feel 'just like the queen' by making a shopping trip a special outing. 'You know he says "Don't you dare open the car, I'll do that!" Opens the car, gets the … I say "Darling, I can put my seatbelt on, I'm not helpless," and he says "You'll do as you're told when you're out with me." And he treats … it's just wonderful, he's such a darling.' (Ward et al, 2012, p 73)

The attitude of her son and his wife results in Grace asserting her independence – she spoke of crawling on the floor rather than asking for their help, while that of her friend enables her to adopt what might be seen as a posture of dependency, but in fact makes her feel she is being well treated and valued, rather than patronised because of her frailty.

Elsewhere studies have suggested that it is the capacity to construct care receiving in terms of reciprocity for care giving that enables older people to accept help without challenging their self-identification as independent adults (Breheny and Stephens, 2009). Forbat (2005) identifies different ways in which family histories are used to frame what is regarded as normal reciprocation of care within families, even in cases where adult children express ambivalence about having experienced care in the past. She also identifies the way in which intimate care for parents can be 'normalised' by reference to similar care previously received. She quotes a son caring for his elderly mother.

> I used to say 'how many times did you wipe my bum when I was a baby nobody complained you didn't complain about that you just did it didn't you?' So that's how I looked at it. (Forbat, 2005, p 145)

In this instance what might be taboo cross-gender care giving is made acceptable by comparing it with the care of a mother for her baby, and by acknowledging the reciprocal nature of care at different stages of life. Care for older spouses or partners is often a continuing expression of love that requires difficult adaptations to changed circumstances. But it is rarely seen as a decision to give care in response to care received in the past. When pressed, spouse carers may acknowledge that they have 'received' benefits from their partners and current care may be conceptualised as a form of 'repayment' (Forbat, 2005, p 146), but this is rarely a calculated exchange. In some cases 'unidirectional' care characterises all or most of married life, as in the case of Eddie whose wife developed depression following the birth of their daughter and who continues to care for her in his 80s (Ward, Barnes and Gahagan, 2012). In other cases, older spouses and partners care for each other through illness and frailty and the contemporaneous reciprocity that characterises such relationships means it makes little sense to identify one as care giver and the other as care receiver. Care arises from and is given through a committed relationship.

In other contexts, for example siblings caring for brothers or sisters in old age, reciprocity is less evident. Lydia responded as follows to a question from me about whether her older sister, whom she was currently caring for, had ever looked after her.

> No. The only time that she, when my son was tiny she would, of course money was very tight with me, she would buy him a suit or clothes. She looked out for [son] but I can't ever remember her sort of looking out for me at all. Perhaps she did and I didn't notice. (Barnes, 2012)

It could be considered that there is reciprocity of sorts here, but it is not the basis on which Lydia is caring for her sister. For her and other brothers and sisters caring for siblings in older age, the primary source of their accepting responsibility to care is the awareness of need in the context of the normative expectations of family life. Diana had never particularly liked her brother and certainly saw no reciprocity in terms of any help she had received from him. She cared for him: 'Because it's family, blood, blood's thicker than water and I promised my mum before she died that I would look after him or keep my eye on him' (Barnes, 2012).

The older people in Breheny and Stephens' (2009) study are younger older people (between 55 and 70), and have not had to respond to the transitions of advanced old age. At 97 Grace spoke with sadness about having to give up the voluntary work that she undertook until the age of 92 because of her mobility problems and the reluctance of the organisation she worked with to continue to accept her as a volunteer. This had contributed to her sense of losing a valued identity. Her feeling that her son and his wife were waiting for her to die in order to move house exacerbated her sense of worthlessness. Breheny and Stephens recognise that the older people they spoke to could still invoke a range of skills and resources to reciprocate help. But they also cite work carried out in an assisted living facility (Beel-Bates et al, 2007) that identified ways in which older people with fewer resources than those in their study could demonstrate reciprocity for the care they received. They did this through participation in community activities, pleasantness to staff and family, and expressions of gratitude.

While an ethic of care recognises that we have all received care at some stage in our lives, the principles discussed in Chapter Two do not 'require' reciprocity as a basis for care giving. It is not a calculation of what may be owed in response to what has been received in the past, but rather attentiveness to current need that prompts care. But it seems that in a social and cultural context in which dependence is associated with worthlessness, reciprocity can become an important resource in everyday care negotiations. Yet, while the notion that care received in old age can be construed as a demonstration of reciprocity for care given when younger is a common one, this is not always the case in practice. As Grace's story illustrates, explicit or implicit appeals to this principle are not always successful in generating care. Nor is it the case that care givers necessarily feel that their actions in giving care are based on a previous or anticipated receipt of care. The idea of care giving and receiving as a straightforward calculus of exchange cannot account for much of the care that is given and received within families. Its resonance is more complex than this and we once again need to understand how reciprocity 'works' by considering actual social and personal relationships.

One aspect of the longevity that characterises contemporary societies is the increased life expectancy of people with learning disabilities (Mencap, 2007). This has generated concern about the capacity of older people to continue to care for their adult children, and a situation in which sibling care is becoming more evident (Dew at al, 2004; Bowey and McGlaughlin, 2005). But another consequence is the emergence of another form of reciprocity – care for ageing parents by adults with learning disabilities who have previously been regarded as care recipients (Walmsley, 1993; Ward, 2011). Ward has argued that an ethic of care can help challenge the positioning of people with learning disabilities as dependent and in need of protection: 'Recognising and acknowledging their role as mutual carers has the power to relocate them as capable individuals engaged in relational autonomy' (p 174). For people with learning disabilities themselves, being able to provide care, and being recognised as someone who *can* give something back, offers a sense of pride and enables them to challenge other people's perceptions of them as lacking in capability. As one mother cited by Ward said of her adult daughter with learning disabilities: 'I don't know what I'd do without her' (p 170). In a rather different context, one of the women interviewed for our study on older people and well-being was a 75-year-old woman with learning disabilities who had moved to live with a family (not related by kinship) after spending most of her life in residential care. For Mary this involved learning to live in a family group for the first time and both receiving and giving care within this context (Ward, Barnes and Gahagan, 2012). In such contexts the capacity to reciprocate care is inflected with a powerful political as well as personal significance. To give care is a liberating experience and care cannot be given without also being received.

Thus while reciprocity can play an important role in caring relationships, we need to consider how it operates in different contexts. Kittay notes that interdependencies of caring relationships are common, but that reciprocity in care does not necessarily fit standard relationships of parity in which the 'efforts I exert on your behalf will be met by some equivalent exertion on your part, immediately, at some specified time in the future, or when need arises' (1999, p 67). Rather she refers to 'a linked and nested set of social relations' (p 68) which captures the importance of social cooperation to ensure support for care givers as well as for those identified as in need of care. The standard dyadic model of reciprocity may not be available and this should not mean that care cannot be given in these circumstances, or if it is given, it should not be at the grave expense of the care givers. Responsibilities for care cannot be encompassed solely within family relationships, even if this is where most of the care giving takes place.

> Reciprocation from the charge may never be possible. The dependency worker is entitled not to a reciprocity from the charge herself, but to a relationship that sustains her as she sustains her charge. (p 68)

It is perhaps the care that is given and received within families to people with dementia that is the paradigm case for a situation in which reciprocation from the person cared for cannot be expected. The changes in behaviours, activities, interactions and expectations resulting from dementia affect the individual concerned, their loved ones and close family members. They have significant impacts on family dynamics, and on social networks. The challenges that these changes offer to assumptions about 'normal' interactions and the basis on which these are built are profound. The moral dilemmas that are posed are both mundane and fundamental to the way in which the status of the person with dementia as a person may be sustained or undermined. For example Daniel, a man interviewed in my study of care givers, talked of his uncertainty about how to respond when he discovered that his wife, who had dementia and had been admitted to residential care following a stroke that left her unable to walk and him unable to carry out the physical assistance with mobility that she needed, had had her mattress put on the floor to prevent her falling from bed (Barnes, 2006, chapter 5). He knew his wife would have been unhappy about this when she was well, but she appeared not to be upset in her current situation. What should he do? Should he challenge the practice on the basis of knowing how his wife would have responded before she developed dementia, or should he accept her current response and the 'best interests' argument of staff? One of the issues for Daniel was that he felt alone both in dealing with the moral dilemmas he faced as her carer in this context, and in adapting to being 'without' her in his everyday life.

> I go home; I don't think anybody knows I'm alive actually. People that come, they come to see you here, nobody comes to see me. I'm there, by myself, looking after myself, cooking my meals and doing everything that's got to be done – the

> washing, the ironing. I have a woman that comes in to do the vacuuming and polishing one day a week, that's all. (p 91)

Daniel sought to retain caring responsibilities for his wife after her move to residential care and this constituted his continued reason for living, but he was also very aware of the absence of care for himself and angry about a lack of reciprocity from a welfare state to which he and his wife had contributed for many years.

The significance of everyday talk within families both about and with a relative with dementia can demonstrate how families are attentive to the need for people with dementia to sustain aspects of their personhood in a context in which this may be a source of harm – for themselves or others (Purves, 2011). Purves's fascinating study of the way in which family members position themselves and their relative with dementia (Rose) through talk within the family demonstrates a particular example of negotiating a previously valued role as grandmother in the context of uncertainty about Rose's continuing capacity to look after her grandchildren. The family members in Purves's study demonstrated considerable moral discomfort as they sought to develop strategies to minimise Rose's distress while also recognising that the key roles she used to fulfil, both as grandmother and as family cook, were becoming problematic. These negotiations took place in the context of a close knit family that lived in geographical proximity and had regular contact with each other. The three adult children recognised the importance of developing new storylines that not only accommodated their mother's developing dementia, but that also embraced their father's role as primary care giver. This family perspective, rather than the more usual focus on the dyad of care giver and care receiver, offers an important insight into the processes by which family members seek to develop their own ethical approach to care and to deal with the messy moral dilemmas that are central to care in such contexts. A key resource for the family in doing this is their intimate knowledge of Rose and what is important to her sense of self. In contrast, Brannelly (2006) identifies the way in which concern over the safety of children is used by professional workers to justify an undesired intervention within a family to remove to a residential home the grandfather who has developed dementia. The worker in Brannelly's study uses apparent concern for the care of children to justify an action that demonstrates little attentiveness or responsiveness to the needs of the elderly man, and which involves decisions apparently based on little specific knowledge of the particularity of the situation.

Judith Okely's (1999) discussion of caring for her mother after she developed what was assumed to be dementia, but was later discovered to be CJD, also emphasised the importance to good care of the intimate knowledge that comes from long-term relationships. That knowledge, she demonstrates, is not restricted to an intellectual understanding, but embraces the emotional significance of the impact of cognitive decline that encompasses the public as well as private persona. A major focus for this in the case of Okely's mother was the loss of her driving licence.

> I identified utterly with her pain and anger as I faced a woman who had given birth to me at the height of bombing and the siege of Malta, who had crossed continents as an evacuee with two infants. As a young widow, with only lower school certificate and a pittance, Bridget had made a successful career, first as a social worker and then as a university lecturer. Her great indulgence was high-powered cars ... Now, confronted by her own frailty and diminishing autonomy, it was my turn to be strong. I had to witness her growing helplessness as fate and, what no one guessed, the fatal illness took their surreptitious course. Bridget's arguments were utterly reasonable. Her still powerful intellect responded with full force: she had had no accident, she drove slowly, whereas the young male tearaways who sped round the corner at the back of her house had caused several crashes. (p 28)

Okely's account reveals the struggles that relatives have in learning how to care when they are faced with the impact of cognitive decline. Knowledge of how the person was before dementia affected them is often key to intimate care, but may not be a sufficient condition for caring well. Sabat (2010) demonstrates how such intimate knowledge of the person can be assisted by exchanges with a professional who can offer psychosocial support, counselling and education to the care giver. In this instance the person with dementia was a man who had had a distinguished career in the US military and the care giver was his wife who was described as both devoted to him, and a highly independent woman. Once again, although this account is not framed by specific reference to an ethic of care, it highlights the significance of the moral principles of care. In particular, it highlights the way in which becoming more attentive to the subjective experience of the care receiver, in response to their need to receive care, can enhance both the care that is given and the flourishing of the care giver. It highlights the relationality of care, and demonstrates the importance of care for the care giver to ensure her well-being, not only to enable her to continue to care, but in her own right. It is also another example of how an initially private experience of care giving can lead to a more public advocacy role. In this case, this emerges out of the woman's growing awareness of the way in which people with dementia are demeaned and a determination to challenge this.

Some close relatives make the decision that they cannot become care givers for a person with dementia. An article published in the Alzheimer's Society's magazine *Share* in 2006 told the story of one daughter who had faced the decision about whether she should become the carer of her mother, with whom she had never got on and whom she did not actually like. June Russell said: 'I've been struggling with feeling resentment, and the need to exercise compassion and do the right thing ... I don't want to do it, and am not at all suited'. In this context June's decisions can be understood as a decision to *take care of* her mother by arranging a care package for her and ringing and visiting on a regular basis, rather than by becoming a hands on care giver. A common dilemma for those who do become care givers is whether they should step back from direct care giving and pass this over to specialist workers in residential accommodation (Banks and Barnes, 2011). As the case of June Russell demonstrates, basing such decisions on an understanding of the particularity not only of the needs of the individual but also of the relationships involved can constitute good care.

Conclusion

In this chapter my focus has not been on the physical tasks of care giving, of tending, or on the organisational aspects of care. Rather it has been on the processes of exploring and negotiating the relational dimensions of care and the difficult ethical decision making that is integral to this. For those involved in relationships with older people and for older people themselves, how do they adapt and respond to changes in physical and mental capacities? How can an increasing need for help be negotiated without an older person's personal identity and sense of worth becoming undermined? How can the relationships between spouses, and between adult children and their parents, retain a sense of enjoyment in each other's company and respect for the person a partner or parent was and is? In the case of parents of disabled children, how do they adjust over a lifetime to their changed expectations of a normal trajectory of growth, development and separation and with their personal sense of loss, hurt and grief, at the same time as enabling their children to become who they want to be? How can families, whose lives are chaotic, and who appear to be careless of their own and their children's needs, negotiate a way of caring in difficult circumstances? All these challenges are both relational and ethical and have to be faced alongside the sheer hard graft of care giving. Both care givers and care receivers are engaged in their own work of adaptation and learning through their relationships with each other. Each is seeking to find the right way forward, the best thing to do in what are difficult circumstances, at the same time as trying to enjoy the everyday pleasures of intimate connections with others and to minimise the everyday frustrations of getting along with those you share your world with.

A major strength of a perspective from within a feminist ethic of care is the recognition that care cannot be 'contained' within the moral boundary and private sphere of intimate family relationships. It recognises that such relationships are constructed within social relations of power and inequality and defined within gendered constructions that have assumed an association between women, dependency and care. This can be problematic for men taking on roles as carers as well as for women who feel guilty if they do not 'accept' such roles. In emphasising the relational character of care, an ethic of care calls attention to the experience of the care receiver as well as of the care giver, and also the impossibility of defining people according to such a binary distinction. People take on different roles at the same and different times throughout their life course and family life encompasses complex caring histories as family composition and relationships change over space and time. An ethic of care names care as a political as well as a private issue and one that demands a response from public services to enable social justice. For the family members who are exploring the intense care relationships that have been the focus of this chapter, the support they get from those who are paid to care can make a big difference. In Chapter Four I develop an analysis of paid care work and consider the interaction between this and unpaid care giving.

FOUR

Working at care

Modern welfare states accept some responsibility for ensuring the well-being of those who become ill or frail, are born or become disabled, or experience difficulties and disadvantage through poverty or other forms of material deprivation. The precise division of responsibility between public and private, state and family, is a matter of ideological, cultural and political debate and both the practice and study of social policy focuses substantially on where this boundary should lie and how this should be determined. Similarly, the question of *who* a state accepts responsibility for is contested and shifting. Attempts under the Poor Law to define the deserving and the undeserving poor have been re-configured in debates about which families, which children, which disabled people, and which older people should be entitled to support and which should be left to take responsibility for their own welfare and well-being. At a policy level an ethic of care analysis can and has been applied to the way in which such decisions are framed, how such responsibilities are expressed and what assumptions are made both about the nature of what it is to be human and what values should underpin policy decisions (Sevenhuijsen, 2000, 2003a, 2003b; Williams, 2004b; Barnes, 2011b).

But here I want to consider what an ethic of care analysis can offer to understanding what it is that the diverse cohorts of 'care workers' do and what they seek to achieve as they work to carry out the state's responsibilities for ensuring welfare and well-being. The range of job titles and responsibilities is vast: social worker, care assistant, nurse, occupational therapist, counsellor, play worker, day-care worker, bathing assistant, domiciliary care worker, personal assistant, doctor and physiotherapist are simply a selection. Care has become qualified: we need to know whether it is medical care, health care, nursing care, community care or social care that is needed, in order to determine who has responsibility for 'delivery' and whose budget should pay for it. As welfare states have developed, as the notion of welfare societies has evolved, and as care work has become more specialised, a number of significant issues have become evident. First, the status associated with such roles and tasks is very variable, including the extent to which they are recognised as 'professional' roles, and how well they are rewarded financially and respected socially. Associated with this is the question of who undertakes these roles: the division of labour according to gender, ethnicity and country of origin of such workers is significant. Second, where are these workers employed? The distribution of care workers between state agencies and private (for profit) and voluntary or Third Sector organisations is fluid and varies between states in relation to decisions about the nature and extent of state responsibility for welfare and well-being. And third, both the terms used to describe the work undertaken and the content of the jobs themselves have changed not only as a result of developments in the knowledge base, but as a result of challenges from the recipients of services and a consequent rethinking of what the relationship between workers and service users should be.

It is also important to note some additional points before applying an ethic of care perspective to care work. Changes in the architecture of welfare states and the proliferation of specialties have generated a need for systems that enable coordination, cooperation, collaboration or partnership between workers employed in different agencies and often in different sectors. This has resulted in the creation of partnership modes of governance and service delivery (eg Glendinning et al, 2002), and is also associated with more participatory modes of policy making (see Chapter Eight). But for the purposes of this chapter, the implications for interdisciplinary working also relate to different ways of thinking about care and the different approaches to ethics and professional ethical codes adopted by different groups of workers (Banks, 2010). As Brannelly (2011) has demonstrated, it is not enough for one worker to apply an ethical sensitivity to care work if others involved in decision making do not share the approach. And finally, the expansion of information and communication technologies into care work have created a situation in which we can no longer assume that 'care' only involves face to face contact between a human provider and recipient. The question of what 'telecare' means for what I have been assuming up to now are the necessary characteristics of care has yet to be fully addressed. We need to consider the ethical and relational implications of an increasing reliance on technology for delivering services intended to maintain independence.

Thus, applying an ethic of care to an analysis of care work requires a focus not only on what care workers do, but also on the circumstances in which they do it, both in terms of their relationships with those to whom they provide care, and their position as workers in agencies responsible for 'taking care of' the needs of those considered eligible for services. Peta Bowden (1997, 2000) has argued in relation to nursing that two versions of care ethics are necessary to encompass these different perspectives: what she refers to as 'feminine' and 'feminist' care ethics. She identifies 'feminine' care ethics as deriving from an interest in the ethical dimensions of personal and informal relationships, whereas 'feminist' care ethics derives from a more political concern with women's institutionalised subordination. I want to develop her argument for the need for a critical analysis of the institutional context for care work, as well as of personal and informal relationships, and to apply this to contemporary challenges to care work and the question of whether this means we should assume that care is 'past its sell by date' (Beresford, 2008). In order to introduce this I need to review key characteristics of the 'anti-care' position that have influenced contemporary social policy and practice.

'Choiceandcontrol' not 'careandprotection'

In a critical analysis of personalisation from an ethic of care (Barnes, 2011b) I deliberately elided the words in this sub-heading in order to highlight the way in which care has become negatively associated with practices addressed towards a marginal group of individuals considered unable to exercise any influence over the help they need to live their lives as they wish. In contrast, choice has become linked to practices that enable individual service users to exercise control over services and over their lives and thus to become empowered. Individuals who exercise choice and control can realise their citizenship; their illness, disability or frailty is not an impediment to their participation in things like the work, leisure and cultural activities that constitute everyday life. The discourse of 'choice' has achieved a dominant position in the UK and elsewhere (eg Barnes and Prior, 1995; Clarke et al, 2007; Mol, 2008; Rabiee and Glendinning, 2010) and in the UK this has been embodied in the policy of direct payments to enable users to purchase their own services, and, more broadly, in the promotion of personalised services (Spandler, 2004; Ferguson, 2007; Duffy et al, 2009). Needham (2011a, 2011b) demonstrates the way in which personalisation has flourished both because of failures in bureau-professionalised welfare states to provide respectful, responsive and effective services that enable people to be well and to do well, and because of the strength of the discourse of the autonomy of the individual. Personalisation appears to adopt both the language and the objectives of disability activists and hence has become the radical option for social care at the same time as it has become official policy. To be against personalisation (although precisely what personalisation is, as Catherine Needham has so eloquently elaborated, is not entirely clear) is to be on the side of paternalistic, overprotective services that do not enable disabled people and others to exercise the same choices that 'you or I' might wish to do.

However, there have always been different positions within the disability movement which have differently prioritised collectivist or individualist responses to the 'disempowerment' of disabled people, and which have recognised the importance of distinguishing influence exercised through 'voice' from that exercised through 'choice'. For example, when I was studying disability organisations in the early 1990s, one high-profile group was deliberately seeking to counter the discourse of 'independent living' by adopting the term 'integrated living'. This was in acknowledgement of the problematic concept of 'independence' and in order to highlight an objective that promoted the integration of disabled people's lives with the lives of non-disabled people (Barnes, 1999). While this coalition of disabled people certainly sought to ensure that disabled people were able to live their lives as they wished, this was framed within a commitment to public services rather than to market-based welfare. At this stage it did not appear inevitable that strategies based in individual control of personal budgets would necessarily be seen as the only or the preferred way of enabling disabled people to receive the support they need to live their lives as they wish. Nor, at that stage, did it appear inevitable that the discourse of individual choice would be whole-heartedly embraced across the political spectrum as the basis on which social and health care, and indeed other services, should be designed and delivered.

A particular critique of personalisation as it has developed within UK social policy and practice is that a model that is based in a position adopted by younger disabled activists may not be appropriate for some other groups of social and health care service users, in particular frail older people (Lloyd, 2010; Lymbery, 2010). I have suggested that Putting People First, the English policy document that is the reference point for the development of personalisation in practice, is in danger of erecting a new moral boundary by constructing people by reference to whether or not they have capacity to contribute to determining the care and support they need (Barnes, 2011b). This is not helpful if the aim is to generate policies and practices that acknowledge the universal need for care and do not devalue both care and those in need of care; that is, policies that recognise that care is both relational and social.

I want to argue that two, very different, ideological positions have been unhelpfully entwined in the way in which choice has become the primary value underpinning welfare services in many Western states. The first is the liberal and neo-liberal assumption of the primacy of the rational, autonomous, self-sufficient individual who places few or no demands on the state for help. Such a person is happy, indeed expects, to shop around for help in those unusual and unfortunate circumstances in which they cannot meet their needs from within their own and their family's resources. The second is a position that claims that it is absolutely right and proper that, when people are in need of help from welfare services, they should be able to influence the nature of those services, when and where they are provided, and that they should expect to be involved in whatever way is appropriate to their capacities and circumstances in the process of service delivery. And that to enable this, collective involvement in processes of decision making and governance is also necessary. This is a position I have argued in many contexts over many years (eg Barnes, 1997a; Barnes and Bowl, 2001). I do not believe that the latter position requires that choice is the primary value or mechanism to enable this (Barnes and Prior, 1995), and nor do I believe that this position requires the concept of care to be abandoned in favour of assistance, help or support. All three terms have been proposed as alternatives to care in order to get away from the association between care and paternalistic or even oppressive welfare practices (eg Shakespeare, 2000), and all have their place as descriptors of what is done in the process of meeting needs. But none carries the ethical resonance that is necessary as a basis on which social policies capable of delivering justice and well-being in situations of dependence and vulnerability can be built. Nor do they embody an understanding of the emotional, social and relational nature of human interdependencies that are necessary to ensuring practices that respect not only the recipients of care, but also both paid and unpaid care givers and the relationships between them.

A conceptualisation of what is required to meet needs as a choice over services is an impoverished view of what is necessary to enable well-being and social justice. And, as Mol (2008) argues, it is not just at the front line, at the point at which people and services interact, that we need to consider the significance of choice as a basis on which services are built. The logic of choice 'carries a whole world with it: a specific mode of organising action and interaction; of understanding bodies, people and daily lives; of dealing with knowledge and technologies; of distinguishing between good and bad and so on' (p 8). Choice emphasises individual decisions at the point of service use and the service systems that derive from this are constructed on the results of such decisions, rather than on the basis of collective political decisions about what we value and how we can organise to achieve this.

Mol's empirical work is specifically focused on health care for people who live with diabetes. But what she has to say about the limitations of choice as a basis for health care in this context has much broader significance. Her discussion of control of, or attentiveness to, a diseased body is a good example to consider in view of the significance of 'attentiveness' as the first principle of care ethics, and the adoption of 'control' as a key principle of personalisation.

> In talk about living with diabetes the word 'control' is frequently used for people's attempts to stabilise their blood sugar level from the outside. But that term is misleading, for attending to one's metabolism does not begin to resemble controlling one's muscles. Face it: sugar is being burned in all the cells of a body. This process cannot be steered from a centre. It is not steered from a centre in a body without diabetes, but neither can it be brought under voluntary control from the outside. It depends on far too many variables. It is impossible to control them all: unexpected things always happen. (2008, p 36)

If 'unexpected things always happen' in relation to the central dilemmas of this specific health problem – the control of blood sugar levels – how much more is this the case in the lives of people who live with mental health problems, with cognitive disabilities, with increasing frailty, and their families? Mol's argument is that rather than learning to exercise internal control, people with diabetes need to learn to be attentive to their bodies and to recognise that their bodies can no longer be contained within the envelope of skin which covers them. The insulin that their bodies need to survive and the instrument (the 'pen') that introduces the insulin into their bodies are external to them. Does this mean that they are a slave to an external source of support? Not so, says Mol.

> Caring is not a matter of control let alone of oppression. It does not involve staying free or making someone else into a slave. Instead, it is a matter of attending to the balances inside, and the flows between, a fragile body and its intricate surroundings. (2008, p 39)

In diabetes 'self-care' (that is, the regular injection of insulin, the attention to content and frequency of what is eaten) becomes essential. The task of the doctor or the nurse and the care workers is not only to educate, to provide information and to teach people with diabetes about their condition and how to self-manage this, but to help them explore how they may lead a good life in a situation in which they have no choice but to take their medication otherwise they will die. What sort of relationship doctors and nurses are able to establish with their patients is central to their capacity to enable the good care necessary for this. The consultation that takes place between a doctor and a patient with diabetes is not about providing the patient with information to enable them to choose, or about pursuing a series of arguments to determine the best option, but being attentive to the 'twists, turns, problems, frictions and complications' (p 87) that characterise life with diabetes and which patients, nurses, and doctors – the 'care team' – need to understand both in terms of what they indicate about what is happening in the patient's body and in their lives as a whole.

Later I consider what care full practice looks like in other contexts. But it is important to consider the effect of the dominance of a discourse of choice, rather than care, on the way in which workers think about their practice and the sensibilities they do or do not develop in carrying out the work of care. And it is also important to think about other aspects of the context in which care work is undertaken that also affect this.

Care work in context

Recently I have spoken at social work and inter-professional events on the topic of an ethic of care. In one case the event had a specific focus on inter-professional ethics and there was considerable interest in what I and my co-presenter had to say about an ethic of care as a language in which discussions could take place across both professional and lay boundaries (Banks, 2010). At another event that also focused on inter-professional practice, but at which the focus was not ethics, there was rather more scepticism about what I had to say, although it prompted an invitation to speak at a third event, a conference specifically for mental health social workers. My presentation there followed that of a man working for the Department of Health on a programme to introduce personalisation in mental health services. His presentation confidently asserted that extending choice to mental health service users would empower them and his style of delivery admitted no uncertainty. Non-verbal responses to my talk which followed this initially registered some surprise and, as I went on, some in the audience made positive non-verbal responses to my rather different contribution. In a workshop session following the plenary, one social worker, a man who had been practising for several years, thanked me for questioning the orthodoxy that the previous speaker's contribution had represented.

I cite this example not in a spirit of self-congratulation, but to indicate the way in which dominant ways of thinking about values and the practices these imply set the context in which practitioners work. At another practitioner event, where I spoke on a similar topic, some participants provided feedback that indicated that they had not thought about the significance of care in their practice and that they had been encouraged by my input to do so. Their response indicated the way in which care has been written out of social care practice. In a similar way Angie Ash has written of the 'silent "ethical voice"' in social care practice (2010, p 203). In research that looked at elder abuse Ash was puzzled at the lack of any construction of the problem of abuse as an ethical issue. She was particularly puzzled by this silence since the agency concerned was considered to provide a supportive and collaborative culture in which to work and it had performed well according to formal inspections. Ash noted:

> ... the social and political context of the work of social workers and their managers mitigated their alertness, or attentiveness, to barely acceptable situations for older people – 'you calibrate what's acceptable to what you know ... you operate in that real world' as one manager put it, became the operant conditions of their 'real worlds'. Constructive critical challenge was not embedded into discussions, whether of elder abuse, or of service planning, management, delivery and regulation. As one manager observed 'all this activity that goes on often doesn't seem to get to the heart of how people are living and being cared for'. (p 205)

An emphasis on activity – 'busyness' – rather than reflection on the core values of practice appears to have the effect of desensitising practitioners and their managers to the ethical dimension of what are clearly unacceptable practices in the care of older people. But I would also suggest that this tendency is exacerbated by a devaluing of the notion that care is and should be at the centre of what such practices are about. What Frank calls the 'demoralization' of physicians (Frank, 2004, p 83) can also be seen to have similar origins (at least in part) in the way in which the work of doctors is circumscribed by a bureaucracy that 'conceives care as a quantity of goods and services to be allocated as scarce resources and/or commodities' (p 79). His use of the term 'demoralization' reminds us that neo-liberal approaches to health services not only embody assumptions about how best to organise services, but have ethical implications. The way in which services are organised, managed and governed impacts the identities of those who work within them as ethical agents. If care is either/both constructed as a commodity to be allocated or/and as a failure to recognise the citizenship and moral agency of those who use services, then how are practitioners expected to develop care full practices that recognise but do not exploit vulnerability?

Bowden (2000) approaches the issue of the institutional context within which nurses work in a rather different way. Arguing that: 'Ethically successful relationships, relationships maintained in ethical care, are mutually empowering and interdependent with other such relationships' (p 39), she identifies the way in which women's experience as carers for those who are more vulnerable than themselves can be appropriated to serve the interests of those who are more powerful – in this instance both doctors and administrators. In a context of unequal power relations within the workforce she suggests: 'What counts as a nurse's autonomous decision may be coerced or internalised subservience; what counts as mutuality between nurses and doctors may be manipulation and self-serving artifice; what counts as reciprocity may be finely crafted deception and deceit' (p 42). This corruption of caring values in the context of structural inequalities within the health system implies that a robust and critical ethic of care has to be focused on the institutional relationships within which care is given as well as on the direct relationships between care giver and care receiver. It is not only the nurse–patient relationship that we need to consider, but the organisational culture within which such relationships are enacted. For example, a paternalistic top-down culture within the institution is likely to be reproduced in the way in which nurses practise. Thus to construct nursing ethics as a matter of individual choices based on 'rational deliberation independent of coercive or disciplinary relations' (p 46) is to ignore the impact of the disempowerment nurses can experience because of their subservient position within the health system. Bowden suggests that an expanded conception of an ethic of care that encompasses institutional and political relations can offer insights about not only what nurses should do, but how health care should be organised to enable its ethical potential to be realised.

In her discussion of 'caring institutions' Tronto (2010) makes a similar point, identifying what she refers to as the 'warning signs' of bad care within organisations. Broadly these refer to an absence of adequate accounts of 'power, purpose and plurality' (p 163), and they include a view of care as a commodity to be purchased, rather than a process in which needs are identified through relational dialogue and care is given and received through relationships. They also include failure to understand the full range of responsibility for care, encompassing not only those who give care, but those who should take responsibility for attending to need. Managerial practices that concentrate on developing systems, procedures and rules, rather than on enabling the competent practice of care giving, cannot support good care. The amount of attention focused on developing systems to calculate and allocate payments in order to implement a system of individual budgets is an example of considerable activity being expended without 'getting to the heart' of care giving, as the manager quoted by Ash (2010, p 205) observed. And in the rather different context of residential child care work Steckley and Smith (2011) consider the way in which a devaluation of care is obscuring the capacity of child care workers to explore the morally challenging work of enabling some extremely damaged children and young people to be nurtured and to grow.

Frank's (2004) discussion of the challenges addressed by doctors who experienced themselves as marginalised in different ways, within a health system that has lost its moral integrity, demonstrates that it is not only those traditionally understood as in powerless situations within the hierarchy who struggle with how they can really care. The doctors whose experiences Frank discusses include a gay Cuban doctor working with AIDS patients in the early years of the identification of the disease, a man who practises 'poverty medicine' and lives in the same locality as many of his patients, a woman doctor with native American heritage who seeks to respect the different values and traditions of her Navajo patients when they encounter the assumptions of Western medicine, and a man with both Indian and African origins who reflects on the differences between his physician uncle's experiences dealing with smallpox in India and the way in which 'risks' are understood in work with AIDS patients in the US. Each seeks to develop his or her own moral practice of what Frank calls 'generosity' in which medical *care* is an essential part of medical treatment. It is significant that all have to deal with their personal experiences of otherness as well as learning to understand the difference that is created through illness. Frank concludes:

> The story which each physician-author finds him- or herself part of is not an AIDS story, or a Navajo story, or a gay story, or an inner-city story. It's a story of unfinalized hybridity, of unceasing attempts to bring together disparate parts, respecting the otherness (constructing identity, as Hall says 'with and through, not despite difference'), but believing in a harmony among these parts. (2004, p 105)

These doctors struggle to care in spite of being in a comparatively powerful position and occupying respected roles not only in relation to their patients, but within society as a whole. Nurses, as Bowden (1997) emphasises, practise within the context of a publicly regulated system, subject to formalised bodies of ethical conduct, and a public respect and recognition that draws its inheritance from popular images dating back to Florence Nightingale. In the UK they are usually public employees, they are represented by professional bodies and trade unions, and they receive professional training and education – from 2013 it is planned that they will have to have degree-level qualifications. In contrast, workers providing care within residential and day care settings, and in people's homes, have limited training, are not recognised as professionals, are increasingly likely to be employed within the private or voluntary sector and to receive pay that is below that of public sector workers. The development of direct payments and individual budgets means they are increasingly likely to be employed directly by older or disabled people or by their families. An increasing percentage of such workers are migrants who were born outside the UK. Cangiano et al (2009) quote what they describe as a conservative estimate that in 2008 there were 135,000 foreign-born care workers in the UK, comprising 18% of all those employed in this capacity. Williams (2010) identifies the way in which the intersection between care regimes and migration regimes is shaping a context in which migrant care workers are increasingly likely to be employed in the provision of home-based care in countries of the North and West.

The position of such workers can be hard. While employers may celebrate their work ethic, the workers themselves may feel they have to accept unfavourable working conditions because they have families in their countries of origin that they need to support, they do not have a local support network to draw on, and their immigration status compromises both their capacity to change employer and their eligibility for public benefits if they become unemployed. Cangiano et al (2009) identified cases where live-in, directly employed workers felt they had to tolerate not only rudeness from those they cared for, but also not being fully remunerated for the hours they worked. Williams (2010) suggests: 'Being treated as a "member of the family" may disarm workers so that they are continually on call and the boundaries between work and privacy become blurred' (p 386). In contrast, cultural stereotypes that identified a 'caring ethos' among some groups of migrant workers were reinforced by the views and experiences of both workers and the older people with whom they worked. Both older people and migrant care workers overwhelmingly emphasised the quality of relationships as defining the quality of care. While language proficiency could be a barrier, there were also reports of very positive relationships being developed, although the amount of time workers were allowed to spend with the older people they worked with acted as constraints on this (Cangiano et al, 2009). Research exploring the different trajectories of care workers both within and across regions, as women (and some men) leave home to work in other people's homes, has revealed the way in which racialised as well as gendered stereotypes intersect with colonial histories and religious identifications to shape the issue of 'who cares where', as well as the way in which care workers are treated (Williams, 2010).

The precise power dynamics that operate in the context of different forms of care work obviously vary. But what is evident is that any analysis of the work of care needs to recognise the way in which both discursive power and structural inequalities impact on the relational dynamics of care. Eva Feder Kittay's description (1999) of her relationship with Peggy, the paid care worker who shared the care of her daughter for many years, acknowledges the privatised nature of the arrangement that she was able to come to because of her privileged position as a professional woman. Kittay expresses some discomfort with the nature of this relationship: 'Sometimes I feel that my relationship to Peggy vis-a-vis Sesha is like the patriarchal relation of husband to wife vis-a-vis their children ... Each time I see the analogies, it makes my feminist and egalitarian flesh creep' (p 160). Yet the understanding and respect between the two of them is very different from the negative descriptions cited by Cangiano et al. What this suggests is that it is inadequate to read off the precise nature of the relationships that can be achieved in any particular system or service context. Employing a care worker privately through direct payments will not necessarily result either in a view of care as a commodity to be exchanged for cash, or in the exploitation of a worker who has neither trade union representation nor personal resources to ensure fair treatment. But to strip care out of such a relationship, to see it as a source of practical assistance embodying neither emotional nor ethical sensitivities and sensibilities to the personal and interpersonal conflicts that come from needs associated with ageing, illness or disability, cannot provide a basis on which to enable well-being for those cared for or satisfaction for those paid to care. Thus we need to return to what care looks like in practice to complete this discussion.

Care work and social justice

The debate about the relationship between care and justice that I considered in Chapter Two takes on a human face when it is applied to the practices through which social policies express the responsibilities of states to those in need who are resident within their borders. Here I illustrate the significance of this by drawing on practice issues in different contexts.

Earlier, I deliberately avoided using the word 'citizen' to refer to those who are or might be the focus of social care practices. Not all those in need are citizens of the state from which they seek help and the way in which the practitioners to whom they are referred construct, interpret and respond to their claims highlights the tensions and possibilities residing in a prioritisation of a rights or care/needs discourse (Paszkiewicz, 2011). In her study of social work and social care practice with refugees in England, Paszkiewicz identified competing discourses among front-line practitioners that reflected not only official policy and populist discourses regarding the rights of those who are not citizens to claim welfare, but also different conceptions of justice. She suggested that a needs/care discourse was more consistent with cosmopolitan notions of social justice that reflected rights deriving from a common humanity than with membership of a specific community that had to be earned in order to make rights claims. Those workers adopting discursive strategies that emphasised needs for care were more likely to explore ways in which they could 'play the system' to the advantage of refugees, than those who prioritised a rights discourse. She cites Morris: 'the conferral of a right can act as an expression of the boundaries of moral obligation for a given society' (Morris, 2010, p 155), reflecting Tronto's identification of the way in which moral boundaries can get in the way of policies and practices that both meet need and enable justice.

A very different kind of moral boundary is the focus for recent work by Kittay and Carlson (2010). A focus on the challenges to moral philosophy offered by cognitive disability is not an obvious place to locate a consideration of care work and social justice, but one of my overall arguments in this book is the necessity for a rediscovery of the philosophical basis of practice in a way that can act as a counterbalance to the functional and economistic influences that have shaped this in recent years. In her contribution to this collection Kittay (2010) confronts the reality that apparently respectable arguments are being made within the discipline of moral philosophy that some people with severe cognitive disabilities have a moral status rather lower than that of some non-human animals – such as pigs, dogs, rats or chimps. The extremity of that argument is shocking to those whose perspective is the everyday lives of people with such disabilities, their families and those who work with them. But it serves to remind us of the realities of practices that are not always that far in the past (Wong, 2010), based on assumptions that it is acceptable to operate with a theory of justice that excludes some groups of human beings from its purlieu. It is often down to those working at the front line to determine what kind of practice will really deliver justice in contexts that challenge our understandings of moral boundaries and of personhood. Such contexts include work with people with dementia (Brannelly, 2006), with people who are near death (Lloyd, 2004), with those experiencing acute mental illness (Pettersen and Hem, 2011), and with those who have murdered children (Stroud, 2008). In such contexts the inadequacy of practices based in assumptions of rational individualism and justice as a matter of rights becomes particularly acute.

From a rather different perspective, it is also important to reflect on the significance of care and justice in relation to the experiences of care workers as employees. This is evident in the situation of migrant care workers who, as we have seen, are often in quite disadvantaged positions vis-à-vis employment status and their power to influence this. But more generally, employment in 'care work' is increasingly subject to the negative impacts of 're-structuring' and 'modernisation' within welfare services (Mooney and Law, 2007). Many of those who do care work are also those who need to use 'care services'. Resistance to the way in which care work is structured, as well as to the way in which those doing the work are employed and paid, is often argued to be in the interests of both those doing the work and those using the services, although the use of strike action and other means of securing workers' rights is always contentious in the context of care work. This enduring tension is likely to be a focus of considerable personal and political conflict in the context of public service cuts and the drive for austerity. But the relational emphasis of an ethic of care reinforces the need to consider how care work can be organised in a way that enables workers both to care and to feel cared for.

Care full practice

The literature on care ethics and different forms of practice is now extensive and it is not my intention to review this as a body of work or to summarise key arguments. In a previous book (Barnes, 2006) I applied the ethical principles articulated by Tronto to social care practice, emphasising the importance of narrative-based practice to their implementation. There is broad agreement about the significance of relational, dialogical and narrative practice to an approach based in an ethic of care (eg Hess, 2003; Wilks, 2005; Brannelly, 2006; Martinsen, 2011) and it is perhaps unnecessary to simply repeat the case for this. Rather what I want to develop here is the contribution that an ethic of care can make to practices that recognise and include the 'care receiver' as an active agent in the care process. In Chapter Eight I consider this in relation to service user involvement in deliberative processes of policy making. My focus here is on the front line where practitioners and service users are engaged in a process of determining how best to meet needs in a way that respects the particularity and the social and cultural context of the person needing help, acknowledges their responses to being in such a position, encompasses their relationships with others from whom they receive and to whom they may give care, and is focused on achieving an outcome that as far as possible meets needs for both care and justice. Such processes must engage with difference and conflict among those involved in caring networks and relationships. They also need to acknowledge the complex power relations that operate within and between the private world of the care receiver and their network, and the public world of the practitioner and the system within which she works.

In order to do this it is important to understand such processes as engaging with:

- the lived experience of the service user and the experiential knowledge they have developed of 'what works' for them in terms of help or support;
- the emotional dimensions of that experience that may sometimes make it hard to make decisions, to accept help or to see a way forward;
- the care that is given by intimate others – both family members and friends (see Chapter Five) and the knowledge generated through such practices;
- the emotional responses of unpaid carers, in particular those whose relationship with the service user is affected substantially by their need for care, and their own needs for care;
- the professional knowledge and skills of the practitioner(s) involved;
- their emotional engagement with the situation and the people that they are trying to help;
- their experience of being cared for and supported (or not) within their work situation.

Thus applying the moral principles of care involves engaging with epistemological issues as well as relational and emotional issues. The narrative and dialogic practices proposed as necessary to embody an ethic of care in practice need to bring together emotional, cognitive, and ethical understandings and perspectives (Nussbaum, 2001). It also usually involves not only a dyadic relationship – practitioner and service user – but a broader network that includes other workers who may be employed in different agencies, and other key members of the service users' network (Brannelly, 2011). In terms of the moral principles articulated by Tronto, this perspective necessitates in particular a development of the principle of 'responsiveness' to recognise the contribution of the care receiver and significant others to the care process. And if we start from Kittay's idea of 'nested dependencies' to recognise the importance of care for the carers, we need to extend this to include the dependency of paid care workers on the support they receive from others. This encompasses not only the 'partnerships' between workers from different professions and different agencies that are frequently involved in a 'care team' working with a particular service user, but also the opportunities for discussion of ethical or other troubling or upsetting issues associated with doing care work among colleagues. Having spaces and times in which such issues can be explored and discussed is an important way in which responsibilities for care become shared beyond a specific dyadic relationship.

The practical and resource demands of care are a matter of collective responsibility. This relates both to the proper remuneration and treatment of care workers, and to the organisation of care work to ensure workers have time both to do care and to discuss this with colleagues. But it is also a collective responsibility to promote ethical debate about the nature of care in order to ensure the good care that will contribute not only to individual but also to collective well-being. A failure to do so is evident not only in the failure of the workers in Ash's study to name as an ethical issue the poor treatment that left older people with dried faeces caked to their slippers, but also in the investigations reported by the Health Service Ombudsman in England (2011). This included cases in which a husband, who had accompanied his wife who had Alzheimer's disease to hospital, was forgotten and left in a waiting room while she died, and a failure to arrange any follow-up care for an elderly lady discharged from hospital following a pelvic fracture. She was found dead a few days later and a post mortem showed death from peritonitis and a perforated stomach ulcer.

What goes on in supposedly caring institutions is not just a matter for those working within them and those seeking help from them.

If it is claimed that workers do not have the time or opportunity to do other than offer the most perfunctory assistance, if practices are evident that, if public, would be condemned as care less, then these are political issues that require public debate to influence what goes on in such institutions and the level of funding required to support ethical care within them. Some years ago I acted as a Mental Health Act Commissioner, visiting psychiatric hospitals to ensure the provisions of the 1983 Mental Health Act were being adhered to and that those detained under the Act were being treated properly. My role included visiting Ashworth, one of the high-security hospitals. During my period as a commissioner there was a public inquiry arising from reports of abuse into the treatment of women patients and this prompted media interest in the usually closed and hidden world of high-security psychiatric care. Two incidents from this stand out. During the inquiry itself, a male nurse gave evidence purporting to demonstrate the quality of care given to women patients. Before they go to bed, he reported, the women line up and we give them a kiss and a cuddle. There was a gasp from the normally impassive legal team. I was subsequently interviewed for a TV programme (the interview was not used, as the focus of the programme shifted). During my interview I described the process of slopping out that happened in the morning after the women had been locked in their rooms overnight. After the interview was completed the cameraman came up to me and asked quietly: "What is slopping out?" Both incidents highlight the way in which practices that shock most people can develop in publicly funded institutions and are simply unknown and not understood (the incidents refer to the early 1990s). Giving care in these contexts is something that only a small number of people will ever do directly, but accepting responsibility that good care is provided is a shared responsibility of all citizens.

So what does this look like in practice? This requires us to look once again at what practitioners actually do, and then at what is in place to support their practice. The starting point is the moral principle of responsiveness since this focuses on the experience of 'care receiving' and calls attention to the fact that this is a necessary part of a care process that is truly relational. Picking up on one of the examples cited earlier, how might we understand the response of a woman in a secure psychiatric facility to being kissed and cuddled by a male nurse before bed? A full understanding of this, I suggest, requires at least the knowledge that over 90% of the women admitted to such facilities have been sexually abused; knowledge of the consequences of sexual abuse; an understanding of the power relationships that exist within closed institutions; attention to the history and personal circumstances of the individual woman; and the ability to be attuned to behavioural and non-verbal as well as verbal responses. That is, it requires professional knowledge on which general psychiatric nursing practice is built, as well as particular knowledge of the individual and sensitivity to his or her reactions. Not to draw on professional knowledge in this context could well be judged to be both uncaring and unethical.

While this might be considered a fairly extreme example, similar principles apply in other contexts. When people turn for help to services that provide specialist help relating to illness, disability or the consequences of ageing, there is an expectation that the practitioners working in those agencies have specialist knowledge that can help those in need understand why their bodies, their minds, their emotions or their interactions with others are doing what they are doing. They expect to get access to knowledge that can help them understand their reactions and responses, as well as help in dealing with this. But they will also expect that their own knowledge and understanding will contribute to the process and, if an unpaid carer is involved, she will also expect that the insights and knowledge she has gained from being with the person and caring for them will be heard, respected and drawn on.

Tove Pettersen and Marit Hem (2011) discuss a similar approach to what they call 'mature care' by developing a particular concept of reciprocity rather than responsiveness (as Tronto has defined this). Arguing that 'mature care calls attention to, among other things, the reciprocity of interests' (p 217) (in the particular case they examine between nurses and service users in psychiatry), they develop an understanding of relational care where the focus is on the interaction between the carer and the person cared for, and transcends 'the traditional demarcations between private, public and professional' (p 219). Thus they consider what I referred to in Chapter One as the danger that care may become self-sacrifice, and that purely altruistic care can lead both to the burn-out of and manipulation by care givers. Care cannot be one-sided and requires at least a dialogue, and at best the active contribution of the care receiver as well as the care giver. In a one-sided perspective:

> From the perspective of the carer, care is thus envisaged as something that can be 'delivered' from one person to another, and from the perspective of the one cared for, care is comprehended as something that can be 'extracted' from the carer. Both images obscure the interaction that actually takes place between two persons in a caring relationship and,

> in addition, the potential aspects of power are neglected. (p 220)

Pettersen and Hem also include an epistemological dimension to their analysis, suggesting that the necessity of including at least two perspectives within a caring relationship implies access to contextual information in order to make good decisions. They also argue that the person cared for needs to recognise the point of view of the care worker, their relatives, and other patients: 'The lack of cognitive flexibility makes it difficult for those cared for to correct, change, nuance or expand their understanding of their own situation in light of other's input. As a consequence, self-reflection, growth and change might suffer, as well as their ability to feel concern for others' (p 221). The authors discuss two contrasting examples from within acute psychiatry to illustrate what can happen when a patient is open to establishing a relationship with workers and where the idea of such a relationship is dismissed.

This suggestion that those receiving care need to take an active part in a caring relationship and that their contribution to the process can be understood as a form of reciprocity has similarities with Noddings' (1996) consideration of reciprocity in caring. However, her focus on parent–child or teacher–pupil relationships leads to a particular perspective constructed around the type of growth and development that is understood as the primary purpose of these particular relationships. The following assertion embodies a highly privatised view of the process of caring and a highly normative view of reciprocity.

> What the cared-for gives to the relation either in direct response to the one-caring or in personal delight or in happy growth before her eyes is genuine reciprocity. It contributes to the maintenance of the relation and serves to prevent the caring from turning back on the one-caring in the form of anguish and concern for self. (p 35)

Pettersen and Hem's analysis offers more scope to consider the contextual meaning of the reciprocity of the person cared for. Similarly, Mullin (2011) invokes the concept of 'gratitude' to refer to the way in which the recipient of care should respond to care that is given with respect for the dignity of the recipient. She does not argue that gratitude should be given regardless of the attitude with which care is provided, or that it should be demanded in what she refers to as 'tit-for-tat reciprocity' (p 118), but that appropriate gratitude 'has an important role to play in generating respect for care providers and care receivers alike' (p 111). She counters the arguments that disabled people do not wish to feel 'grateful' for the support they have a right to receive, and argues that gratitude is one contributor to the type of 'healthy relationship' to which a feminist ethic of care is aiming. The values associated with being independent frequently generate a reluctance within individuals to feel dependent and this, in turn, can lead to a resistance to receive care in situations where it could both benefit the care recipient and relieve anxiety in the care giver. Learning to receive care positively could, as Mullins suggests, contribute to the valuing of care per se, as well as enabling the type of dialogue through which good care can be given and received. However, gratitude is a difficult concept and one that is not sufficient to the development of a concept and practice of reciprocity in care. I suggest it is still necessary to further develop a useful conceptualisation of this.

I cited Noddings' work to demonstrate the importance of a contextualised understanding of both the significance of reciprocity and the ways in which it might be expressed and demonstrated. Peggy's story of how she learnt from Sesha Kittay what worked for her in terms of exercises to aid her development (cited in Chapter Two) illustrates how care workers need to be open and receptive to reciprocal contributions to the care process that might not be immediately obvious. This is particularly the case when the person cared for has cognitive or communication difficulties, but there are other contexts in which a non-verbal gesture or an apparently disconnected story may carry an important message from which the care worker needs to learn, both emotionally and cognitively, how, say, an elderly woman likes to be bathed and dressed. In other contexts a more equal exchange of information, arguments and experiences might characterise the interaction between an 'expert patient' who has lived with an illness over many years and a doctor who is a specialist in that disease. As Mol (2008) describes, aspects of such interactions might superficially be comprehended through a logic of choice: doctors who specialise in diabetes give patients information about blood sugar levels, what happens when they become too high or too low, how they can be monitored and how they can be raised or lowered. Patients learn to observe how their bodies respond and how they can best manage insulin injections. Doctors have access to the latest research evidence about effective technologies; patients want access to that information. But to understand the reciprocal relationships involved here as designed to facilitate patients to make the best choices of treatment, diet etc for themselves is to understand facts as separated from values, and that choices made in the consulting room involving a doctor and her patient may not 'work' in the context of the everyday lives patients share with others.

> In the logic of care facts and technologies are more fluid than the logic of choice takes them to be, while will and wishes are more constrained. Less fluid. Control is not on offer. The world may well be adaptable and adjustable, but only up to a point. There are limits to what can be changed – but these limits are not obvious at the beginning. It is difficult to predict what may work and what will fail. Thus, the logic of care wants us to experiment carefully. Try, be attentive to what happens, adapt this, that or the other, and try again. (p 61)

Such experimentation involves a collaborative relationship in which both patient and doctor are active participants and is better understood as 'mature care' that involves reciprocal relationships than as a process of enabling choice.

I am arguing here that a developed understanding of reciprocity, which is itself a development of the principle of responsiveness, needs to encompass unpaid carers as well as the relationship between care worker and service user and to take on board the knowledge and expertise of all those involved in caring relationships. Current UK policy names unpaid carers as 'expert care partners', but only if they promote the citizenship of those they care for (HM Government, 2008; Barnes, 2011b). The way in which the relationships between paid worker, unpaid care giver and care receiver are constructed in this policy document emphasises tension between individual needs and perspectives, rather than a relational understanding of the interconnectedness at the heart of care. This is a policy discourse that apparently offers recognition to carers, but devalues care. Here, as elsewhere, the concept of partnership is invoked as a mantra without comprehending what this might mean in terms of care full practice. Brannelly's study of the work of community psychiatric nurses and social workers with people with dementia and their families reveals the dangers of workers making assumptions about relationships and contexts in which people with dementia and their families are trying to work out how best to live together in a difficult situation (Brannelly, 2006; Barnes and Brannelly, 2008). Morris's study of families negotiating how to care for their children in the spaces provided by family group conferences (FGCs) suggests a more positive model for ways in which those involved in what may be networks of caring relationships can make an active contribution to the process of care with paid workers, but also highlights strategies by which workers can undermine this (Morris and Burford, 2009).

Supporting care full practice

The FGC model offers an example of a form of practice that is relevant not only to ways of enabling service users and unpaid carers to play an active role in the care process, but also to supporting workers to explore the messy moral dilemmas that are frequently part of care work and to develop their ethical sensibilities and skills. Ash (2010) concludes her review of the absent ethical voice within care for older people with a call for cultures that require critical thinking and questioning 'where staff would feel professionally confident in constructively challenging each other, their agency and other professionals' (p 207). Tronto (2010) also concludes her discussion of caring institutions by identifying the need for 'well conceived spaces' (p 169) in which ethical conflicts relating to care can be addressed and resolved. There are examples of recent practices intended to enable the critical reflective space for workers to address both ethical issues and those that offer particular emotional and other challenges to good practice. This includes work being developed at the Ethox Centre in Oxford where Michael Dunn is leading a project in practical ethics involving social care workers (www.ethox.ox.ac.uk); the Schwartz Center Rounds that enable multidisciplinary care workers in hospitals to present and discuss cases that have challenged them emotionally or ethically rather than clinically (http://theschwartzcenter.org); and work developed at the King's Fund in England within the Point of Care programme to improve patient experience (www.kingsfund.org.uk/current_projects/the_point_of_care).

One significant point about these developments is that they are all based in institutional contexts – hospitals or residential care homes – where it is easier to bring workers together to debate such issues than it is in relation to practitioners whose work is conducted in people's own homes or in dispersed community settings. In a situation in which social work supervision is now focused on performance, rather than being a space in which to reflect and review difficult issues, and in which domiciliary care workers are only paid for direct contact time with service users and limited to 15 minutes' contact time with them and are thus unable to develop conversations with them, it is harder to see how spaces for collective ethical reflection can be created. Our collective responsibility to enable workers to consider the ethical dimension of the work they do depends in part on our collective willingness to provide the level of public funding for care services that means that limited resources cannot be claimed as a reason for not doing so.

This also relates to the way in which we see the role of inspection and regulation. If this is focused on financial, procedural and performance issues it will not serve the purpose. It is useful here to reflect once again on a relevant experience while I was a Mental Health Act Commissioner. Nursing staff on a psycho-geriatric ward were concerned to explain to visiting commissioners why some patients were in chairs which constrained them from getting up. Effectively they were pinned down. The reason for this, we were told, was that it was visiting time and these patients were so restless that they wandered constantly. Without some means of keeping them still it would be impossible for their relatives to converse with them and thus to sustain a relationship. I am not making a specific judgement about this practice; I am using this to illustrate the importance not only of reflection on the particular circumstances being faced in order to reach decisions about what is ethical in particular cases, but of opportunities for public scrutiny of such practices, in this instance by a body that reported to parliament and had powers to influence public policy as well as specific practices in particular institutions. The Mental Health Act Commission has since been abolished.

Conclusion

Care work has become specialised, dispersed and fragmented. It encompasses work that attracts very different levels of recognition for the skills involved and is undertaken by workers who occupy very different positions within organisational hierarchies and social class relations. The intersection of welfare regimes and migration regimes means that the distribution of care work, the experiences of care workers and the relationships they can establish with care receivers also need to be understood through the lenses of global movements of labour – what has been referred to as the 'global care chain'. A critical ethic of care needs to address not only the interaction between care workers and those to whom they provide care, but also the social and economic relations through which care work is organised. But whatever the type of work involved and whatever the context, care work requires ethical sensibilities and relational as well as practical skills. The organisation of care work needs to enable workers to reflect on the ethics as well as the work of care.

Poor care is not simply something that can be blamed on individual workers, but knowledge that poor care is not uncommon contributes to a reluctance among many to seek the help they need. It thus has an impact beyond the direct experience of those subject to it. Poor care – that may be incompetent or paternalistic rather than abusive – is not a reason for abandoning care, but rather for promoting a better understanding of how an ethic of care can be applied to develop practices that respect and include those cared for in the relational practices involved. It can also highlight the networks in which care is given and received beyond the formal system, how multiple relationships need to be accommodated within the decisions that are made about the way in which help may best be provided, and what strategies are best adopted to deal with personal and interpersonal challenges. As an ethic that derives from everyday lives rather than from any specific professional body of knowledge or practice, an ethic of care can provide a language in which debates between workers from different disciplines, as well as between workers, service users, their lovers, friends and family, can take place.

FIVE

Friends, neighbours and communities

An ethic of care highlights the relational nature of what it is to be human. As I have argued in Chapters Three and Four, this necessitates an understanding of different types of relationship and of the characteristics of relationships in which the giving and receiving of care contributes to nurturing, growth and well-being, and to making a world that we can live in together as well as possible. The two previous chapters have focused on the types of relationship which are, in a social policy context, typically considered as the main contexts within which care is given and received: within families, and between users of services and those paid to do the work of care. In this chapter I explore rather different types of relationship – those that are explicitly identified as friendships or those which may be considered 'friend like'. Some ethic of care theorists have explicitly addressed the significance of friendship in the context of care (Friedman, 1993; Bowden, 1997). Both the forms and role of friendship have been the subject of sociological analysis (Spencer and Pahl, 2006), and the particular significance of friendship in the context of relationships between women (Raymond, 1991) and LGBT people (Roseneil, 2004) has been the subject of both empirical research and theoretical analysis. However, friendship receives little attention within mainstream social policy. I want to argue in this chapter that this is an unfortunate lacuna and that it is important to understand the significance of friendship in order to develop social policies which can support a diversity of caring relationships, and which recognise the role of collective support as well as individualised services. I start by outlining the way in which friendship has been defined and understood and then consider three contexts in which this has particular relevance for my argument concerning care and care ethics.

What are friends?

Pahl and Spencer (2004) suggest that one reason for a rather limited body of research that takes friendship as its starting point is that it is hard to pin down precisely who 'friends' are: 'Whereas relative, neighbour, workmate and colleague are all categorical concepts, implying an ascribed status, friend is a relational, achieved label: to call someone a friend hinges on the quality of the relationship with that person' (p 203). The assumption that categorical fluidity is problematic as a basis for empirical research implies an approach to research that requires initial categorisation to determine its focus. In practice, as they go on to show (Pahl and Spencer 2004; Spencer and Pahl, 2006), virtually everyone can identify not only who their friends are, but what it is that makes them friends. In doing so the diversity of different types of friendship emerges, reflecting not only the different roles that friends may play at different life stages, but also the way in which friendship may map on to other types of relationship, including kin relationships: for example, Dorothy Rowe's (2007) book on sibling relationships is called *My Dearest Enemy, My Dangerous Friend*.

Rather than offering a specific definition of friendship, I want to highlight key issues that have been identified as important in considering friendship and how it may differ from other types of relationship. These can be summarised as relating to the voluntaristic nature of friendship – friends are chosen, rather than ascribed – and the extent to which a friendship relationship is understood as one that is reciprocal and largely equal. One particular perspective on friendship concerns its significance to those excluded from kin relationships formed through marriage. This offers one context within which what has been identified as the political significance of friendship can also be understood (Raymond, 1991). Spencer and Pahl summarise the nature of friendship as follows.

> The tie between friends is defined as an informal one: friends are people who can relax with each other, who feel comfortable in each other's presence; there is a sense of being off duty with friends, free from work or family responsibilities. Friends are also perceived as people who offer each other practical help, or give emotional support, sharing in each other's highs and lows, and friends are often defined as people who can confide in one another, who know each other's secrets. (2006, p 59)

The characterisation of friendship as informal, voluntaristic and reciprocal suggests a basis for caring that is untainted by the cultural and social expectations of familial relationships, or by the rule-bound, professionally dominated provision of care from within 'caring institutions'. Peta Bowden suggests that:

> Friendships call up a sphere of social activity that is both exhilaratingly free from regulation and profoundly fragile. The lack of publicly administered roles, activities, responsibilities and boundaries imbues friendships with liberating possibilities for interpersonal caring, unmatched by the more clearly defined structures of other social relations. But at the same time the potential for relatively unrestricted expression is hedged in by the constraints of its own uncertainty ... The friendship that is given in freedom can also be withdrawn with impunity. (1997, p 60)

This rather asocial interpretation of the nature of friendship relationships reflects key aspects of the way in which friendship has been theorised that need to be examined. While it is certainly the case that one can choose one's own friends in a way that one cannot choose family or work colleagues, for example, in practice friendships are made in the context of other social relationships (including family, work and relationships based in physical proximity), and the capacity to sustain friendships interacts with broader social and economic circumstances. Thus, friendships across different social classes may be comparatively rare because many friendships are made within social contexts that are still structured by class differences; and sustaining friendships over time is affected by mobility, time and financial resources. We may have more freedom to choose friends than siblings or other kin, but our capacity to both develop and sustain friendships is contingent on a range of social factors. And the suggestion that withdrawing friendship can be done with impunity rather neglects the social norms that operate within relationships and the sanctions that others might impose in response to perceived neglect of responsibilities to friends from within social networks. Commitment and trust are also key characteristics of friendship (Friedman, 1993), which questions the notion of friendship as free from any form of 'regulation'. Trusting involves being confident that we can demonstrate our vulnerabilities and let down our defences, and we cannot do this if we fear that friendship will simply be withdrawn on a whim. It is the nature of the way in which the 'rules' of friendship emerge, develop and are negotiated and how these are different from within other types of relationship that is more the issue here.

For Friedman (1993), a key characteristic of friendship is its focus on specific others in all their particularity and uniqueness. It 'takes as its focus the unique concatenation of wants, desires, identity, history, and so on of a particular person. It is specific to that person and is not generalizable to others ... We show partiality for our friend by attending selectively to her particularity in all its detail and variety' (pp 190–1). Both Friedman and Bowden link the particularity of friendship to the centrality of taking the best interests of one's friend as the starting point and focus for actions through which we express our friendship. And since friendship, perhaps more than any other relationship, can only be understood in terms of mutuality and reciprocity (if the other person claims that I am not her friend, can she be my friend?), then acting in a way that promotes the well-being of a friend involves both giving and receiving care. It also requires the sort of attentiveness and responsiveness that ensure that the way in which we do care is prompted by the way she would want us to care, not the way that being in a particular familial relationship causes us to think we *should* care, or that our formal role as a care worker tells us we *must* care. Friedman also suggests that the intimacy and disclosure that characterise friendship can contribute to moral growth through opening up standpoints other than our own. Attending to what may be different views, attitudes and responses of others whom we know well, trust and respect can cause us to reflect on our own positions, and 'When we do not know exactly what to believe, we can try to determine *whom* to believe' (p 200). In this way friendship can be a source not only of practical care and support, but also of ethical development that contributes to our capacity to respect the preferences and commitments of others.

The mutuality and reciprocity of friendship reflect the significance of equality as a defining characteristic. The openness and trust that exist among friends are not inflected by the status or power differences that operate in many other social and familial relationships. Thus it is hard for friendships to develop among work colleagues who are in a hierarchical relationship to one another; and while mentoring/supervisory relationships may develop into friendships, this is usually after the initial focus of the relationship has been superseded – for example, when a research student has completed their studies. Those who identify friends among kin relations are suggesting that their relationships with spouses, siblings or even parents have the characteristics of equality, trust and reciprocity over and above the socially defined purposes and expectations that accompany the kin relationship. 'Family as friends' (Spencer and Pahl, 2006) can be identified both within and across generations among those with whom people can confide, who enjoy each other's company and help each other out.

A final, rather different characteristic of friendship has been considered in both historical and contemporary accounts. This is the potential of friendship to support unconventional ways of living and what are seen to be 'deviant' or challenging ideologies; hence, for example, the importance of friendships within LGBT communities. By so doing, friendship has been seen to support social change (Friedman, 1993). The significance of this and other characteristics outlined here become relevant as I consider contexts in which the relationship between friendship and care needs to be understood.

Caring for and receiving care from friends

A close friend of mine, one with whom I had previously lived and with whom I have been friends for over 20 years, had a serious accident. Judy fell and damaged her pelvis and neck. This meant that she was unable to walk without assistance for some time and had to have serious and invasive surgery to treat her neck injury. The fall happened when she was staying with another friend who lived in another town. Judy lives alone on the top floor of a four-storey block of flats that does not have a lift. She has a very small family, and her close relatives are very elderly and live in another part of the country. As I was preparing this book I asked her about the help she received from her friends at this time. She responded with a list of different types of help that included:

- one friend living in her flat for the first week to enable her to come out of hospital;
- friends bringing flowers, chocolates and food for lunch that they cooked in her flat. "This was hugely cheering and went on for four months";
- driving her around, including to medical appointments;
- cutting her toenails;
- talking through problems and making suggestions;
- taking her car out to keep it charged;
- notifying her family about what had happened and making sure that they were kept informed but were not too alarmed;
- many other forms of practical help, and help in identifying and negotiating clinical support.

For Judy, help from family was not an option. Not all her friends got it right in terms of the way they offered help – one was described as rather "overbearing" in her need to help and another as rather assertive in her demands to visit. However, after her initial requests for help, the help that was offered was suggested by friends themselves as well as being given in response to requests. Judy reflected that: "The whole experience made me glad of my single years. I have built up an army of friends over the years. They naturally seemed to take on different roles which was perfect, particularly alongside the professional help I was getting." When I asked her whether she thought the help she received was evidence of care from her friends, she reflected that it was never a "one hit piece of help", that people came back again and again, and when she talked with one close friend about having an event to thank those who had helped her, he advised against this as the help she had received was evidence of how much people cared for her. She also noted that others said they thought she would do the same for them.

Judy's story is a very practical example of 'what friends are for'. It highlights the emotional and practical dimensions of care giving from friends; indicates that it is not only family members who need to take care not to make those in need of care feel helpless; and also indicates that while giving care is not based on an expectation of exchange, a sense that it is within the context of a mutual relationship in which reciprocation is likely means that care giving is not experienced as a 'burden'. The intimate knowledge of friends enabled them to care for her (in most cases) in ways that reflected her preferences and pleasures, as well as to understand what was necessary to avoid anxiety among her family.

It is also a particular example of a circumstance in which care from friends effectively replaces care from family. There are many individual circumstances in which family are not able to care, where there are no family members to care, or where the strong preference is for care from friends. It is also the case that social changes in the way in which people form and change interpersonal relationships, and in which they practise living together and apart over a lifetime, mean that assumptions about 'who cares' cannot be defined within kin relationships. Not only is there a need to 'rethink family' (Williams, 2004a; Murray and Barnes, 2010) in terms of who constitute family members and how people do family, there is also a need to think beyond family to recognise the caring roles that non-family members can play and how these can be recognised and supported. In the early days of the development of community care policy the emphasis was on challenging the way in which reference to 'community' care rendered invisible the fact that, in practice, care was provided primarily by women within families (Parker, 1990). I am not suggesting that that analysis is redundant, or that much remains to be done to enable a more equitable division of caring labour within families. But restricting an analysis of both how care is given and received and how social policies need to be shaped to a focus on families is to fail to recognise the diversity of the contexts in which care happens, and to exclude from consideration the situations of many different people for whom family care is not an option. To build social policies solely on the basis of assumptions that it is only family that cares is to close down the possibilities of diverse forms of care giving that more completely reflect the diversity of the ways in which people live their lives and the values they hold.

Women like my friend who have lived alone for much of their adult life are one group for whom care from friends takes on a particular significance. But older people in diverse circumstances identify the role of friends in maintaining their sense of well-being. Some of those in Breheny and Stephens' (2009) study (see also Chapter Three) were reflecting not only on care from family but also from friends as they highlighted the significance of reciprocity in negotiating the receipt of care in ways that did not cause people to feel passively dependent. Exchanging support of 'equal value' (2009, p 1301) and experiencing mutual benefit from giving and receiving care were identified as important in caring for friends. And the role of both friends and neighbours was a significant theme in our research on older people and well-being (Ward et al, 2012).

In Chapter Three I told the story of Grace and the contrast she drew between the functional help from her son when he took her shopping, and the care that was evidenced by a younger friend when he assisted her with the same task. We cannot know why it was hard for her son to demonstrate care for his mother, but we do know that the care she experienced from her friend was an immensely valuable source of affirmation of her identity and personal value, as well as a practical support. While some older people in the Ward, Barnes and Gahagan study spoke of the increasing importance of friends because partners died and other family lived far away, others spoke of the negative impact on well-being of loss of friends. They identified difficulty in forming new friendships that embodied the qualities of those that have continued over many years because they do not include the shared histories, and perhaps the potential for reciprocity, that characterise long-term friendships.

> I think I've always got a lot out of, I suppose, personal relationships ... particularly friendships because I have no brothers or sisters you see, and I miss them, ... miss having close friends in my peer group ... I meet all these different people and some you take to and some you don't and that's life isn't it, but it's ... not so deep in a way, is it, it's a superficial sort of thing. (Margaret, 83, divorced) (p 31)

While objectively Margaret was living in a context (sheltered housing) where there was the potential for other friends to be made, it is the particular qualities of friendship, rather than acquaintance, which are lacking for her as well as the caring support that friendship enables. But some forms of care can be experienced within less intimate or intense relationships. For example, neighbours can play an important role in providing emotional support and security, checking that curtains are opened in the morning, and offering companionship simply by offering a cup of tea or chatting as they sit together outside (Ward, Barnes and Gahagan, 2012). In early work on community care, Philip Abrams and his colleagues adopted the term 'neighbourhood care' to highlight the significance of support available from others living nearby (Abrams et al, 1989). As Wenger (1993) has demonstrated, older people have very different types of support network, some of which comprise mainly kin, and others in which friends and neighbours are important sources of help. She also emphasises the reciprocal nature of such relationships.

> Friends are people you can confide in, reminisce with and spend time with, who may help in emergencies. Neighbours are seen as generally helpful but most important is their proximity, availability in emergencies and their awareness of problems leading to interventions. Elderly people are themselves friends and neighbours and so these relationships are expected to be reciprocal. Reciprocity between non-kin, as described above, tends to be specific and immediate. In long-established communities, however, a generalized ethos of helpfulness may be observed which approximates to generalized serial or long-term, delayed reciprocity and receiving help may depend on being perceived as having been helpful to others. (p 33)

Wenger's empirical study emphasises the diversity and contextuality of friendship relationships and their significance as sources of care for older people. In our study of well-being (Ward et al, 2012), Peter's story offered a particular perspective on this. Peter is a gay man in his 70s who had lived with HIV for over 20 years. He described the way in which friendships had been important to him throughout his life. Friends are the source of shared activities such as visiting the theatre, and going out for meals, and friends are also people with whom he can share experiences of medication. He is sad that he gets tired and can no longer travel to visit friends as he used to, but he likes writing letters and was scathing about Twitter as a means of keeping contact.

He has lost friends to AIDS, but he keeps their pictures on display as it is important to him to preserve their memories. Friends also help him with some of the practical things that he now finds hard to do, such as cleaning his flat. He prefers to receive this help from friends rather than from service providers who have to stick to their rules about ways of doing things. Peter's narrative of friendship reflected not only the personal significance of friends to his well-being, but also his experience of being a gay man and part of the gay community. He spoke of ageism within the gay community, linking this to an emphasis on hedonism. Nevertheless he feels a commitment to the community and to supporting those within it – both old and young. From the perspective of an ethic of care he sees himself as a care giver as well as care receiver. He likes to encourage young friends who are not familiar with the theatre to get to know it and to share his love of it; and he spoke of a dream of buying a big house to let out to gay older men, particularly those with HIV, who are in need of support. Because he has survived with HIV for a long time, he would like his body to be used for research when he dies. Thus he demonstrates a sense of wanting to reciprocate for the support he feels he has received and that has contributed to his well-being.

The way in which care and intimacy are practised among those whose lives have not been lived within heterosexual or solely kin relationships is an important focus for understanding care and friendship. As Adam (2004) has noted, one result of the emergence of AIDS as an illness identified with gay men was the emergence of a group of 'non-traditional' care givers in the partners and friends of those who became ill. Some of those in this situation, like MacIntyre (1996), see themselves as 'non-traditional' family members whether or not they are currently the partners of those they care for. In other contexts those who have written about care and intimacy among LGBT people from a more sociological or political perspective have emphasised the way in which their lives should cause us to think 'beyond the family' (Roseneil and Budgeon, 2004), to understand care between partners who do not live together, friends who do live together and those who do not. Thus it is not only among those who may identify themselves as lesbian, gay, bisexual or transgendered that we need to think about care and friendship, but rather we should recognise the diversity of ways in which people share their lives and do care within this. And for Davina Cooper (2007), applying a feminist ethic of care to the unusual context of a women's sexual bathhouse offers a way of challenging normative notions of care as a 'largely sanitized and idealized approach to human connection' (p 244) and instead to include within such a conception the 'frequently conflict-laden, intense, gritty, and fleshy character of relationships' (p 257). Considering friendships and intimacies in different contexts can expand our appreciation of care as an embodied as well as affective and emotional practice.

Heath (2004) has explored the increasing significance of a diversity of shared living arrangements that do not involve kin among young people. While the nature and quality of relationships within such households vary considerably Heath noted 'the central importance of close, supportive friendships within the everyday organization of many peer-shared households' (p 172) and suggested that they constitute an example of an ethic of care in practice. Similarly Roseneil's (2004) study of networks of care, intimacy, friendship and support among those who did not live with a partner highlighted that:

> A good number had moved house, or had persuaded friends to move house, with the aim of creating local friendship networks that could offer reciprocal childcare and help in times of illness, as well as pleasurable sociability. It was friends far more than biological kin who offered support to those who suffered from emotional distress or mental health problems, and who were there to pick up the pieces when love relationships ended. (p 413)

The examples that Roseneil, Heath, Adams and others offer of care among friends illustrate ways in which people are developing caring capacities and negotiating ethical practices of care within relationships that are not defined by the specific role expectations that exist within families. There appears to be no hesitation about using the language of care in these contexts, indeed Roseneil suggests we should 'queer the care imaginary' (p 409). It is the significance of 'family' that is questioned, not the significance of care, reflecting alternative practices of care based in equality, mutuality and reciprocity in diverse contexts, rather than obligation deriving from normative family ties. Spencer and Pahl's (2006) empirical work also suggests that, in people's everyday lives, drawing hard and fast distinctions between kin and non-kin may not reflect the way in which people both think about and behave within what they call their 'personal communities'. This all serves to remind us of the limitations of overly narrow conceptions of care restricted to specific familial relationships. It suggests that fuzzy distinctions between kin and non-kin that exist in some other cultures, for example the Maori concept and practice of *whānau* that includes both kin and non-kin who live in proximity and share feelings of responsibility for individual and collective well-being, may have increasing relevance in thinking about how caring relationships might be promoted in other cultural contexts.

Collective care: the value of groups

This discussion of the role that friends play within networks includes examples where friends have made a decision to live together as well as examples of care within non-resident friendship networks. These examples highlight the tensions and negotiations that exist between maintaining privacy in a context of collective living, and attentiveness to individual needs and the needs of the group. They also provide an important counterargument to the highly individualised assumptions underpinning much policy regarding social care in the UK and other Western societies. The horrors of 'institutional care' that became evident in the 1960s were one driver for the closure of residential establishments and the move to care provision within community settings for people with learning difficulties and those with mental health problems (Barnes, 1997a). The widely cited preference of older people to remain living in their own homes underpins the expansion in private and voluntary sector domiciliary care services and the importance that is attached to 'befriending' services that offer some human contact for people who would otherwise rarely even talk to someone else. One consequence of staying at home is that this often means staying at home alone. Particularly for older people living in rural areas, living alone can mean loneliness and isolation (Scharf and Bartlam, 2008). More recently, the advent of personalisation and individual budgets has been promoted in part as a way of enabling both older and disabled people to use money to pursue individual leisure pursuits, rather than attending day centres that are characterised as lacking in stimulation and outside the 'mainstream'. At the same time as collective solutions to care for older people are being marginalised, alternative services, usually operating at the margins of formal service provision and dependent on uncertain and insecure financing, are being developed precisely to provide opportunities for older people to meet together and take part in shared activities that offer the benefit of reciprocal support (eg Smith and Barnes, 2011).

What is in danger of being lost in this wholesale promotion of individualised solutions is the value of more collective ways of doing care. Indeed, it is in some of these contexts, particularly day care, that the concept of care itself has been declared redundant. But in some cases we can see people making conscious decisions about how to live their lives in anticipation of future needs for care and deliberately drawing on collectivist solutions in doing so. For example, some women who lived through the substantial social and cultural shifts of the 1960s and 1970s and are currently reaching post-retirement and older age are exploring the potential of housing cooperatives, co-housing schemes and 'intentional residential communities'. These embody the collective ideas that shaped much of women's campaigning during the 1970s as collective solutions to meet their own personal needs and to avoid the isolation and social exclusion faced by many older people (see, for example, Older Women's Co-housing: www.owch.org.uk). These women experienced friendships as important in enabling them to live the lives they wanted when they were younger and are recognising their potential in enabling them to give and receive care in old age.

Thus in this section I want to consider a number of rather different examples that embody an understanding of care that is not restricted to a dyadic relationship between two unequal people, but as something that can be generated through living and being together in contexts in which young people, older people, disabled people and those who are experiencing mental health problems or emotional difficulties live and sometimes work together. These examples often involve friendships or friend-like relationships and challenge the possibility of drawing clear distinctions between care giver and care receiver.

The first example is offered by an ethnographic study of young people living in two residential homes in Scotland (Emond, 2003). As Emond notes, the received wisdom is that 'the group' is a negative force in such homes and something that both adults and young people should fear. Her study, which involved living in the homes over a period of a year, generated rather different insights into the way groups operated among the young people who were resident there. Most fundamentally the young people regarded the resident group of which they were a part as 'an important force in their day-to-day lives, their view of themselves and their social world' (p 326). The 'competences' young people demonstrated as they developed interpersonal relationships with other residents contributed to the fluid and interchangeable positions they were accorded within the group, and those competences included ones that we can understand as care. For example:

> ... after a difficult telephone call with her dad, Sharon entered the group room tearful and distressed. Hilary immediately comforted her and began cuddling her and smoothing her hair. For that moment in time, Hilary was granted a high position within the group; they admired her

> and respected her appropriate skill of support and allowed her the opportunity to demonstrate it. (p 326)

Caring competences within the group appeared to derive from a capacity to understand and empathise with how other young people were responding to what was happening to them because group members were familiar with the difficulties others faced. Responses to the support offered were based in an ability to trust other young people because, unlike staff, they did not exercise any particular power over them. Evidence of a lack of trustworthiness (taking possessions without permission, for example) which could undermine support within the group led to group sanctions.

The latter evidences one example of the problematics of group life. Working out how to deal with bad behaviour as well as how to support and encourage other members of the group through good and bad times was a characteristic of group interactions. These young people had not chosen to live with each other and thus their relationships do not fit the emphasis on voluntarism that characterises definitions of friendship. But young people in general do not choose whom they go to school with and it is among fellow pupils that friendships are often formed. Emond writes: 'whilst the young people could not control *who* they lived with, they had a sense that they could control *how* they lived with them' (p 332, emphasis added). Once again we can suggest that part of this process of learning how to live together is about working out an ethic of care appropriate not only to the way in which to respond to individuals within the group, but also to support the capacity of the group collectively to live well together. This was explicit in circumstances in which group members discussed individual predicaments resulting from the way in which they had been treated by staff and/or by family or others outside the home. Such discussions demonstrated awareness not only of the way in which individuals were responding to things that had happened to them, but also of the impact of such events on the group as a whole. The demonstration of attentiveness and responsibility to meet need on the part of group members helped the young people living in these homes to live in this particular world, which they had not chosen, as well as possible.

Emond's conclusion is that fellow residents have a significant impact on the care experience of these young people and that there is a danger that such impacts become marginalised or ignored as the benefits of individualised responses dominate social policy and social care practices. This conclusion is one that can be applied in other contexts. A study of people with dementia living in residential care (Surr, 2006) identified the way in which relationships with others in the home played an important role in enabling the older people to maintain their sense of self in the face of the processes of decline that accompany the disease. For some, being in a group was a way of feeling included and sociable and they generated narratives that enabled them to locate their current relationships in their former lives. Hilda, for example, identified them as former school friends: 'Well, I've found it's been pretty ... friendly. Er, I knew some of the people from er, you know, when we went to school, but of course when you leave school you alter a bit, don't you [chuckles]. But I've got on very well with them and I've enjoyed it' (p 1725). Other residents made new, important relationships within the home that contributed to their sense of self. Surr says of one woman's relationship with a male resident: 'John's friendship also accorded her the opportunity to be looked after and cared for, a role she relished' (p 1725). Not everyone in the home developed such supportive relationships, but the general point once again is that residential accommodation can provide a context in which care among peers can play an important part in contributing to well-being in difficult times.

But it is not only in the context of shared living arrangements that we can see the significance of care among friends and within friend-like relationships. The much maligned day centres in which some older people, people with mental health problems and other disabled people spend some parts of some days can offer spaces in which they can develop friendships and supportive relationships. For example, colleagues and I were surprised when a consultation event we organised for women with mental health problems was used by one group to seek support for their campaign to keep what they regarded as 'their' day centre open in the face of plans to close this down (Barnes, Davis et al, 2006). For them the centre was a space where they could retreat from many of the pressures they experienced in the 'mainstream' locations of their lives – in particular their families. Like the young people in residential care, an important aspect of the day centre was the support they received from other women who had similar experiences to their own, and this was not something they thought they would be able to find in the 'mixed' settings they were being encouraged into. Similarly, older people attending a day centre that they refer to as their 'club', which they do not 'use', but of which they are 'members', are threatening to march on the town hall if changes in policy result in its closure. They understand the policy changes that may threaten the centre because they meet regularly with the staff to decide on activities and policies regarding its running. Most of the older people who attend this centre (I am a Trustee) attend because they risk becoming socially isolated. Satisfaction surveys demonstrate that one of the main things they value from their attendance is the friendships they develop with others.

Other distinctive ways of creating contexts for collective care and support are found in 'care farming' initiatives (Dessein, 2008; Di Iacovo and O'Connor, 2009). 'Care farming' or 'Green Care' involves small groups of disabled people, people with mental health problems, or others who are experiencing emotional turmoil staying with farmers to experience the benefits of mutual support and participation in the rhythms of growing food and working with animals as well as with other people. Such projects, which exist in Belgium, France, Italy and other European countries, break down the moral boundaries that separate care values from, for example, economic values that guide agricultural production. They emphasise values of solidarity and the necessity of regenerating relationships as core to an understanding of care. The benefits of care farming from the perspective of service users often relate to the sense of community as well as the respect that they receive because of the contributions they make. They experience themselves as valued members of a community, contributing real work to a collective purpose. Their connection is with others with whom they share similar background/experiences; with farmers who approach them as they would any other worker, rather than as someone with a particular problem; with the natural world through activities based on the natural rhythms of times and season; and through their contact with animals and with nature. Care is not a separate process in such contexts. Rather it is embedded within the way in which people live and work together.

A key characteristic of these examples of the experience of care within collective contexts is that the 'recipients' of care are involved in and contribute to the process of making things happen, either through formal participation in decision-making processes, or through collective effort in the everyday operation of these initiatives. In the context of earlier discussions about the principles of care, this can be understood as another expression of 'responsiveness' or 'reciprocity'. Those receiving care are not passive recipients, but are actively engaged in the process not only of giving care, but of making decisions about how they and others will live, work and spend time together. They are not made to feel helpless, a burden or capable only of receiving care from others. But neither are they engaged in processes where what happens is based on individual choices in order to exercise individual control over their lives. They are taking responsibility for other people's well-being as well as their own and their everyday lives reflect the emotional, ethical and practical truism that we are relational beings.

Collective action and solidarity

In her treatise on affection and friendship among women Janice Raymond (1991) explores different cultures of female friendship in different places and times. While not romanticising either example, she considers the role of both religious orders for women and an organised movement of 'marriage resisters' among Chinese women as spaces within which both friendship and political action have been important to challenge the dominant order. Closer to home in terms of groups that are the focus of social policy concerns, Groch (2001) has identified the way in which the separate spaces in which some disabled people have lived and been educated have been significant in the genesis of an oppositional consciousness that has led to collective action among disabled people in challenging 'ablist' assumptions. In addition to the personal care and support that may develop within residential living, this may also enable a more political awareness to develop, in spite of, or indeed because of, the oppression experienced in such contexts.

From another perspective we can look at examples of collective action among disabled people and survivors of mental health services, among people living within deprived and neglected neighbourhoods, among older people seeking a voice in policy making and in other forms of collective political action and ask if friendship and care have a role in such contexts. Drawing on research into different examples of collective action and officially initiated forms of participatory governance (Barnes et al, 2007) I have contrasted the way in which official discourses of civil renewal and social cohesion might seek to account for and promote such initiatives, and how we might view them from an ethic of care perspective (Barnes, 2007). Official discourses based in communitarian exhortations to act responsibly in the public sphere – 'The ethos here is one of something for something – of rights and responsibilities going hand in hand' (Blunkett, 2003, p 2) – highlight the very different meaning of responsibility invoked in this context from the way in which Tronto and Sevenhuijsen have applied it. In Blunkett's communitarian ethos, responsibility is a requirement to conform to obligations defined by reference to the common good, rather than arising from awareness of our moral responsibilities for others: 'the moral subject in the discourse of care always already lives in a network of relationships in which s/he has to find balances between different forms of responsibility (for the self, for others and for the relationships between them)' (Sevenhuijsen, 2000, p 10).

If we consider how those who take part in these different forms of collective action talk about their motivations we get a much stronger sense of care than of obligation. For example, young people involved in a Single Regeneration Budget initiative in an inner city area with high levels of deprivation cared about what it was like to live in the area, not only for themselves, but also for their family and friends.

> I was brought up in [locality] and have been in [locality] for the last 25 years. I don't see myself moving out so obviously I will probably get married in the next couple of years. I don't want my kids to grow up in an area where I know every corner they turn there is going to be a drug dealer or a really deprived area. If we can change that now, hopefully when my kids grow up, my family, my friends, they won't have much to worry about. (Cited in Barnes, 2007, pp 67-8)

Similarly, those campaigning for improved health services in another deprived inner city area were motivated by concern about evident injustices and lack of care.

> Our area where I live is the highest cancer rate in the country ... I have been concerned quite a long time, basically because my family were heavily destroyed by ill health. Cancers and things. And it always used to fascinate me that a person dying of cancer could go into the likes of the X Hospital, and they would be waiting hours just to get a bed. (Barnes, 2007, p 68)

Activists in this area saw themselves as people who were in a position to take up these issues on behalf of friends, family and neighbours. Their activism was located within their commitment and relationships to the area and to the people living within it (see Chapter Seven). For others collective action can be a source of friendship and a way of establishing relationships with others. For example, some older people who have become involved in forums to give a voice to older people in local policy making identified their primary motivations as developing friendships rather than political campaigning (Barnes, Harrison and Murray, 2012). In other contexts the relationships that develop among activists embody relational characteristics of friendships that not only model the type of social relations that reflect the objectives of the group, but also sustain the action necessary to achieve them. This is particularly evident among those who can experience most exclusion from 'community'. Fiona Williams (2004c) has identified this in relation to support groups of parents of young people who use drugs (see also Chapter Five) and it is also evident among participants in groups of women who have been sexually abused and in mental health user groups.

Thus, a woman involved in a mental health advocacy group spoke both of her satisfactions in being able to achieve changes for others, and the support that the group offered her.

> ... it's just nice for people to be heard and I love that. I love putting that across. And then when things actually change for that person you get terrific satisfaction, ... I know there is a sympathetic response here (within the group) and sometimes that's enough from people here, to know that you're not really well but you're coming in anyway. I know that I'm going to get all the support here and people will help me all they can. (Barnes, 2007. See also Barnes and Gell, 2011)

This sense of being among others who understand what it is to live with mental illness and thus can provide appropriate support when needed reflects the experience of young people living in residential care discussed by Emond (2003). The way in which people involved in different forms of action to achieve social change speak about their motivations suggests the importance of understanding the way in which personal biographies generated a sense of responsibility for action. Responsibility is not an abstract concept but is rather grounded in relationships with particular others: those living in the same area and sharing in the disadvantages associated with that, or others who shared experiences as disabled people, mental health service users or older people, for example. The expression of responsibility is related to attentiveness – which can be understood as an openness to understanding the circumstances and needs of others, and a preparedness to take action on this basis. Attentiveness to the circumstances of others involves recognition of issues of vulnerability and power and the necessity of giving voice to the perspectives and experiences of those who are often marginalised or stigmatised. The relationships among those involved in these groups share the characteristics of equality, reciprocity and voluntariness that distinguish friendships and it is these relationships that help sustain action among the group and offer a vision of what broader caring relationships might consist of.

Conclusion

Friendship has a low profile in social policy and social care practice which belies its particular significance in the everyday lives of many of those who use social care services. Relationships with other service users often develop into friendships and embody care for peers that is grounded in the understanding that comes from shared experiences. In this way friendship can play an important part in the care experiences of service users. The care that is provided through these relationships may look and feel different from that which is given and received either within families or through paid care work and this suggests the need to broaden our concept of care. In some situations we need to understand friendly care as contributing to the collective political challenge offered by groups of service users. Friendship can both motivate and sustain such action.

But the significance of friendship to care goes beyond relationships between those who might be identified as users of social care services. Normative assumptions about the significance of the family as the collective in which care for children, for those who become ill or have accidents, and for those who become frail in old age is provided have drawn attention to unequal gender and age relations in care in this context. But arguably they have obscured the significance of what might be more equal caring relationships provided within voluntary friendships, and what might be characterised as 'contingent' friendships emerging out of more collective forms of support for people in times of difficulty. Social relations beyond as well as within family offer a more inclusive picture of care giving and receiving among those who do not live their lives within 'traditional' family groups.

The different examples considered in this chapter also highlight the way in which an emphasis within current policy on individual solutions provided to people in their own homes and in 'mainstream' social settings devalues the potential of more collective forms of care in practice. Theorisation of care as occurring only or primarily in the context of unequal dyadic relationships misses the collective nature of care giving and receiving that can occur among friendship networks or in groups that may be formed for purposes other than care giving and receiving, but in which care becomes a key part of everyday relationships.

SIX

Civility, respect, care and justice: the 'comfort of strangers'?

In his analysis of the 'hierarchy' of obligations for care, Engster (2007) includes in his identification of the 'special relationships' which constitute the second level of responsibility (after care for self), a stranger in need for whom we are the only source of succour, for example an injured walker in a deserted landscape. By so doing, he disentangles care from intimate relationships and links it also with what he refers to as 'circumstantial dependency' (p 57). He also names 'general duties to care for all others in need' (p 57) as the lowest level of obligation, but nevertheless one that is necessary to a complete theory of care. This does not mean that in all these cases a responsibility to care should lead to what Tronto calls 'care giving', that is, the hands on provision of care. That, Engster argues, should take place according to the subsidiarity principle – at the level at which familiarity and proximity mean that the best knowledge and understanding are available to ensure the 'best' care.

An ethic of care reminds us of the relational ontology of humanity. It reminds us that to live in the world as well as possible we have to do this with others. As Doyal and Gough (1991) have elaborated in their 'theory of human need': 'Whatever our private or public goals, they must always be achieved on the basis of successful interaction, past, present or future, with others' (p 50). An ethic of care provides a basis on which to develop an understanding of the sort of relationships that are necessary to survival, nurturing, well-being and justice. It also offers a framework within which we can assess the capacity of social policies to enable and support such relationships and achieve such objectives. But we are involved in a wide range of relationships throughout our lives and the interactions in which we necessarily engage in order to meet our private or public goals encompass very different levels of intimacy, intensity and duration. Many are with people whose names we do not know, whom we may never meet, or whom we may encounter only fleetingly. Does it make sense to think that all such encounters can be understood by reference to care? Tronto anticipates critical reactions to her and Berenice Fisher's broad definition of care.

> The range of care is very broad. In fact, when we begin to think about caring in this way, care consumes much of human activity. Nonetheless, not all human activity is care ... Among the activities of life that do not generally constitute care we would probably include the following: the pursuit of pleasure, creative activity, production, destruction. To play, to fulfil a desire, to market a new product, or to create a work of art, is not care. (Tronto, 1993, p 104)

Thus, from this perspective, we can fulfil many of our public and private goals in interactions that do not involve or constitute care. Many of our necessary interactions with others can be considered to be purely functional: they do not embody the 'reaching out to something other than the self' (Tronto, 1993, p 102), or the action that follows attentiveness to need that is necessary to care. We have needs that can be met without care: I need someone else to fix my car when it goes wrong, but I do not expect or require that the mechanic will demonstrate care for me as he attends to my car. However, I do hope that he will treat me with respect during our interactions. Some of the recent critiques of care in practice have suggested that a wide range of needs, including those typically included under the rubric of care, such as personal care of disabled people, can be met through relationships that do not embody care. I have argued against this on the basis that to strip care out of such relationships ignores the emotional and ethical dimensions of such interactions. At worst treating such encounters as purely functional can result in abuse, and, as Grace's story (Chapter Three) shows, functional help can leave needs unmet because needs are not purely functional.

To accept that human beings are relational is to require a better understanding of the different types of relationship in and through which we live our lives. We need to interrogate the significance of care in different types of relationship. For example, writing of well-being as a relational concept, Taylor (2011) has argued the need to distinguish close and distant relationships, although both are implicated in the experience of well-being.

> ... by close relationships I refer to those which are closer in an inter-personal and/or locational sense. They tend to have a richer or denser structure with high emotional content and are often associated with friendship, family, care or community. By distant relationships I mean those which are more formalised and impersonal and may include those

> with providers of public or private services, consumption and market exchanges or even the more chance relationships experienced in open social milieu. (p 780)

Drawing on Misztal (2000), Somerville (2009) distinguishes what he refers to as 'realms of interaction' ranging from 'accidental encounters' to 'pure relationships' and the very different types of process at play within them. Such processes may relate to, for example, the style of interaction, the identity of those involved, the motivation underpinning the interaction and the content and quality of the relationship. The focus of Somerville's analysis is 'respect' and his argument is that mutual respect is crucial for all the types of interaction he distinguishes. Unlike Taylor, whose starting point is well-being, Somerville makes no reference to care as a characteristic of relationships, even though he includes 'pure' relationships involving intimacy and commitment.

In this chapter I move away from a consideration of different types of 'close' relationship – those between family members, friends, and relationships in the context of service delivery that involve rather more than the formal, impersonal type of relationship Taylor suggests characterises service provision – to consider what I refer to as 'stranger' relationships. My definition of stranger relationships includes, but goes beyond, what Taylor identifies as 'distant' relationships. It includes chance encounters in public spaces, interactions with public officials that do not involve personal service delivery, and market exchanges (my encounter with a car mechanic, for example). But it also includes relationships that are not face to face, via different forms of information and communication technology, and, more distant still, it includes relationships with people we do not know, with whom any ties we acknowledge derive from our shared humanity and recognition of need and whom we will never meet. What I aim to do in this chapter is to consider if and how we might think of 'care' in relation to such relationships.

Complete strangers

I noted in Chapter Two that more recent developments of care theory and care ethics have moved beyond an understanding of care as solely applicable to particular, primarily intimate relationships. Indeed, it could be argued that a fundamental principle of an ethic of care is to breach the moral boundary between public and private in terms of the relevance and applicability of the values of care. Many of the moral dilemmas of social policy, and public policy more generally, concern the way we do, and the way in which we should, treat strangers. Strangers are not only those who are 'outsiders' to our immediate communities, whether we think of that in terms of physical proximity or shared identities, but also those in places far away whose lives are interconnected with ours not only because of a shared humanity, but through the interdependencies of contemporary global economic, social and political institutions. The way in which we think about these unknown others, the extent to which we feel and accept responsibility for them, and whether we care about what happens to them, influences the way in which we shape policies, allocate resources and, indeed, even whether we notice them when we are setting out policies that are intended to be universal in their coverage.

Natalia Paszkiewicz, a research student who worked with me and a colleague to study social care provision for refugees in England, was genuinely surprised at the absence of any specific reference to their particular needs and circumstances in official policy documents (Paszkiewicz, 2011). Her analysis of social care policy documents drew on Sevenhuijsen's (2003a) Trace approach. Not only did this not uncover any explicit reference to refugees as potential recipients of social care services, but references that she originally considered might implicitly refer to the particular circumstances of refugees, in fact concerned sub-groups of the indigenous population considered to have particular levels of need. This lacuna left individual practitioners with little guidance about what to do when faced with someone who, for example, had mental health problems and who was in a legal limbo in terms of their refugee status. Practitioners had to negotiate between the legal requirements and regulations deriving from provisions designed to regulate the entry of refugees into the country, their personal and professional values concerning the provision of services to those in need, populist views of deserving and undeserving migrants and official discourses that swerved between appeals to 'fairness', rights and system abuse. Paszkiewicz's analysis of practitioner discourses as they sought to determine what they should do in the particular cases they were invited to consider (through the use of vignette-based interviews) revealed understandable and perhaps inevitable inconsistencies and tensions between rights and care discourses. Workers who emphasised rights discourses drew on formal regulations and appeared constrained by the limitations they imposed. Those emphasising a care discourse were responding to the immediacy and the particularity of the situation they were asked to confront and, like the young women in Gilligan's research, sought to make judgements based in a contextual understanding rather than by reference to formal rules. Paradoxically perhaps, a care discourse was invoked in order to refuse help in the first instance because, suggests Paszkiewicz, it would have been too hard for practitioners to terminate support once a relationship had been established – that is, when they had started to give care. From this insight she suggests that the increased contact between 'strangers' may lead to a situation in which the moral boundaries between justice and care are necessarily undermined.

> ... taking into account the scale of migration in the contemporary world, cultural diversity in global cities, the growing importance of the internet, and social media in particular, and travelling made more affordable, we are indeed given an opportunity to meet distant Others, and possibly develop an ability to *compati*, in Latin 'suffer with' those people and build solidarity embedded in those acts of compassion. (Paszkiewicz, 2011, pp 224-5)

Whether this effect is evident in different contexts may be an empirical question – and I consider aspects of this later. But this study is one example of a number of ways in which the relevance of care ethics to stranger relationships and to issues of global or cosmopolitan justice has been argued.

Virginia Held (2006) argues that there are a number of ways in which an ethic of care provides more nuanced and more complete resources to address issues of global justice than liberal rights-based concepts of justice do. Unlike moral theories based in universal rules: 'The ethics of care has resources to understand group and cultural ties, and relations between groups sharing histories or colonial domination or interests in nonmarket development' (p 157). Its attention to the context in which need is experienced requires us to understand not only personal contexts, but also those defined by cultural, political and global inequalities and experiences of domination. Rather than seeking to adjudicate between competing rights and interests, an ethic of care encompasses the shared interests of carers and those who are cared for and fosters positive involvement, social bonds and cooperation. All these characteristics, Held argues, have implications not only for the way in which states around the world treat their citizens, but also for the responsibility of wealthy societies to those living in poverty elsewhere, for international politics and relations between states, and for international responsibilities to ensure the proper treatment of women subject to violence, rape, forced marriage and exclusion from education and health care.

Held's critique reflects Robinson's (1999) application of feminist ethics to the field of international relations. Robinson sees in both liberal cosmopolitan justice arguments and in communitarianism applied to the international sphere, a failure to recognise the concrete conditions within which difference generates inequalities: 'Any account of global ethics or global justice which ignores these patterns of exclusion, and their economic causes, will be, by definition, inadequate' (p 99). Recognising how people live in relation to one another, the core relational ontology of an ethic of care, is fundamental to an international politics and international relations capable of pursuing justice in a context of difference: 'what is morally significant about globalization is that it highlights the need to think of new ways of responding to difference – ways that resist the compulsion to homogenize and assimilate, but also, importantly, ways that do not approach difference as absolute but as existing only in relational terms' (p 102). Social relations that are characterised by power differentials are also moral relations and moral decision making requires attentiveness to the way in which the potential for exploitation and coercion exists within all relationships. These insights need to be applied to decision making about state autonomy and sovereignty, and when and how to make humanitarian interventions. But decision making in relation to specific humanitarian crises needs to be embedded within a recognition of the way in which 'everyday processes, practices, and social relations in international relations often lead to devastating levels of human suffering' (p 147). In other words an ethical approach to international relations based in an ethic of care needs to encompass an understanding of the way in which power relations between, as well as within, states create the conditions for everyday suffering caused by poverty and social exclusion, as well as the particular crises consequent on war, famine or other disasters.

In the final chapter of her book Robinson offers concrete examples of forms of grassroots development based in 'partnering' not 'partnership' that she suggests embody an ethic of care in practice. These examples reflect what, in a UK context, might be distinguished as local initiatives based in community development approaches, in contrast to community engagement designed to deliver officially determined objectives. In a later article she links paternalistic concepts and practices of care with liberal notions of development through aid (Robinson, 2010). She argues that liberal discourses of humanitarianism can be invoked to promote the responsibilities of benevolent Northern states in 'developing' the impoverished and dependent South. In contrast:

> A critical feminist ethic of care grows out of a recognition of the role of power in constructing relations of dependence, upholding the myths of autonomy and concealing the needs and responsibilities of care. Thus, it recognizes the complex interdependence and relationality that characterize relations and individuals even in distant geopolitical regions. (p 137)

While she rejects 'reciprocity' as defined by contrarian notions of liberal cosmopolitan justice, Robinson's argument about international relations of care reflects the importance of a developed notion of reciprocity that I explored in Chapter Four. Recognising people as both givers and receivers of care, and acknowledging both the response and contribution of care receivers to the practice of care, means that we should not interpret care for strangers in foreign lands as implying a donor–recipient relationship. Rather we should understand how Western or Northern states, international institutions, global economic relationships, and international flows of labour contribute to an apparent dependency in the first place. We also need to explore how practices such as those promoted and developed by Kabeer (2005) and her colleagues can offer alternative models for development based in collective agency and the strength of relational attachments. (See Chapter Eight for an application of similar ideas to the process of policy making.)

This perspective requires us to consider the everyday lives of those who are complete strangers. As I suggested in Chapter Four, the' global care chain' is an obvious example of interdependencies in which those at the wrong end of global inequalities are themselves bereft of care in order to meet the 'care deficit' in the West. Ehrenreich and Hochschild's (2003) collection of accounts of women from the Philippines, Sri Lanka, Mexico and other 'Third World' countries who have left home and travelled to undertake care work in the North and West starts with the story of Josephine and her children who are left behind while she earns money to support them. One has attempted suicide on two occasions; another lives in an orphanage, does poorly at school and picks fights with others. Applying an ethic of care at a global level requires us to be attentive to the needs of Josephine's children, as well as her needs as a care giver in a foreign land, and the needs of those for whom she cares. Kittay's 'nested dependencies' are evident here, but it is Josephine's children, the weakest in the chain, who miss out. We (in England where I live; in the West generally) will probably never encounter people like Josephine's children directly, but the policies we adopt create the conditions in which there is an insufficient supply of indigenous care workers, encourage a view of care as a commodity to be bought, and make it apparently beneficial for women like Josephine to leave her children to earn money elsewhere. These policies affect *their* access to care and they suffer injustice as a result. We need to care about them when we make policy decisions.

Allison Weir adopts this perspective in arguing for an imagined future in which:

> An adequate public policy would have to eliminate global care chains, eliminate the conditions that force women to leave their families behind in poor countries to do carework and domestic work for wealthy families or leave their children in substandard care in ghetto neighbourhoods while they spend their days caring for children in wealthy homes. (2005, p 313)

Theories both of cosmopolitan justice, and 'post westphalian democratic justice' (Fraser, 2009, p 29) remind us that it no longer (if it ever was) sufficient to think of justice bounded by the borders of nation states. But a liberal rights concept of justice is insufficient to achieve the aspirations of social justice at a global level. For Weir's dream of global liberation for women to be achieved, care must be valued as a social good rather than, at best, treated as a private value and, at worst, devalued as a constraint on the autonomy of independent agents. As Williams has argued (2004a, 2010) an ethic of work needs to be balanced with an ethic of care, not only within states, but also at a global level.

As I indicated earlier, in addition to the migration from East to West and from South to North in order to undertake care work, the other flow of people around the globe that focuses attention on the significance of care for strangers is the situation of refugees. In the early 2000s the Australian government adopted a much criticised and exclusionary policy in response to 'boat people' seeking refugee status in Australia (eg Porter, 2006). Not only were refugees initially put into detention centres on arrival, the Australian government subsequently reached agreement with Pacific island states that, in return for subsidies, potential refugees would be shipped out for processing elsewhere so they did not touch Australian soil. In his critique of both the policy, and the moral vacuum it demonstrated, Desmond Manderson wrote:

> It appears to be the government's relentless goal to avoid that face-to-face moment in which our responsibility dawns in the light of another's need – by hiding them behind

> barbed wire fences; and by hiding behind the language of 'breaking the law' and 'illegal' immigration which attempt [sic] to prejudge the issue ... the strategy developed by the Australian government is designed to undertake their surgical removal from the body politic. The boat people that are the subject of this legislation are to be *excised* – both from the community that might prompt from them a claim of legal rights, and from the consciousness that might prompt from us a recognition of ethical responsibility. (Manderson, 2002)

This critique highlights the strategy that Paszkiewicz identified of othering in order to avoid caring. The government not only refused to care about what happened to the people it turned away, it also actively prevented the Australian people from caring for them. Drawing on the work of Levinas, Manderson points to the limitations of a rights-based approach in this context. To be secured, rights have to be claimed and the refugees seeking to enter Australia are not in a position to make this claim since they are forcibly prevented from arriving at a place where it can be made. In contrast, responsibilities to those in need do not depend on a legal definition of rights: 'Since the responsibility is ours to undertake and not theirs to claim, it is proportional to their vulnerability and not our choice' (2002). That is, it is we who should care, rather than they who should have to claim their rights. Justice requires an acceptance of responsibility to care. Writing in response to the same policy Porter (2006) locates the Australian response in the context of the post-9/11 move to ever more fixed dichotomies, such as citizen/foreigner, like us/not like us, with us/against us, friends/enemies. She says: 'Absolutist dichotomies are blind to nuances, middle ground positions, particular contexts, and connections, all the considerations needed for wise, compassionate decisions' (p 110). Unless we feel such compassion, she argues, we cannot reach just decisions about how to treat people. And the impact of both popular and official discourses that embody these dichotomies is to foster racist attitudes and actions beyond the specific treatment of refugees. Porter points to racist graffiti, mosques being subject to arson, and women wearing the hijab or headscarves being spat at and tormented in Australia following the decision regarding refugees.

Strangers in our midst

As Porter's discussion demonstrates, othering also can and does take place in relation to those who are not outsiders in terms of having 'moved in' from one country to another, but who are seen as 'different' because of culture, ethnicity, lifestyle, or because of disability or mental illness. The everyday lives of those who live with mental illness, for example, are characterised by multiple experiences of stigma and discrimination and for those who are from minority ethnic groups or who are lesbian, gay, bisexual or transgendered, the experience of stigmatisation can be multiplied (Wahl, 1999; Gary, 2005). The survey of people with mental illness reported by Wahl, for example, identified people affected by overhearing hurtful or offensive comments about mental illness and by similar media portrayals. More than half of those who responded to the survey had experienced being shunned or avoided, and nearly three quarters said they avoided telling others about their mental illness because of such experiences. Such stigmatisation can have material effects. Many avoid situations in which direct discrimination is possible or likely: like the lesbians in a study by Ward (2005), 'self exclusion' was a strategy used by survey respondents to avoid rejection by others. But a third of those in Wahl's survey reported being turned down for jobs for which they were qualified when they revealed a psychiatric diagnosis and others said they had also been turned down for volunteering positions, even within the mental health field. Both the predominantly white population included in Wahl's survey and the different minority ethnic groups in the studies reviewed by Gary (2005) include those who actually avoid mental health services because they do not wish to identify themselves as mentally ill because of the response this evokes – within services and beyond.

One policy response to this situation has been the adoption of anti-discrimination legislation that makes it illegal to discriminate on the ground of disability or mental illness (as well as race or ethnicity). But studies of the effect of such legislation (eg Barnes, Brannelly et al, 2006) have demonstrated that legislation alone is inadequate for overcoming everyday experiences of discrimination or stigmatising attitudes and responses, not only from strangers, but also colleagues, and even friends and mental health workers. Hankivsky (2004, p 59) draws similar conclusions from her analysis of the application of equality rights legislation in Canada. She concludes that a liberal rights approach fails to give attention to the wider social, economic and political contexts in which women's claims for equality arise and hence fails to effectively overcome discrimination.

One effective way of addressing discriminatory attitudes and behaviours has been awareness raising and training provided directly by people living with mental illness. For example, one of the early initiatives of the Nottingham Advocacy Group (NAG), one of the first user-led groups in England, was Mental Health Awareness Week (Barnes and Gell, 2011). This adopted the strategy of 'normalising' mental illness by linking it with the familiar effect of stress. As the following quote from one of those involved in this work reveals, service users developing this strategy encountered very basic incomprehension about those who live with mental illness.

> ... a vicar's wife once said 'What if I invite these people into my home? How would they be?' And I said 'Well, they'll be like you, they'll have two eyes, and a nose and mouth and two ears'. You know they think they're going to see something weird and they don't know that perhaps they will have a nervous breakdown and start with a mental illness. (Quoted in Barnes, 2007, p 9)

Once again, this strategy is based on breaking down the separation that marks out particular groups of people as other, as strangers even though they are within the same physical space. It can be understood as part of a process of 'transformative recognition' (Fraser, 1997) in which the non- or mis-recognition and disrespect experienced by people who live with mental health problems are challenged not by defining a specific set of rights and protections for people who can be defined as mentally ill, but by destabilising the processes that lead to people with mental illness being defined as different (see also Barnes et al, 2010). I agree with Fraser that this is a process through which a deeper and less competitive concept of social justice can be realised than one based in either affirmative redistribution or recognition. Anti-discrimination legislation is necessary but not sufficient to overcome the stigma experienced by people who live with mental health problems. But I would also argue that a care perspective further enriches the way in which we might both understand and respond in this situation. Gladys Bombek, the woman quoted earlier who was a volunteer with NAG, articulated a lay understanding of what Porter (2006) and others have discussed as 'compassion': 'Compassionate co-suffering presupposes a sense of shared humanity. "The other person's suffering is seen as the kind of thing that could happen to anyone, including oneself" (Blum 1980, 511)' (pp 101-2). For Gladys, this understanding has come from lived experience and sharing that experience with others similarly affected, rather than through philosophical debate and reflection. In yet another, rather different, expression of responsiveness or reciprocity from those considered up to now in this book, Gladys (and other service users involved in awareness raising) offer to those who do not know at first-hand what it is to live with mental illness an insight both into the pain of this experience, and into our shared humanity through such experiences. And in so doing she encourages us to care about both the particular individuals affected and the broader issue of mental illness as part of the human condition. She suggests we should be attentive to the needs of particular individuals, and also to the way in which mental illness is generated through the ways in which we live together. But she does not invite pity because she also demonstrates that those who are directly affected are people capable of acting on their own behalf, of supporting each other and making a significant contribution both to mental health policy and to lay understanding. She invites us to care and to do what we can to demonstrate that we do not reject 'people like her' as 'other', but also not to condescend, or to act or feel superior.

Living with mental illness is objectively hard regardless of the way in which known and unknown others respond on the basis of stigmatising attitudes. Treating people the same is not always adequate. A care perspective requires us to be attentive to particular needs, without devaluing the person who has these needs. It encourages a positive and proactive response based on understanding that, for example, someone may be isolated and withdrawn not because they want to be or because they have a reserved personality, but because they are experiencing a severe depression. A care perspective encourages a responsibility on all to care enough about others to recognise that behaviours that we may find strange or unusual could indicate a need for help, or at least understanding, rather than the 'discomfort and unease' that Mark Brown identified in stranger responses to his learning disabled son (see Chapter Three).

The comfort of strangers

Many of our day to day interactions involve stranger relationships. Indeed for some isolated older people, interactions with strangers may comprise the majority of their human contact. The conversations they enter into on buses, in shops, or in the park may be the only conversation they have in a day. The way in which they are treated when they go to make an appointment at the hairdresser, at the doctor's surgery or when they pay a bill at the bank can have an important impact on their sense of well-being. Can we include such relationships, which comprise relationships that Taylor (2011) has described as 'distant', within an analysis of the significance of care in everyday life? Does it stretch the meaning of care too far to suggest that encounters such as this, which may be fleeting, one-off, and impersonal in the sense that they take place between people who do not even know each other's names, could be understood as constituting a form of care if they demonstrate an awareness of and concern for the other?

In order to address these questions it is useful to consider other ways in which such encounters between strangers have been considered, both theoretically and in policy terms. Most attention to stranger interactions has been prompted by concerns about a perceived breakdown in everyday civilities characterising contemporary social life (Buonfino and Mulgan, 2009). It is not my purpose here to engage with the debate about whether, empirically, things are worse now than they were 20, 50 or 100 years ago, but it is useful to consider the language that has been used within public policy about this and how the perceived 'problem' has been conceptualised.

The concept of 'respect' has been invoked in the context of policies intended to counteract the perceived incivility of public behaviour – particularly among young people. In policy terms this is closely related to the introduction of the term 'anti-social behaviour' as a means of seeking to characterise what might be understood as 'sub-criminal' behaviour that is virtually impossible to define, but which, for a period of more than 10 years in the UK, was the focus of a raft of policy initiatives (Squires, 2008; Millie, 2009; Prior, 2009). One of the problems with respect, as it has been invoked in policy terms, is thus the way in which it has been employed to counter a perceived disrespect among particular groups within the population towards the 'majority' population. Although not exclusively concerned with the behaviour of young people – referred to in extreme cases as 'feral youth' – in practice most anti-social behaviour policies and initiatives have been focused on young people.

As elaborated by former UK Prime Minister Tony Blair, respect is something that has to be earned by the demonstration of proper behaviour – but only when there is evidence of particular forms of 'disrespectful' behaviour on the part of those who, for example, drop litter, queue jump or harass neighbours. There is no suggestion that either government or the 'respectful majority' need to earn respect (Millie, 2009). However, respect like care carries a lay resonance that means we cannot reject the concept out of hand because of the way in which it has been employed by particular politicians. In Chapter Two

I identified the way in which Daniel Engster has named respect as a principle underlying care:'the recognition that others are worthy of our attention and responsiveness, are presumed capable of understanding and expressing their needs, and are not lesser beings just because they have needs they cannot meet on their own' (2007, p 31). This would suggest that young people, and others, who are identified as behaving in ways that earn an 'anti-social' label, should also be accorded respect and that there should be attentiveness to the needs that may lie behind their behaviour. And, in spite of his work being invoked by Prime Minister Blair in support of government initiatives in this area, Richard Sennett (2003) was much more concerned with linking both material inequalities and the behaviour of institutions with an absence of respect, rather than with identifying sub-groups of the population as to blame for a breakdown in social order.

Respect carries with it notions of mutuality and reciprocity and is also linked with recognition. Disrespect is one aspect of the cultural and symbolic injustice that Fraser (1997) identifies in relation to the recognition dimension of justice. Honneth (2005) draws on different philosophical traditions that identify respect for the other as a person as fundamental to any concept of recognition. Respect for someone means we value them, at a minimal level as another human being, and thus reciprocal respect is a necessary basis on which to build social as well as personal relationships. At both individual and collective levels, people need to experience positive recognition to feel that they are being properly and justly treated. Care is not possible without respect.

Older people's fear of the disrespect (or worse) that they might encounter in public spaces is understood to be one factor that isolates them in their own homes. Subjective perceptions of the way in which people interact in public spaces generally, as well as the way in which they personally are treated, were cited in our study of older people and well-being as having an impact on their sense of being well, or not, not only within the specific localities in which they live, but existentially within contemporary society. For example, in a rather nostalgic reflection on the past, one man in our well-being study said, "When I look at the days before the war, people were friendly. They'd stop and chat to you. Now you just get a hello and walk on. Miserable looking creatures."

However, the positive encounters with strangers in their everyday lives can contribute to a sense of being connected with others and the outside world. The following quotes from first a man and then a woman reflect this.

> ... because I like the human contact you know, the same as I never use the, down in the supermarket, I never go to this place where you book yourself in I go through the check out cos you can have a bit of banter with the checkout people and there are certain checkout people I have, I have struck up a relationship with down there, so that's good ...
>
> People will often talk to me actually. It's strange. People will ... I otherwise will chat to people if they look down and out and sorrowful at the bus stop where I'm waiting. I tend to open up the conversation. (Ward, Barnes and Gahagan, 2012, p 32)

Such encounters certainly suggest recognition, both on the part of others and on the part of older people themselves towards others, but can they be considered care? There are perhaps two ways in which we might characterise them as such. The first is suggested by the first of these two quotes which implies that what might start out as stranger relationships can, in some cases, develop beyond this. The elderly man who is speaking is relieved that his shopping trips have enabled him to 'strike up a relationship' which might carry the possibility that it would at least be noticed if he failed to appear. Another example of this is a personal one. Following the death of my mother in law, the chemist from whom she used to receive her medication asked about her because she had not seen her for a couple of weeks. More generally the importance of these encounters may be understood as greater for those who have few other contacts than they might appear to those whose busy lives are substantially taken up with a range of different types of interaction. The narratives of the older people in our study were full of stories of loss of the intimate relationships they had with family and friends who had been important to them. In this context encounters with strangers which involve attentiveness to their feelings and circumstances may be experienced as evidence that someone else cares enough about them to spend time over a conversation, and thus the subjective experience may take this beyond respect or recognition to encompass a form of care.

Virtual strangers

I also want to reflect briefly on the potential for care among strangers who never meet because they encounter each other through electronic communication. This is a huge topic that I do not attempt to offer any comprehensive perspective on, but it is relevant both to a developing theory of care and to practices that might promote this. There are different aspects to this. Telecare and telemedicine are technologies through which information, advice, support and occasionally interventions can be offered in the context of formal service provision. This is not the focus of my discussion here, although the ethical significance of such developments has received some attention (eg Ganyo et al, 2011). More relevant to my discussion in this chapter are exchanges that develop or are deliberately stimulated among those who share experiences (such as living with cancer) in order to support or care for each other; to express support and solidarity for unknown others experiencing suffering or oppression, and among those who come into contact through Web-based media such as YouTube.

One of the best known examples of a Web-based support group is that hosted by Macmillan Cancer Support in the UK (www.macmillan.org.uk). Known as the Macmillan Online Community, it offers those living with cancer, sufferers and their families and friends, an opportunity to engage in an online exchange of information, advice and support. The following extract is from an exchange prompted by a daughter whose mother was in the final stages of bowel cancer and who was dealing with uncertainty about whether she was getting the best advice from clinicians. She was also uncertain about how much she and her sister should tell their mother about the seriousness of her condition. One response, from a woman called Tracey, was as follows.

> I can only feedback my mum's latter weeks if that helps? ... I was told that the family is the best judge of deterioration and that you instantly know when it is happening. I think this was very true you do. I would say trust your instincts. I would like to say something more positive but I think often you just know when the end is nearing.
>
> I so feel for you Diane because the journey is horrendous but if you want the truth the medics need to be communicating with you ...
>
> Sorry but I get a bit stuck when knowing what to say to somebody like yourself because I know how tough it is and nothing makes it any easier. All I can add is I will be thinking of you. I find that each person's story at this stage I can relate to because it was only a few weeks ago when I was living it. (http://community.macmillan.org.uk/forums/p/37471/419361.aspx)

Tracey had never met Diane, but Diane's response indicated they had exchanged communications before and in one response said she 'sent her love'. It could be suggested that it is easy to make entries on a website and that do to so is simply evidence of superficial intimacy. It requires no action beyond typing a few paragraphs of text. But the fact that exchanges do build up, that Tracey is responding within a few weeks of experiencing her own mother's death, and that she is thinking what it is from her experience that might be helpful to Diane, can also be seen as being both attentive and taking responsibility, trying to act competently and being aware of how what she is offering is being received. And both this exchange and others prompted by Diane's original post certainly demonstrate reciprocity as those who engage are both offering and receiving practical suggestions and expressions of emotional support. These 'virtual' exchanges may augment or replace the support given and received within self-help groups which also characterise groups like NAG (as discussed earlier) and the self-help groups organising around different aspects of parenting that Williams (2004c) considers.

Harley and Fitzpatrick (2009) have explored an interesting example of spontaneous communication among strangers using YouTube as a conversational medium. The story of Peter, or Geriatric1927 as he calls himself, is unusual in that the majority of those 'vloggers' who post video blogs on YouTube are young people for whom information and communication technology is a usual part of their everyday world. Peter, in contrast, was born in 1927 and is one of the few older people who make regular use of this medium. Peter's vlogs started by telling the story of his life, but he developed a following among younger people who started to contact him and ask him for advice, for example about drug use. In their article Harley and Fitzpatrick consider aspects of the multimodal communication enabled by vlogs in terms of their capacity to reproduce aspects of face to face communication, in this context specifically in relation to intergenerational communication. They conclude that:

> Web 2.0 technologies such as YouTube represent an untapped resource for intergenerational initiatives aimed at re-engaging generations and that people are able to creatively construct effective communication even within the constraints of this medium. By understanding the ways in which vlogging can be appropriated, we can look for opportunities to more proactively facilitate and support this as a form of social engagement, eg, through guidelines for how to use video

> blogging, through creating specific opportunities for more older and younger people to connect online such as via local initiatives, and through designing accessible tools that can make it easier for conversational partners to interweave their video contributions. (2007, p 689)

We might also ask what contribution such developments might make to enabling care giving and receiving among those who do not come face to face. The time Peter spends seriously considering and responding to his young followers' questions indicates ways in which he cares about what happens not only to those young people themselves, but to young people in general. He is attentive to what they say and considers carefully how to respond to them. While this was not the objective of the study, in a personal communication Dave Harley suggested that this was an example of the potential for caring for unknown others through the internet. And this example is a good one of an older person in a care-giving rather than a care-receiving role.

Finally, organisations like Amnesty International, which has since its inception mobilised people to express care and concern for both named and unnamed strangers across the world, are using internet communication to increase the scope and size of response to human rights abuses. Joining up and paying a membership fee, signing an email petition or making an entry on Facebook are limited but cumulatively effective demonstrations of care for strangers, employing new technologies to more effectively achieve already established objectives. It is well established that expressions of concern and support from strangers can make a qualitative difference to the experiences of those unjustly imprisoned. Information and communication technology can both encourage more strangers to feel able to express such concern and put a 'human face' to collective injustices. As Silk (1998) observes: 'mass media and electronic networks play a significant part in extending the range of care and caring beyond the traditional context of shared spatio-temporal locale and our "nearest and dearest" to embrace "distant others"' (p 179). But for such practices to address issues of injustice and inequality they need to be embedded within a broader attentiveness to the processes that produce them, rather than remaining focused on individual human rights.

Conclusion

An ethic of care that takes the mother–child relationship (Noddings, 1984) and maternal thinking (Ruddick, 1989) as the basis on which to build a concept of moral practice in the public sphere can offer only a limited way of addressing the challenges of how we can live well together with strangers, both those in our midst and those who are physically distant from us. In this chapter I have considered the way in which an inclusive, political theory of care needs to encompass relationships that go beyond those of intimacy and to address relationships with unknown others as well as with those we encounter fleetingly. Different writers have addressed this and offered convincing arguments for why care is necessary to theorising the just treatment of strangers as well as known others. A global perspective on interdependencies and the way they impact on the everyday lives of people we will never meet encourages a concept and practice of global social justice that embodies the relational sensibilities of an ethic of care. As the work on the treatment of refugees demonstrates, how we treat strangers from other parts of the world also impacts on the way in which we treat strangers within our midst. It takes more than anti-discrimination legislation to generate just treatment of those regarded as 'different' or 'other'. This becomes clear when we consider the limitations of such legislation in overcoming the exclusions experienced by people who live with mental health problems as well as by disabled people.

In Chapter Four I considered the position of migrant care workers and the implications for the practice of care within care work in the West. In this chapter I have also drawn attention to 'those left behind' – the way in which the 'care deficit' is transferred to those who are least powerful within global socioeconomic relations. The more frequent and diverse movements of people that characterise contemporary life necessitate an awareness of care needs and the relationship between care and justice at a global level. But this is also an issue for the way in which international relations are conducted, and for the way responsibilities to poor and oppressed people are enacted by rich states and transnational bodies. The sources of such exclusions and oppressions are relational as well as material and an ethical response demands attentiveness to the way in which they are produced as well as to how they may be ameliorated. Care ethics requires attentiveness to the cultural, social and political, as well as individual, contexts in which needs are both produced and experienced and this attentiveness enables a more holistic response than that offered by liberal notions of human rights, and a more critically effective response than that of an international communitarianism.

The development of a vast array of means of communicating with those we never meet face to face may mean that we are more aware of strangers and that there are more possibilities for expressing care for strangers than ever before. Many of our everyday interactions are with people we do not know. The quality of those encounters can make an important difference to well-being. For some, such interactions evidence a lack of recognition and respect, and for some they involve discrimination and stigmatisation. In Chapter Two I identified respect as one of the principles underpinning care and here I have suggested we need to retrieve respect from the very partial and exclusive ways in which it has been invoked in UK social policy, to reinstate its importance as a relational value. From the perspective of everyday lives, we can see examples of an absence of care in stranger relationships and the consequences of this and indications of how the comfort of strangers can make a difference to subjective well-being. This is not to propose that it is desirable or possible for everyday encounters with strangers to embody the intimate and intensive care that characterises either family or friendship relationships. But the development of a critical and holistic ethic of care requires that we think about care not only in terms of intimate relations, but in terms of attentiveness to and responsibility for others in more distant relation to us.

SEVEN

Places and environments

> On the most general level, we suggest that caring be viewed as a species activity that includes everything that we do to maintain, continue, and repair our 'world' so that we can live in it as well as possible. That world includes our bodies, our selves, *and our environment,* all of which we seek to interweave in a complex, life-sustaining web. (Quoted in Tronto, 1993, p 103, emphasis added)

In this chapter I consider Tronto and Fisher's inclusion of 'the environment' within the life-sustaining web of care. This has potentially very broad implications, encompassing our relationships with the micro environments in which we live, through to the global level and the relationship of humanity to the planet on which we live. As we will see, adopting this perspective takes us into some similar territory to that addressed in the previous chapter in relation to care for distant others. 'Care for the environment' is one of the familiar, everyday ways in which the concept of care is invoked. In this context it reflects increasing concerns that a lack of care for the 'natural' world in which we live is in danger of putting the sustainability of that world at risk and, in the process, increasing tension and conflicts between those whose lives are lived in different places on the planet, and between those who have the material resources to avoid the worst of environmental degradation and those who do not. There are also times when 'care for the environment' is seen to conflict with prioritising care for people.

Consideration of the relationship between social policies and environmental issues has moved beyond a rather marginal and minority interest. For example, Michael Cahill has written on transport policy and social policy, and on green social policy generally (Cahill, 2003, 2010), and a recent special issue of the journal *Critical Social Policy* (Aldred, 2011) reflected a range of ways in which environmental and social policy issues need to be brought into conjunction in policy making. Articles in that issue considered, for example, flood risk and its differential impact on more deprived coastal communities (Walker and Burningham, 2011); the distributional impacts of climate change mitigation policies (Buchs et al, 2011), and the relationship between capitalist political economy and environmental injustices (Bell, 2011). The contested concept of 'environmental justice' employed here introduces another dimension of the complex nature of social justice and suggests additional ways in which we need to think about the relationship between care and justice.

Walker and Burningham (2011) highlight the way in which the devastating floods caused by Hurricane Katrina in the southern states of the US not only demonstrated the highly uneven impact of such disasters, with those in already disadvantaged situations disproportionately affected by them, but also the way in which this called in to question a straightforward distinction between 'natural' and 'technical' problems. Lawson (2007) refers to Katrina as an example of an 'unnatural' disaster. The focus of Walker and Burningham's article, however, is on the differential impact of flooding in the UK, drawing on two key questions that frame a concern with environmental justice (or injustice). The first is a distributional issue: the relationship between social inequalities and environmental 'goods' and 'bads'. The second involves an evaluation of such patterns: 'in the light of what is expected to be a just and fair situation, in respect of, for example, how the inequalities are being produced, who is responsible for them, how relevant decisions have been made and how government policy and practice are enacted' (pp 217-8). It is possible to relate a variety of dimensions of inequality and disadvantage to the disproportionate impact of flooding. These include: social class; levels of social capital within communities; health status; gender and age. However, Walker and Burningham argue that a justice frame is more useful than an inequality perspective in developing an understanding of why such patterns exist and thus in focusing attention on where and what type of action is needed to mitigate or indeed prevent such injustices occurring. Such a perspective exposes the way in which the most technically efficient solutions of flood risk management may not be the fairest solutions. From the perspective of my argument here, we can suggest that in order to develop solutions that both deal with the environmentally problematic issue of flooding (or, indeed, other effects of climate change), and are socially just, there is a need to care about both the environment and those most adversely affected by environmental catastrophes. And as Lawson (2007, p 6) has suggested, in an argument that resonates with the discussion in the previous chapter about global interdependencies and the importance of care for distant strangers, such responses cannot just be short-lived, humanitarian reactions to crisis, such as floods, drought or earthquake, but require continuing caring responses to ongoing violence, racism and poverty in places like New

Orleans, Haiti or Sub-Saharan Africa. She links an ethic of care to an international politics of responsibility.

> Care ethics then, challenges us to be attentive and responsive to our own location within circuits of power and privilege that connect our daily lives to those who are constructed as distant from us. For example, how are long-term relationships of inequality structured through our individual and collective stances on global climate change, on international debt forgiveness, on immigration, on free trade policies, on global health research and action, on fair trade and organics movements; and how might these be restructured as relations of care and mutuality? (p 7)

Particularly when financial resources are seen to be strained, the tension between local caring responsibilities and those prompted by global interdependencies is seen to require the type of ordering of obligations that Engster (2007) has argued for. But Lawson is suggesting that it is not possible for us to separate out 'near' and 'far' caring responsibilities in a straightforward manner. Catney and Doyle (2011) also apply a North–South perspective to a political perspective on environmental issues. They argue the limitations of a liberal cosmopolitan view of the relationship between North and South on environmental (as on other) issues, not least because of the failure to take into account the responsibilities of 'past citizens' in the North for creating the conditions in which carbon-intensive industries have created the problem faced by present citizens. They thus introduce a temporal as well as spatial dimension to the issue of environmental justice and offer another perspective on the issue of interdependencies and the importance of contextual understanding of 'rooted communities of space and place' (p 190).

Space and place are clearly vital to an understanding of individual and collective well-being. We live our lives in particular physical locations and it is necessary to go beyond the notion of 'good fortune' (Smith, 2000) to understand how and why those spaces and places impact on our lives to good and bad effect. Not only have social policy academics developed an increasingly sophisticated and critical analysis of the significance of place and of environmental issues to the core concerns of social policy, geographers have also explored the significance of care, ethics and social justice in their analysis of place and space (eg Silk, 1998; Smith, 1999; Lawson, 2007). I draw on such work in this chapter, but my starting point is a rather different one.

The questions underpinning my analysis start once again from the relationality of care, the importance of including both care giving and care receiving within an understanding of the significance of care in our everyday lives, and the way in which social policies and policies concerned with place and space can support or undermine that. Thus, firstly, I am concerned with the importance people attach to being able to care for their environment, and, secondly, the extent to which they feel cared for by the way in which their environment is designed and maintained. My argument reflects an understanding of the spatial as inherently relational; that concepts of space and place need to be formulated in terms of social relations, and that social relationships cannot be fully understood without locating these in space (and time) (Massey, 1994, 2005). Looking at the issue of care in the context of people's relationships with their environments once again highlights the significance of a reciprocal understanding of such relationships, including the impact of inequalities and other power relationships.

In order to interrogate the significance of care ethics to a better understanding of how we can live well in the environments we inhabit, I have once again selected three different contexts to consider. These examples offer a rather different perspective from some of the work cited earlier as they are all concerned with environments that are directly created by human activity. While it is not possible to think about any 'natural environments' that are unshaped by human intervention, one aspect of the way we live in the world involves designing, creating and shaping specific environments for different purposes. The three examples that I consider here all emphasise the everyday interactions in which we may both give and receive care within different spaces and places. The first focuses on older people's relationships with the immediate places in which they live. The concept of 'home' is an emotionally charged one and one that is central to the practice of care within families as well as the construction of social care policy and practice. Thus it is important to understand home as a contributor to the experience of receiving care, and as a focus for care giving. The second example pulls back to consider the neighbourhoods and public spaces that surround people's homes. Here I am concerned with the messages that they send about the extent to which people feel that the public authorities that are responsible for these environments care about them, and the extent to which different groups of people feel comfortable within them. These are physically constructed spaces that embody collective decisions about resource allocation, design and 'what sort of people' are prioritised as inhabitants and users of public spaces. My interest here is both in the messages that public officials as representatives of the state give about care for citizens and residents, and how residents themselves seek to demonstrate their care for their broader environment in the way in which they use and seek to shape spaces and places. The third example is rather different. Most adults spend much of their lives in work environments. In Chapter Four I considered the importance of the particular context in which care work is undertaken in terms of the capacity of workers to practise ethical care. Here I consider other types of work environment as well as the place of work in the construction of active citizens from a care perspective.

Older people and home

Home has both functional and symbolic significance. The social geographer Graham Rowles has conducted extensive research on older people's relationships with the places in which they live, developing sophisticated ideas about the person/environment fit. He refers to a sense of 'being in place' which, in the case of older people, refers to a lifetime of experiences that reflect different dimensions of 'insideness', encompassing familiarity with the physical setting, social integration and historical legacies associated with living life in a particular place (eg Rowles, 2000; Rowles and Watkin, 2003). Home is much more than a physical space in which to eat, sleep, pass time, entertain family and friends – although all those are important as well. When older people say they want both to stay living in their own homes and that they want to die at home, they are expressing the relational importance of home. Home embodies aspects of both current and former identities: it is important in terms of people's relationships to themselves; to significant others with whom that space has been and continues to be shared; and to adult children, for whom it is a base to go out from and return. In their study of environment and identity in later life, Sheila Peace and her colleagues (Peace et al, 2006) consider the symbolic meaning of the way older people present themselves through the way in which they present their homes. Homes embody memories of who we and others close to us have been, as well as who we want to tell others we are.

The capacity to shape the immediate environment is important. Peace and her colleagues suggest that:

> It seems very likely from our data that older people take a lot of pleasure in and maintain confidence levels through the continued power they have to create, alter and adapt the fine details and routines of domestic daily living. Even for those who have become very frail and sometimes immobile,

> arranging and re-arranging small objects and ornaments is important because it demonstrates the importance of agency that can be seriously eroded when others take over tasks that can still be managed. (2006, p 98)

As well as physically shaping their environments through placing, arranging and rearranging objects within the home, the routines that older people develop in organising aspects of their home environment serve to enable them to integrate aspects of their lives. The way older people in Peace and her colleagues' study talked about aspects of their home environments, and objects within these spaces, enabled them to present themselves as complex, multifaceted and creative individuals. Such arrangements, and the life shaping that they embody, may be challenged by the rearrangements necessitated by increasing frailty and the sometimes major upheavals of, for example, moving a bed downstairs, or installing equipment to move the person from bed to chair, into the bath, or up the stairs. Some people may resist the idea that their home effectively becomes a treatment location, invaded both by the technologies of medical care and the presence of multiple practitioners. As access to space becomes more limited, key items may be arranged within easy reach of a favourite chair. An older person's physical world may be reduced to what they are able to reach within a few steps and, to an outsider, this may appear to create visually messy and physically dangerous clutter. The temptation may be to 'tidy up', to remove things that appear to be 'unnecessary' from a pile on a table, to shift things from floors because there is a danger that they create a 'fall hazard'. But this may interfere with the ordering of physical space within the home that embodies an older person's sense of who they are and what is important to them at this stage of their life.

If homes, the objects within them, and the way in which both internal space and external space (gardens, yards or balconies) are arranged embody such emotional and symbolic significance for older people, then their capacity to care for their immediate environment is significant. In some instances this requires getting others to do the practical work of 'looking after' house or garden because the physical capacity to do so has gone. In some cases there is a strong wish for someone to come and 'take over' as the work not only of physical care for home, but also the management of repairs becomes too much (Ward et al, 2012). The ability to secure this help depends in part on other relationships that can be the source of practical help, and in part on whether people can afford to pay others to do this work. In both cases there is a danger that such 'looking after' will not be done in the way the older person wants. One woman in our study of older people and well-being spoke of the way in which her husband anticipated his death by getting everything in the house repaired and decorated so that his wife would not have to worry about this. His care for her was expressed through his care for what would be her home environment when she was on her own (Ward et al, 2011).

A physical incapacity to look after the home environment is one reason for deciding to move elsewhere and this can be experienced as a significant loss. Talking about the impact of her husband's stroke, one of the women interviewed in our study of older people and well-being noted that this:

> ... had led to a decision to sell the big house they used to own and to move into a flat and 'he absolutely hated the loss of a garden'. Jennifer described the house itself as a loss, but one she recognised was part of other life changes as it had become too big for the two of them and too hard to look after. (Ward, Barnes and Gahagan, 2012, p 72)

Losing the capacity to care for the home environment can mark a significant shift in older people's lives. This links with their capacity to care for themselves, which in turn reflects their confidence that there are people nearby whom they can call on if necessary. Another woman who lived alone spoke of deciding to leave the home she had loved for many years following an incident when she needed to call for help and could not find anyone nearby to respond to her.

Homes are also places of security and feeling insecure can also mean feeling uncared for. Lack of any relationships with those living close by can mean homes are also places in which it is possible to feel shut away from others. One 97-year-old woman interviewed for the Ward et al study said: "Oh I'm here on my own. Absolutely. A week can go by and I don't speak to anybody at all. Not a soul; not a living soul." In discussions among members of the older people's research team conducting our well-being study, there was a lengthy consideration of the tension between maintaining privacy and a hope that others would be sufficiently concerned about them to check up if they had not been seen for some time. This was prompted by interview responses that indicated that, even among those living in housing schemes designed specifically for older people, people often did not know their neighbours, and by information about a sheltered housing scheme where it was a matter of policy that staff did not go into residents' rooms. Most members of the research team liked the idea of the 'relational security' associated with a concierge system that still operates in some properties. This involves someone having overall responsibility for the property and for ensuring the security of not only the building, but also the people within it. Such a system carries the possibility of the development of trusting relationships which can minimise the tension between a formal rule-based system that seeks to define the boundaries between respecting privacy, and demonstrating care and concern for residents' safety.

I started this section by noting the reluctance of many older people to move from their 'own homes' into residential or nursing homes. This again was an important feature of discussions among our research team and one which participants found very hard and quite depressing. Many of those interviewed had some experience of residential care – either directly or through friends or relatives. One couple in their 90s had been exploring future options and had tried out residential homes by taking one week respite breaks. While one experience was quite positive, another had been very negative. It was less the physical environment that was the problem than a sense that staff 'did not care'. This was reflected more broadly by research participants, with accounts of pills not being administered properly or being left for the resident to take herself rather than seeing that she actually took them; and one person, just out of hospital and sent for convalescence, saying she was "dumped" in the room with no help offered, and the food put on the table where she couldn't reach it. Team members discussing these issues noted the low status of care staff working in these places (see also Chapter Four). The following extract comes from the notes of this discussion.

> Management should be looking at this – private homes are about making money, and a culture can develop where staff don't feel valued. The human demands of care work are such that the profile of the work should be given – it should be recognised that the work is really important you are working with people at the end of their lives, it can mean that there are difficulties you can't always resolve things, therefore the staff need to be well supported otherwise you de-humanise you stop seeing residents as people which is the worst thing that can happen, and you can become immune to how de-humanising it is – lack of recognition of personhood and how really bad actions can be normalised and not noticed. Care is not valued in whatever context it's given – the devaluation of care.

This discussion illustrates, in a very specific context, Doreen Massey's argument that: 'The very acknowledgement of our constitutive interrelateness implies a spatiality; and that in turn implies that the nature of that spatiality should be a crucial avenue of enquiry and political engagement' (Massey, 2005, p 189). Consideration of residential homes as places in which to live cannot be separated from an evaluation of the social relations within them; and these are political issues concerned with the collective valuing, or otherwise, of care.

Sheila Peace and her colleagues also looked at the experiences of older people who had made this move to residential care (Peace et al, 2006). They noted what they referred to as the 'pared down' environment in which older people live in residential homes, but that within these reduced horizons there is an importance attached, as in people's own homes, to the capacity to arrange and rearrange objects, whether memorabilia, clothes or other belongings. But the capacity to do this is usually limited to the rooms people are allocated for their bedrooms and individual sitting space; it does not extend to the areas where people are expected to share communal activities with other residents. Because both the physical and temporal ordering of these spaces is controlled by others, the scope that remains for older people to practise identity construction is much reduced (Peace et al, 2006, p 125). Not only do older people have a much less secure tenure of the 'home' in which they are now living, they have had to discard many of the material objects that were important to them. The consequence is that:

> ... as concealment of frailty becomes very unlikely, revealing oneself as a complex person with decades of antecedent events 'laid down' as the basis of identity, also becomes very difficult. Life is lived in a unicellular setting, associations are reduced for many reasons and activity that links an individual with life and people beyond home is infrequent. There is little left to order and we argue it is the paucity of space, objects and routines that leads to identity becoming more fixed than dynamic. In this sense, environment can be said to inhibit the production and reproduction of identity. (p 125)

What Peace and her colleagues are describing here can, in the terms in which I am approaching this issue, be understood as an impoverishment in the person–environment relationship consequent on an inability to shape the environment in order to live in it as well as possible. In this context the importance of interpersonal relationships is perhaps even more significant. Some of the residents in this study enjoyed being cared for and not having to bother to look after their environment: 'we see here older people, weary from the effort of not managing routine daily life within the mainstream, finding much to appreciate in settings that offer care, support and kindness' (p 124).

This reminds us of the impossibility of separating out experiences of the physical and interpersonal environment in which people live in terms of both care giving and care receiving. In Chapter Five I discussed the potential of interactions between residents in the care experiences of both young and older people in residential settings. In discussing 'homely residential care', Peace and Holland (2001) identified the importance to many residents in small homes of being able to combine privacy with enjoyment of 'the ebb and flow of ordinary life around them as the family, staff, and other visitors dropped in, brought the shopping or exchanged gossip' (p 404). Writing of the meaning of home in the lives of people with dementia Robinson and her colleagues argue that: '... [it] is embedded in human, and in particular, family relationships ... For example, Frank (2005) argues that when a dementia resident says "I want to go home", they don't want to literally go to a physical place they knew as home. They are, rather, seeking validation of their personhood, of their identity, which can only occur in relationships' (Robinson et al, 2010, p 492). Assessments of the quality of small residential homes for people with dementia by relatives pointed, once again, to the centrality of relationships, the capacity to be attentive to individual needs and the importance of time and space to developing relational connections with both residents and their families. The physical design is a necessary, but not sufficient, indicator of the embodiment of care within spaces built for care.

Caring for people/caring for places

Both the design and maintenance of public spaces offer evidence of the extent to which public bodies care for their citizens – or otherwise. They also suggest which sort of people are assumed to be the 'users' of such spaces and contribute to the social construction of relationships within them. In so doing they indicate the extent to which those with responsibility for designing and maintaining public spaces are attentive to the different needs of different users. This has been a major focus of disability campaigners who have quite successfully argued that physically and sensorily disabled people have been designed out of many public spaces that assume a capacity to get up steps, hold open heavy swinging doors and negotiate streets cluttered by street furniture. Responsibility for ensuring physical access is now included within disability discrimination legislation in the UK and elsewhere. But there are many ways in which environmental design can include and exclude, and many ways in which lack of care for physical environments can contribute to a sense that these are risky spaces from which people may wish to exclude themselves. For example, some of the families whose experiences of living in inner city neighbourhoods are discussed by Power (2007; see also Chapter Three) decided during the course of her research to leave those neighbourhoods because they felt that their local councils did not care enough about them to listen to them or to act to ensure a safe environment in which to live. One of the mothers in her study summed up the sense that a failure to care on the part of public officials resulted in a lack of care from local residents as follows.

> The appearance of the area is very bad and sad. It reinforces the opinion [that] it's a dump – because it is a dump. They don't want to improve it so they trash it. I blame the council a lot because they take the attitude that we're only gutter sweeps ... that we deserve less services. If you don't get treated with good quality services, why should you care? (p 22)

Others had tried to play a part in shaping their local areas. Another mother cited by Power had become a school governor, and worked with others to try to improve the local park, but felt "You end up thinking nothing you say'll make any difference, so I'm not entirely sure .... " (p 26).

Here I want to consider how we might consider relationships between people and places not only as civil rights issues, but also from within an ethic of care framework.

One of the problems of legislation designed to ensure the civil rights of different groups of citizens and of resident non-citizens is whether this can be framed in such a way as to include all possible situations. Thus, for example, does disability discrimination legislation require public authorities to ensure sufficient public toilets and publicly provided seating to enable older people to make use of a shopping centre with confidence, as well as requiring that those in wheelchairs can access it via slopes and lifts rather than by steps? How specific can legislation be about the diverse exclusions experienced by different groups and thus the actions necessary to overcome them? This is similar to the type of problem that Hankivsky (2004) addresses in her discussion of Canadian gender equality legislation. Her work demonstrates the gap between legal definitions of rights and attentiveness and responsiveness in particular situations. For rights that are apparently enshrined within such legislation to be realised, it requires an understanding of the contextualised experience of inequality, and it often requires the law to be invoked in legal challenge to already existing practices. While such legislation is important as both a symbolic and a judicial means of ensuring justice, a care perspective would suggest that attentiveness to need and awareness of different groups' experiences of public spaces should inform design and planning in the first instance. And the particular contexts of specific environments require not only a generalised attentiveness to the needs of different groups, but also a real understanding of needs in context. Thus, for example, many of the older people in our study of well-being enjoyed Brighton as a place to live and, in particular, liked both to be able to see the sea and to be able to walk by it. But Brighton is a very hilly town and, even for older people living not far away from the seafront, the sea is inaccessible because of this. Public officials cannot even out the terrain, but they could care enough to ensure that public transport is available on routes to the seafront. And this, in turn, suggests that not only should public officials be responsible for attending to diverse needs when planning the physical environments within which people live their lives beyond their homes, but that they also need to enable different groups of people to contribute to that planning process (see also Chapter Eight). Not only should public officials care about those they are designing for, they should also enable residents to demonstrate their care for their environment by contributing to shaping it.

The history of public policy, in the UK and elsewhere, includes multiple 'special projects' intended to address physical, social and economic need for regeneration and renewal within designated deprived locations (eg DETR, 1999; SEU, 2001). The precise political, social and developmental ideologies underpinning community development projects; urban and neighbourhood renewal initiatives; health, employment and education action zones, and sustainable communities initiatives have varied; however, one perspective on these is that they demonstrate the importance attached to focusing on specific needs in particular contexts and developing a holistic response in which local residents are not only recipients of 'care', but also givers of care through their participation in the process of renewal. However, it is also possible to argue that the necessity for such 'special' programmes is in itself evidence of a failure to care sufficiently, both about and for those places and the people living in them. The fact that they are in need of a 'special project' to rescue them from environmental and social degradation is indicative of a lack of ongoing care on the part of national and local politicians and public officials about the consequences of economic and social policy making. There has been little attentiveness to their needs and evidence of substantial incompetence in creating and implementing policies that can enable people to live well in those areas. Most of these place-based initiatives were also established on a competitive basis, that is, public authorities and their 'partners' in the voluntary and community (and sometimes private) sectors had to prepare sophisticated proposals to make the case for why they should receive special project status. It could also be argued that setting up such initiatives as competitions that required the local area to be presented in bleak terms, to demonstrate the level of neediness necessary to qualify for the attention on offer, is insensitive to the way in which local people respond to how others view them. It also requires considerable activity on the part of those preparing proposals without any guarantee of success, and gives a message to those who are not successful in achieving special project status that they are not worthy of attention.

Victoria Lawson (2007) identifies the reduction in the Bush administration's funding of community development in the United Sates as evidence of the privatisation of social goods and lack of care for poverty and inequality. I am also suggesting here that it is not only the amount of resource made available for the maintenance and development of the environment in which people live that evidences care, or the lack of it, but also how such initiatives are set up. The experience of 'community engagement' in a host of initiatives ostensibly designed to enable local people to influence local decision making and shape the environment in which they live is often one of time-limited commitment on the part of public officials who have to meet externally imposed targets, rather than prioritise responding to local concerns (Barnes et al, 2007). And one extreme case demonstrates how local people experience wariness if not scepticism in response to attempts to engage them in solving 'local' problems (Prior et al, 2007). In this instance residents in a highly deprived area were invited and encouraged to come up with proposals for dealing with an increase in gun crime and other forms of criminal activity in a context in which they were experiencing the direct impact of years of neglect on the state of housing, poor public services and low levels of educational qualification.

It is important also to consider everyday experiences of using public spaces from the perspective of different groups of people. Kristen Day

(2000) has applied care ethics to an analysis of women's experiences of public spaces. Her analysis considers the constraints on such use that arise from women's caring roles, suggesting that women may privilege others' needs over their own because they subsume their own needs and interests over others' preferences for 'which spaces' to engage with as consumers. Thus they go to places because their husbands or children like them rather than because they do, and they choose to live in suburban areas because they are good places to bring up children, but which they can experience as socially isolating for themselves. But as well as offering a rather essentialised view of women, care and place, Day's analysis also has important insights into the issues with which I am concerned here: the way in which public policy decisions interact with people's experience of place as giving or withholding care. She also offers important insights into the way in which an ethic of care perspective can contribute to a positive view of public space as a source of possibilities for care.

Thus, she reviews research which indicates the link between planning decisions that separate residential accommodation from public services and retail facilities, and which limit public transport, with an increase in the functional burden of caring for children. She highlights how 'repressive or restrictive care-giving from others' (p 109), including admonitions not to go out alone at night, can further serve to isolate women from public spaces. And she offers a distinctive view of ways in which women's relational sensibilities may enhance fear and vulnerability in public spaces. There are two ways in which she suggests this can happen. First, behaviours that women interpret as courtesies and friendliness towards strangers, such as smiling, being more emotionally expressive and listening, may be misinterpreted or preyed upon. She identifies the way in which women noted that 'niceness' in public spaces prompted fear for their safety. Second, women's concerns are not only for themselves, but also for others: 'Because their experience of public space is often one of interconnectedness and responsibility for others, women may not neatly separate fear for themselves from other feelings of fear ....' (p 116). Thus when women express concern about the safety of public spaces they may be thinking not only of their personal safety, but of that of children and of concern for the preservation of the community as a whole. This was very evident in the stories told by inner city mothers in Power's (2007) study.

This is an issue explored from a rather different perspective by Murray (2009). Her study of children's journeys to school utilises the concept of 'risk landscapes' to understand the experiences and decisions of both children and their mothers regarding their movements through public spaces. For the mothers, the way in which they seek to minimise the risks their children face during such journeys is tied up with their constructions of being a 'good parent'. While Murray does not use the notion of an ethic of care, her work suggests yet another way in which relationships with everyday environments interact with how people care, as well as whether they feel cared for. We can understand an experience of 'risk' as including an absence of care. From the children's perspective, risk factors as diverse as the amount of dog muck on the paths they have to traverse, the amount of traffic on roads they have to cross, and the messages they have picked up from media and their mothers about 'pervy people' can affect their sense of confidence as they make their way to school. But her work also highlights the intensely personal issues that can also affect this. For one brother and sister it was the place where a pet dog had been attacked that they sought to avoid. This illustrates the emotional responses to places and spaces that cannot be controlled or anticipated by policy makers, but which demonstrate a need for attentiveness to the particularity of people's lives and the way in which they relate to places as well as people in order to ensure appropriate support.

Day (2000) argues that an ethic of care can offer a useful perspective on the contribution women can make to the design of environments. She cites research that has looked at feminist utopian plans for housing, neighbourhoods and public spaces, highlighting ways in which they both blur the boundaries between public and privates spaces, and prioritise ways of sustaining relationships and extending care giving beyond the family home (p 113). Women's relational preferences challenge the separation of public spaces designed for discrete 'user groups', and affect their judgements about what are good spaces.

> Women described preferences for public spaces that demonstrated caring and kindness, through design and through employees and others in the space. Descriptions often emphasized social aspects of favoured places. Preferred public places graciously accommodated interaction with friends, family, and strangers. Such places anticipated and met women's needs, including their psychological needs. (p 114)

Krenichyn (2004) similarly links public spaces with women's experiences of the relationships they can develop within them to consider the interaction between space, gender and well-being. She is concerned to counter an emphasis on the constraints women experience through fear in public spaces and her focus is on women's use of a particular public park for physical activity. This study offers another example of the way in which interactions with strangers, as well as more intimate contacts with friends and family, are valued. Sometimes the women developed a sense of friendliness with people they saw regularly; in other cases a quick smile and hello to those they saw regularly were considered enough to build a sense of 'familiarity if not intimacy' (p 123). Because those who jogged regularly in the park tended to do so at the same time of day, women saw the same people regularly and had a sense that if anything happened to them someone would come to their aid. Being with others engaged in similar activities enables women to feel supported. 'Strangers' notice when women drop out of activity for a while because of injury. Companionship offers both security and enjoyment and helps women to take part in physical activity that is a source of health and well-being. The park offers a space in which women can pursue their own interests as well as both give care to and receive care from family members – one single mother described how her young son was teaching her to skate and taking care to ensure she did not hurt herself in the process. Krenichyn does not address specific issues regarding the design of the park that may facilitate the relationship building she describes, but it is evident that the availability of this space within an urban environment makes a huge difference to the women who use it regularly. Whether consciously or not, by making this space available urban planners have both evidenced care for those who use it, and they have made it possible for the women who use it to develop caring relationships with others.

I have considered the importance of home for older people, but it is also the case that older people's experiences of well-being are affected by their relationship with the places in which they live and the extent to which those places indicate attentiveness to their needs and preferences. If older people feel that the needs of young people are prioritised, it can deter them from making use of public leisure spaces (see Ward, Barnes et al, 2012). Both Valentine (2004) and Vanderbeck (2007) have explored power struggles between older and younger people over the use of public spaces. Relationships with place are also significant in older people's decisions to get involved in forums to give a voice to older people in policy making. Barnes, Harrison and Murray (2012) compared motivations to participate among older people in two towns in the south of England that were physically very close, but culturally very different. One was described as 'fancy middle class', quite affluent and a place that prided itself on being 'stroppy' and 'a little bit of a revolutionary'. Many of those involved in the forum had moved to the town quite late in life, often attracted by this reputation. Here, while local issues *were* the focus of campaigning, motivations to get involved were described in terms of more generalised references to 'public service' or to interest in public issues. In contrast, older people in another town that has higher indicators of deprivation than are common in the region generally were motivated much more by concern about local issues. And in particular they were driven by a sense that the town had been neglected and poorly cared for by policy makers: the town centre had been left to die as a result of the creation of a ring road; a community centre that acted as an important base for all sorts of activities was under threat; and plans to build a waste incinerator represented a threat to people's health. Thus older people were drawing on a strong sense of collective identity and affection for the town in which most had lived much of their lives, but their input was not directed solely at issues of concern to older people. They cared for the town and the people living in it and were prepared to take action to defend it.

Valentine (2008) has cautioned against assuming that better familiarity resulting from encounters with different others in urban spaces will automatically generate 'an ethics of care and mutual respect for difference' (p 329). Drawing primarily on research addressing white majority views of different ethnic groups within urban spaces, she suggests that civility and etiquette in the way in which such encounters are conducted represent a tolerance that conceals power relations without altering prejudice. Spatial proximity alone cannot solve the problems generated by inequality of resources, opportunities or the ability to exercise voice. Nevertheless, ideas about 'shared spaces' in which different generations, different genders and different cultural groups can interact have been influential in recent urban and transport policy. One of the key characteristics of such spaces is that they are based on attentiveness to diverse needs and experiences, including those of children and disabled people. Another is that it is an approach to policy which draws both from an understanding of the interaction between the spatial and the social and which is based in a concern about how people can live well together. It offers an attempt at urban design based in principles compatible with an ethic of care.

What about the workers?

My third, brief, example of the significance of care in relation to environments reflects the importance of the way in which work is organised in terms of people's experience of being cared for and their capacity to care – for themselves and others. I illustrate this with a highly selective review of work in this area. In concluding her review of findings from the CAVA programme (see Chapter Three) Fiona Williams (2004a) called for an 'ethic of work' to be balanced by an 'ethic of care'. What she was reflecting there is the way in which in many Western states people have come to be valued on the basis of their contribution as workers, rather than their contribution as care givers. Paid work is *the* route to citizenship and the way in which unwelcome dependency is avoided. Thus parents should not only undertake paid work in order to ensure that they can provide for their families without assistance from the state, but also to model for their children, the future citizen-workers, the proper way of living one's life as an active, responsible citizen. In their empirical work the CAVA researchers explored the moral decision making in which mothers were involved in deciding whether it was best for their children for them to undertake paid work, or to spend more of their time directly caring for them. Their decisions were based on how they viewed what it means to be a 'good mother' and how they could fit work in to that, rather than on an assessment of the financial rewards of work. Williams poses the following challenges for public policy.

> If work/life balance is actually to *mean* balance, then instead of paid work being the starting point and the question being how, as a society we are to fit our life around our paid work, we put it the other way round and ask: how do we fit our work around our life? Balancing these two ethics, of work and care, enables us to think about how we organise time and our environment – our space – differently. Rather than care needs being fitted in with the traditional requirements of work, we can start by asking what is important for the following areas of our lives: .... (p 77)

She then goes on to list: care of others; care of the self, care of the world, and work time and space as all requiring policy and action to follow, to support our capacity to care in each context.

The CAVA research focused on care in the context of partnering and parenting. We can pose similar challenges in relation to the dominance of a work ethic over a care ethic in later life. Contemporary policy in the UK and elsewhere is focused on delaying the age at which people can retire from paid work. This is justified both by the wish of some older people to be able to make their own decisions about when to stop work, rather than being required to do so because they have passed the age at which they are 'entitled' to be employed, but more significantly by the concern of governments and financial institutions that the state cannot afford to pay for the retirement pensions of large numbers of older people who are living longer. In their responses to the eurozone crisis of 2011, governments in Greece and Italy were proposing a delay to retirement age as one measure intended to convince the banks to continue to lend to them. In this context as in others, financial independence from state support is linked with the health and social benefits of active ageing, through the construction of an autonomous subject exercising choice over how they live their lives. But this policy neglects care in a number of ways. First, those whose working lives have been physically harder and less financially rewarding are often those who feel forced to continue in paid employment in order to retain some material quality of life. A policy that discourages earlier retirement demonstrates a lack of care for the impact of a hard and unsatisfying working life. Second, the majority of those who provide substantial care for others (over 50 hours a week) are over the usual working age (HM Government, 2008). In spite of this a key element of the strategy for carers launched by the previous New Labour government in England was focused on encouraging and enabling carers to also pursue paid work. The message is that care giving is not enough: carers should also consider how they can combine paid work with care. And third, many of those who care through acting as volunteers in diverse contexts are older people. Prime Minister David Cameron's promotion of volunteering as a central part of the 'Big Society' (www.cabinetoffice.gov.uk/big-society) conflicts with the promotion of an ever-longer working life: if older people are to continue in paid work they cannot also act as volunteers.

These particular policies regarding expectations that parents and older people will prioritise work over care are located within broader neo-liberal assumptions about progress and prosperity linked to unregulated labour markets. It is not only paid work, but a particular type of worker, that is valued. This worker is flexible; continually developing a portfolio of skills that can be adapted to changing circumstances; willing to be spatially mobile to follow work and temporally flexible to work split shifts in the interests of economic efficiency. Unlike workers of a previous generation, they should not expect to identify with a place-based trade or industry, nor should they expect to work for the same employer for all or most of their adult life. Nor should they expect to benefit from the support of a trade union that not only represents workers' collective interests to an employer, but also offers its own source of welfare and solidarity.

One consequence of changing labour market patterns is that young working class men are less able to establish themselves in the family breadwinner role (McDowell, 2004). Many working class families are unable to manage on one wage, a fact that has shifted the gender balance in terms of breadwinner roles, but which also means that 'the work of social reproduction must be squeezed into a shorter and shorter time or redistributed among other networks' (p 150). And it remains the case that it is usually women who have to do the everyday work of managing crisis and contingency, and the long-term planning associated with balancing care for others with work commitments (McKie et al, 2002). The culture of ever-longer working hours also means that middle class and professional workers have less time for the care of family and friends or for self-care and this can have a number of negative impacts on individual health and on relationships between family members. For example, Chatzitheocari and Arber (2009) explore the link between shift patterns, long working hours, lack of sleep and health, while in a review of research into working hours and health, Sparks and her colleagues (Sparks et al, 1997) identify the impact of women's long working hours on men's anxiety and depression, considered to be consequent on the 'unavailability' of women to act as buffers for the stress experienced by their male partners.

While employment in the UK and other Western economies is increasingly within the 'service' sector, this does not mean that work experience is characterised by an experience of 'service' values – there is little evidence that work organisation and working practices are characterised by the values of care. In Chapter Four I discussed aspects of the work environment that inhibited care workers' capacity to promote ethical care and suggested that workers' experiences of being cared for were important to this. If we extend our perspective to include workers in other parts of the service industry we get an even more pessimistic view of care for workers. Barbara Ehrenreich's (2010) experience of such work in the US offers a vivid view of this. Work servicing others in bars, restaurants and hotels is characterised by poor pay, assumptions of a high turnover, low skill and no attempt to provide training in order to develop skills. But even at a higher end of the employment spectrum Gosling (1996, p 149) contrasts an appeal to 'community' among employing organisations with business practices that 'constantly threaten any sense of collective responsibility or common sympathy'. McKie et al's (2008) work explores employing organisations' care for employees, through policies on equalities and diversity issues such as maternity/paternity leave and nursery access; through action taken in relation to health and well-being, such as bullying and harassment measures and time off to care for dependents; and policies on holiday entitlement, working hours, and staff appraisal. They use the metaphor of 'organisation carescapes' to consider the way in which such practices interact with experiences of caring responsibilities beyond the workplace, at the same time noting how the term 'care' is largely absent from the lexicon of managers – including human resource managers (Smith and McKie, 2009). There is little evidence of an ethic of care informing the way in which work is organised or being viewed as significant in shaping relationships with colleagues within the workplace.

Conclusion

The relational perspective of care encourages attentiveness to the significance of people's relationships to their environment as well as with other people. This reflects an understanding of the spatial as inherently relational. As we have seen in different contexts throughout this book it is important to adopt a perspective that encompasses reciprocity in such relationships: it is not only a question of whether people feel 'cared for' through the way in which others attend to their environment, but also the extent to which they are able to care for both their own immediate environment and those environments they share with others. But as I have demonstrated in this chapter, people's relationships with their physical and work environments and their relationships with other people are closely connected. It is a truism to say that interactions with others 'take place in place', and the way in which people feel about and are able to relate to others is hard to disentangle from their experience of being in different places. An ethical sensitivity towards such relationships is necessary to the development of place-based policies and practices that contribute to care.

Both geographers and social policy academics have developed concepts of environmental justice, but, with the exception of some work on women and public space, there is little developed analysis from an ethic of care that relates specifically to how that might be applied to people's everyday relationships with their environment. This chapter is an attempt to offer such an analysis. Once again, while distributional concepts of justice are relevant in promoting the spatial and temporal dimensions of social justice, they are not sufficient to encompass the embodied and emotional relationships people have to the places in which they live and work. A care perspective can offer a way of viewing such relationships. We need not only to understand the significance of spaces and places that are designed as locations in which care is given and received (such as hospitals or nursing homes), and both the environmental and relational quality of those spaces, but also the everyday spaces in which people live and interact. Hence it is not only those responsible for designing specialist environments, such as residential homes in which people with dementia can wander safely, who need to think about care and space, but those responsible for creating physical and social spaces in which people of different ages, and with different need and interests, interact in their everyday lives.

EIGHT

Spaces of policy making: deliberating with care

Here I turn to a different type of space from those considered in the previous chapter – the spaces in which social policy decisions are debated and made in the context of participatory modes of governance. Thus the relationships with which I am concerned here are those between politicians, public officials, service users and citizens as co-producers of public policy. In previous chapters I have considered the significance of care in the context of different types of interpersonal relationships, and in the context of relationships between people and certain types of environment within which they live, interact with others and work. Here I address the issue of care as a perspective from which to view social policies, and the processes by which those engaged in the development or formulation of such policies consider what might be the 'right' or 'best' position to adopt in determining their content.

The study of social policy has traditionally focused on policy processes, the changing institutions and architecture of welfare states and the analysis of policies themselves in terms of the different welfare ideologies that they embody. Thus social policy perspectives on care address issues such as the political economy of care, gender, individualism and collectivism in assigning responsibilities for care, and changing policy orientations and how they impact specific social care policies (eg Dalley, 1988; Means et al, 2002; Glendinning and Kemp, 2006). Work that engages with the lived experience of ageing, of being in poverty, of living with illness or impairment, or of being involved in caring relationships within families has tended to occupy a rather different part of the academic terrain, being located within sociology or more specifically being designated as 'health and social care'. And issues of practice and the type of ethics most useful to the development of respectful care work are largely dealt with in the context of specific professional courses such as nursing and social work. My argument throughout this book is that these different foci need to be brought into interaction with each other as well as with the work of moral and political philosophy. This is important not only to develop policies and practices within the worlds of social and health care, but also to understand the broader significance of care in social relationships and in social policy generally.

In this chapter I also draw from another body of work, one that has its origins within political theory, in order to interrogate the idea that 'care full deliberation' is necessary to produce social policies that can deliver social justice and well-being. Both Fraser (2009) and Young (2000) have argued that one dimension of social justice is the right to be heard in the process of public policy making. In this chapter I am concerned with what type of processes of participatory policy making are necessary to move beyond procedural rights to take part, and to enable care full and respect full relationships between those engaged in deliberative practice. I am thus addressing what happens when those who are the subject of social policies enter official spaces of policy deliberation, and how care does, or does not, get brought into policy. But first I develop some of the issues addressed in Chapter Two about the constructions of care within social policies in order to make the connection between policy making and the substance of policy.

Social policy

Social policies are concerned with the welfare and well-being of those whose health, financial, personal or social circumstances mean they have particular needs for help and support on a temporary or more long-term basis. As previous chapters have demonstrated, we need to go beyond national borders and beyond policies that are defined narrowly by reference to care if we are to undertake a comprehensive analysis of the significance of care to social policy. My experience is primarily within health and social care policy, although my work on participative policy making extends beyond this. My analysis in this chapter is shaped by such experiences.

As I noted in Chapter Four, a key aspect of social policies is what they indicate about the balance between public and private responsibilities for such support at different times and in different places. Another is the way in which those who are the targets of policy are viewed; for example as deserving or undeserving of welfare, as active, responsible citizens who not only can, but should, contribute to their own and others' welfare, or as passive recipients unable to make choices for themselves. This is one perspective from which critics adopting an ethic of care perspective have interrogated specific policies. Selma Sevenhuijsen developed a method she refers to as 'Trace' in order to:

> trace the normative framework(s) in policy reports in order to evaluate and renew these from the perspective of an ethic of care. The background motivation to this approach is the wish to further develop care into a political concept and to position care as a social and moral practice in notions of citizenship. (2003a, p 1)

Thus this is not neutral policy analysis, but an approach based in feminist scholarship that has sought to 'de-privatise' and 'de-gender' care, and to expand our concept of citizenship through including care within it. As I explored in Chapter Two, Sevenhuijsen and other political philosophers see care as equally important to the development and analysis of public policy as it is for an understanding of ethical practice in meeting needs within people's private lives. Policies inevitably embody values. The questions from an ethic of care perspective are how care is conceptualised and applied within such policies, what assumptions are made about both where responsibilities for care giving lie, and how care givers and care receivers are distinguished and characterised. And key to this is whether people are conceived as autonomous, rational individuals, or as relational, interdependent, embodied and emotional social beings. Such distinctions are also relevant to an analysis of the design and conduct of participative policy making.

The Trace framework is an articulation of the process that Sevenhuijsen adopted to interrogate a number of Dutch policy documents: 'Choices in Health Care', equal opportunities policies and reports on ageing societies and family politics. She has also applied it to analysis of South African welfare policy and UK parenting policy (Sevenhuijsen, 1998, 2000; Sevenhuijsen et al, 2003). Others have applied this approach more or less explicitly. For example, Williams (2004a, 2004b) has considered New Labour policy relating to children and families from this perspective, and both I and Kirstein Rummery have applied it to the personalisation agenda in English social care policy (Barnes, 2011b; Rummery, 2011). Williams' work has demonstrated the dominance of the work ethic over care ethics in family policy and she argues the importance of a 'radical repositioning of care in political thinking and strategy that will resonate with what matters to people in their family lives and personal relationships' (2004a, p 84). My analysis of personalisation has highlighted ways in which policy that is ostensibly built around care (in this instance social care policy) adopts a discursive construction of care that locates this as marginal and appropriate only in cases where service users are not capable of exercising choice and control. Sevenhuijsen's (1998) own analysis of

Dutch health care policy similarly highlights the centrality of choice as the normative concept around which the policy is built, concluding that 'choice is conceptualized as a shield against an inordinate need for care' (p 139). And as I discussed in Chapter Four this is a theme that is further developed in Mol's (2008) analysis of the dominance of the 'logic of choice' rather than the 'logic of care' in health. Mol's work emphasises not only the emotional content of disease experiences but also the embodied nature both of illness and the care required to respond to it (one chapter of her book is called 'the citizen and the body'). While her focus is primarily on health care practice rather than health policy her analysis is a powerful critique of policies that do not engage with the messy and emotional realities of illness.

One of the characteristics of policy texts that Sevenhuijsen (2003a) calls attention to is the claim that they derive from factual evidence and are value neutral. She suggests that moral concepts and arguments are concealed – sometimes within empirical statements – rather than made explicit, and that where reference is made to values and moral arguments, they are often taken as self-evident rather than being subject to explicit discussion and examination. She also notes that what appears in policy is often the result of complex compromises. A key consequence is that there are likely to be contradictions and inconsistencies in the normative frameworks of policy documents. Such contradictions are familiar to those engaged in the analysis of policy discourse. Policy contains within it different and sometimes competing discourses that may enable cooperation or alliances in service delivery between those who adopt rather different ideological positions, but which may also contain the seeds of unsustainable differences (Barnes and Prior, 2009; Prior and Barnes, 2011). Thus we need to look at what practitioners do as well as what policy makers say in order to fully understand how specific policies may embody care in practice. However, we can establish how different normative frameworks are at work within policy texts, in order to construct the possibilities within which front-line negotiations take place and to understand the specific dilemmas that practitioners need to negotiate in the moral reasoning involved in everyday practice (see Chapter Four; see also Paszkiewicz, 2011).

But what I am concerned about in this chapter is how care 'gets in' to policy in the first place (if it does). We assume that policy makers, who may include public officials, politicians, front-line workers (Lipsky, 1980) and others, have some knowledge and understanding of the lived experience of ageing, care giving, living with physical or cognitive disability and other experiences that provide the focus for policy. We assume that they, in some way, know what they are talking about and that, even if their decisions reflect a value position that is not shared by those affected by the policy and are constrained by assumed resource limitations, those decisions are based in an account of such circumstances that is at least recognisable to those whose everyday lives are the subject of policy. But is this always the case? Kittay (2010) has offered a forceful critique of bioethicists who argue that people they describe as 'severely retarded' should be accorded no higher moral status than certain animals. One of the bases of her critique is the empirical inadequacy of their case, which she names as an ethical problem. She argues that what she refers to as 'epistemic responsibility' and 'epistemic modesty' (that is, recognising what you do not know) is itself morally necessary because policy is built on the positions taken on such issues. So how do policy makers know about such things? Well, some may have been or still be practitioners who have come face to face with service users and have developed a store of experiences on which they can draw as a result. Some may have direct personal experience – they may themselves be disabled, be caring for a parent with dementia or a child with learning disabilities, or share a cultural or ethnic identity with those affected by the policies they make. How public officials negotiate their personal as well as professional identities in participative policy forums is not straightforward (Barnes, 2009). One of Kittay's challenges to Singer and McMahan, the bioethicists arguing about the relative moral status of animals and people with severe learning disabilities, was to actually visit the place where her daughter now lives and to meet those who live there. Direct contact with lived experience can be a powerful learning process. For elected politicians, contact with their constituents through regular surgeries can play a vital role in shaping their ideas. However, for many public officials involved in making policy, knowledge is likely to be indirect, based in research that they have read themselves, or, a more likely scenario, which has formed the basis for policy briefings in which findings are filtered to offer a particular slant on the evidence.

The promotion of evidence-based or informed policy making generated a substantial body of applied research during the period of the New Labour governments in the UK from 1997 to 2010. But these governments also promoted participative governance designed to enable those affected by policies to contribute to the process of policy making (Barnes et al, 2007). Thus, deliberation about policy can include people who have direct personal experience, or representatives who speak on their behalf, in order to inform policy makers at the point of deliberation. Such participatory processes, in which those who use services, or who are the subject of policy have a voice in order to give direct expression to lived experience within policy-making forums, is increasingly common. A key justification for such practices is to enable access to local or experiential knowledge so that this can be taken on board alongside professional or technical knowledge. This has been argued both on the basis of ensuring 'good' or better decision making, and that recognition of this form of knowledge is necessary for 'cognitive justice' (Visvanathan, 2005). But my argument is that more than knowledge is at stake here. Participatory policy making has the potential to enable not only access to a broader range of *knowledge* that is necessary to good decision making, but also better *understanding* of the issues, and potentially can prompt public officials to *care about* the issues that are the focus of policy. At the same time, it is not solely public officials who can learn to care through participation in policy processes.

> The activities and experiences of bringing new issues and insights connected with the significance of relations of care into the public arena are themselves part of the process of learning what it is to be a citizen, participating in collective, inclusive and generalised relations and deliberating over issues of common concern. (Bowden, 1997, p 162)

Here Bowden is suggesting that both citizens and public officials are engaged in a reciprocal process of understanding how to do care in public policy. But in order to realise the potential of participatory policy making in this respect, deliberation has to be conducted *with* care and it is what this might mean in practice that is the focus for the remainder of this chapter.

Deliberative democracy[1]

How then do policy makers engage with and respond to knowledge of lived experience and how does this affect the positions they come to about the right or best policy to respond to different needs? How do they combine an awareness of the realities of the private lives of those their policies are intended to benefit (if we assume a benign

[1] What follows is based substantially on an article previously published in the journal *Critical Social Policy* (see Barnes, 2008) and on my inaugural lecture at the University of Brighton (www.brighton.ac.uk/sass/publications/Barnes_Inaugural.pdf).

intention) with their perceptions of their public responsibilities to ensure appropriate use of public finances and to take into account those who are directly and indirectly affected by decisions reached? In what follows I develop an argument that brings together insights from critical perspectives on deliberative democracy with those from care ethics in order to propose a framework within which the way in which public officials engage with the lived experience of service users may be assessed. My particular objective here is to explore how an ethic of care perspective might help in understanding what participative policy making should look like if it is to both embody and deliver care.

Traditional conceptions of democracy are based in the election of representatives to speak on our behalf in those forums in which decisions are taken about social and public policies. But the practice of representative democracy has come into some disrepute because of lack of trust in elected politicians and low turnouts in elections, and thus the ideal has also been questioned. Instead political philosophers have turned to a rather earlier conception of democracy – one in which citizens debate directly with each other without the mediation of elected representatives. The case for deliberative democracy is made on the basis of a number of principled arguments:

- It will create a more informed citizenry who are better able to engage with the complex issues which form the substance of policy making.
- It will generate better decisions that hold greater legitimacy because they are more open and informed and focused on the general good.
- It will bring decision making out of the hidden back rooms in which bargaining takes place between interest groups, and enable 'ordinary citizens' to engage in dialogue with both the issues and the decision makers.
- It will open knowledge previously restricted to specific scientific or other communities to lay scrutiny, as well as open up political arenas to more direct processes of citizen involvement.
- Technical or expert knowledge alone is inadequate for the resolution of policy problems, since the issues such problems raise are also political and ethical.
- Deliberation will make transparent the reasoning behind positions that are adopted and enable reflection on the differences that emerge though the process of debate.
- *Transforming* views, rather than simply aggregating preferences (as happens in voting), will increase the likelihood that people will move from positions based in self-interest to positions that are more

> likely to deliver social justice as a result of having to listen directly to others whose needs and circumstances are different from their own.

(See, for example, Dryzek, 2002). Theorists of deliberative democracy frequently base their analyses in the work of the German social theorist Jurgen Habermas (1984, 1987). Habermas's contention was that formal economic and political systems operated on an entirely different basis from what he referred to as the 'lifeworld' – the shared common understandings and values that emerge from everyday interaction and communication among people. The former is based on what he referred to as 'instrumental rationality'; the latter on value rationality. Thus he argued for what he called 'communicative rationality' – a set of principles that would guide deliberation between 'ordinary citizens' and public officials in order to prevent the lifeworld being colonised by state institutions. This requires that anyone who is competent to speak and act is allowed to take part in the process of deliberation; that all those taking part in the process of deliberation are allowed to introduce any assertion they wish to make and to question any assertion made by others; that all are allowed to express their attitudes and wishes; and that no speaker should be prevented from exercising those rights – either as a result of internal or external pressure. This in turn has led to a series of normative criteria for assessing deliberative practices based on the notion of communicative competence. This is seen to comprise:

- cognitive competence – the ability of an individual to master the rules of formal logic
- speech competence – mastery of linguistic rules
- pragmatic competence – mastery of pragmatic rules and
- role competence – mastery of rules of interaction.

In spite of their origins in critical theory that was directed at improving the legitimacy of social and state institutions through enhancing democratic processes, the demands made by these criteria imply a somewhat exclusionary approach to deliberation. For example, Webler (1995), an advocate of deliberation in policy making who proposed these criteria, suggested that in the case of 'obvious mental illness and inability to use language' (p 55) it might be ethical to exclude people from deliberation on the basis of cognitive incompetence. We can suggest that basing the principles of deliberation on these criteria is equivalent to basing a theory of social justice on autonomous, rational individuals (see Chapter Two). In both cases, many of those who are the subject of social policy, and whose voices participative methods should be designed to include, may struggle to reach the high bar set for communicative competence within this formulation.

Deliberative practices draw attention to the assumptions we make about who has legitimate knowledge to contribute to policy making, what is the source of such knowledge and what are legitimate ways of contributing to a process of dialogue. I am leaving on one side for now the question of 'representation', which is also regarded as hugely contentious in relation to deliberative democracy (see, for example, Barnes et al, 2003; Smith, 2009). Here I want to highlight the epistemological assumptions and implications of such an approach: what types of knowledge are legitimate and necessary for good decision making and how can these enter into dialogue with each other for this purpose?

There are two ways in which processes of deliberation are seen to enhance the potential for policy decisions to be made on the basis of good or strong knowledge. One argument for deliberative democracy is its capacity to open up expert knowledge to lay scrutiny – for example in the process of witness questioning that takes place in citizens' juries which became popular during the 1990s and the first decade of the 21st century (eg Parkinson, 2006). Citizens' juries involve recruiting a 'representative' sample (or better, a cross-section of the relevant population) to meet over a period, usually of three days, on a specific question for public policy. Citizen jurors hear from a series of expert witnesses and can question them. They may also call their own witnesses. They then deliberate among themselves in order to come up with a consensus solution to the question ('charge') or policy problem they have been posed. Such practices are designed to enable lay citizens to access knowledge that has previously been accessible only within professional knowledge communities or bureaucratic systems, to question it and perhaps to expose the partial or self-interested basis on which it is claimed as 'truth'. But this is within a context in which a key aim is to educate citizens in order to enable informed contributions to policy deliberations. Thus the assumption is that citizens need to be exposed to expert knowledge in order to be educated and to reach good decisions.

But another perspective on such processes stresses their importance as a means by which experts can be exposed to what has variously been referred to as lay, experiential or local knowledge. The case for user or citizen participation in policy making rests not only on enhancing democracy through more direct participation, but also in epistemological assumptions about the type of knowledge necessary for good decision making and for offering the recognition necessary for social justice (Barnes et al, 2010). As well as expert knowledge it is also important to access what Yanow (2003) calls local knowledge: 'the very mundane, but still expert, understanding of and practical reasoning about local conditions derived from lived experience' (p 236). This has also been referred to as 'ordinary wisdom' or experiential knowledge such as that which comes from experience of living with mental illness or other chronic health problems; living in poverty; or negotiating the everyday challenges of being a single mother. Yanow offers a good illustration of what can happen if the importance of local knowledge is not recognised. Northern experts proposed the 'obvious' solution of digging more wells in an area in Africa where there was longstanding drought. More wells were dug and in consequence people living in the area increased the size of their herds of goats and cattle. The animals used more water so no more was available for local people. The reason that herds were increased was because this was what determined people's standing and reputation within the community. Taking action without understanding this failed to solve the problem.

This example illustrates the way in which local knowledge encompasses meanings, values and beliefs as well as cognition. Rational actor theories and purely technical solutions fail because they do not recognise the significance of meanings and values in affecting social behaviour – as in the case of the wells. Examples such as that cited by Yanow illustrate that it is not enough to *know*; it is also important to *understand*. Related to this is the other characteristic that distinguishes local from scientific knowledge. While scientific method produces claims for universal explanations or solutions, local knowledge is situated and contextual. Thus the solutions that are proposed on this basis are particular, embedded in understandings of how things work in specific contexts, and based in practical reasoning. This can be challenging in the case of deliberation that is intended to generate universal or broadly based solutions to policy problems.

This analysis is important in the context of the advocacy and critique of evidence-based policy making. What constitutes 'evidence' is inadequately understood as constituting the outcomes of scientific research. In many ways this is now a familiar argument, although in practice the designs of participative practices do not always reflect the conditions necessary to enable effective dialogue between those bringing different types of knowledge to the policy process (Barnes et al, 2008).

But I also want to suggest that if we are concerned with good decision making we need also to be concerned with moral decision making –

which implies more than ensuring that those able to contribute different types of knowledge to the policy making process can do so. Not only do those making policy need to know and understand, they also need to demonstrate that they *care;* at least to the extent of 'caring about' the lives of those that policy is designed to address – what Tronto refers to as 'noting the existence of a need and making an assessment that this need should be met' (Tronto, 1993, p 106). Harvey (2007, p 25) makes a similar point when she talks about the difference between 'sheer information and empathetic understanding' as a basis on which it is possible to build solidarity between privileged and oppressed peoples. I want to suggest that participative modes of policy making have a particular contribution to make to generating this moral sensibility among policy makers – but only if it embodies ethic of care principles within the way in which it is practised.[2]

Beyond argument

The privileging of reasoned argument within deliberation is a source both of advocacy and critique. Even if we recognise the value and necessity of different forms of knowledge in the making of social policies, we could still argue that the process of deliberation is defined by the capacity to enable arguments to be put, questioned, and explored on the basis of different kinds of evidence. Decisions then become a result of dialogue over the comparative merits of different types of knowledge in coming up with a workable solution in the particular context. But from a perspective that addresses forms of democratic practice in relation to notions of justice, Iris Marion Young (2000) suggested that assuming that deliberation has to be based solely in *reason* – which she argued is usually defined as neutral and dispassionate, and conducted solely through rational argument – will exclude many people. Those who express their views and opinions in a rowdy or dramatic manner are ruled out of order. Expressing views in disruptive or demonstrative ways risks not only the person expressing views in this way, but also the views themselves, being labelled as 'extreme'. Thus, Young argued instead for the importance of recognising and valuing different styles of speech in deliberative processes. In particular she argued for the inclusion of greeting, rhetoric and storytelling as ways of enabling and recognising diverse contributions. 'Greeting' gives public acknowledgement to

[2] Being able to care is also affected by the extent to which public officials are themselves cared for in their work context. This is an issue I address in Chapters Four and Seven.

individuals or groups who have often been ignored or stereotyped, and who are trying to make claims in public forums. Telling individual stories of experiences (narrating) is often dismissed as 'anecdotal' rather than being recognised as an important way of capturing and making sense of shared experience. Rhetoric, a committed and passionate attempt to persuade others, is usually regarded as aiming to manipulate rather than to reflect a genuine expression of the emotional meaning and content of the position being represented. Young argued that situating deliberation, rhetoric, narrative and greeting in relation to one another provides a more sophisticated understanding of what is necessary to enable dialogue between citizens and public officials in a way that is capable of transforming policy making. Fischer (2009) similarly addresses the need to encompass emotional experiences and expressions as part of the deliberative process, but the practice model that he discusses is designed to separate out such expressions from the rational argumentation that leads to decision making, rather than to encourage officials to recognise what they can learn directly from the emotional content of experience.

Kittay's account of her exchange with the bioethicists offers an illustration of a similar point to that made by Young. In describing her emotion-laden intervention in the debate she spoke of the struggle she experienced between her identity as a philosopher and as a mother. As a philosopher she sought to counter arguments she found both offensive and distressful with an alternative logic. But that in itself she recognised was problematic. Instead she concluded that:

> … in laying bare the intensity of my relationship to a daughter who has such profound intellectual disabilities, and the depth of my revulsion to the sorts or arguments made by Singer and McMahan, I am effectively *showing* what it is impossible to argue. That Sesha is as much a daughter as any other beloved daughter to a loving parent. That in showing this, I am carrying out my role as her primary caregiver, because I am attempting to win for my daughter the respect and regard that other mothers try to secure for their children. (Kittay, 2010, p 410)

And Kittay is also making the point here that part of the process of care giving is precisely to engage in public action that can secure the recognition her daughter and others who may not be able to speak on their own behalf deserve. She is arguing that the private virtues of care need to be included in the public sphere of policy making in order to develop practices that embody and enable care.

I discuss other examples that demonstrate the significance of storytelling in the process of policy making elsewhere (Barnes, 2008a). These examples not only highlight the importance of narrative as central to the expression of experiences through which local or experiential knowledge can be contributed to the process of policy making, but also emphasise the significance of emotionality in conveying the substance of the message. While it is possible to recount highly charged emotional experiences dispassionately, this will usually be when they are sufficiently in the past, sufficiently well worked through to no longer hold the emotional charge. If people are engaged in social policy making because they can bring to it direct and immediate experience that needs to be understood to ensure appropriate policy responses, then it is important to understand the emotional content of such experiences and this may only be contributed by emotional expression.

Writing of the 'intelligence of emotions' Martha Nussbaum (2001) argues that it is wrong to regard emotions as non-rational. Rather, she says, they have complex cognitive structures that express powerfully the relationship between the person and the object of their emotion. They offer judgements of the value of the object to which they are directed and beliefs about it (understanding 'object' as referring to a person, an idea as well as a 'thing'). If politics and policy making are concerned with determining action that will support human flourishing, understanding the relationship between emotions and concepts of human good is important for political thought.

Empirical work by Celia Davies and her colleagues who studied the Citizens Council of NICE (the National Institute for Health and Clinical Excellence) identifies the way in which emotional engagement with a topic (on the part both of 'witnesses' and citizens) can enhance cognitive engagement and thus deliberation (Davies et al, 2006). Their study indicated that exchanges were more deliberative in style 'when the content under discussion concerned concrete cases and when they were responding to strong invested statements from witnesses and could identify and mobilise their own strongly held opinions in response' (p 129). This offers empirical evidence in support of Nussbaum's arguments.

How then might we incorporate these insights into both the analysis and development of deliberative practices that can include both diverse knowledges *and* emotional expressions in the making of social policies? And what can an ethic of care contribute to this? 'Good' social policy decisions are not only those that generate workable solutions, but also ethical ones. Deliberative theorists Amy Gutmann and Dennis Thompson (1996) argue that deliberation requires moral argument with the aim of reaching provisional moral agreement on issues of social and public policy. I would argue that this has to encompass what I have referred to as 'emotional morality', by which I mean recognition and respect for the emotional content of experiences and values and the authentic expression of these as a necessary part of dialogue on issues that are directly relevant to such experiences and values.

So how might we understand the moral processes of deliberative practices that can encompass emotional morality? Gutmann and Thompson do not consider emotionality directly, but they do emphasise the necessity of recognising that moral arguments take place in specific contexts and that the arguments that are pursued begin from where we are and have to appeal to those with whom we now live. Not only is it necessary to engage with knowledge that allows understanding of the particularities of local contexts and cultures, a relational and situational ethics is also required. Aristotle argued that moral deliberation involves practical wisdom. There is a link here between arguments relating to ethics and knowledge – the importance of local knowledge vis-à-vis the universalising claims of scientific knowledge is equivalent to the importance of situational as opposed to universal ethics.

I want, then, to propose a different set of normative criteria to be applied to deliberative practices than those that focused on communicative competence that I outlined earlier. Where deliberation is intended to enable the development or assessment of social policies capable of creating the conditions for well-being and social justice, I suggest that such deliberation needs to be undertaken with care. In offering this way of describing what such practices might be, I acknowledge the influence of Sevenhuijsen (1998) whose Dutch version of her book *Citizenship and the Ethics of Care* was entitled *Judging with Care*. As the title of this chapter indicates, what I am concerned with here is 'deliberating with care'. In the next section I set out what this might involve.

Care full deliberation

As I have explored in different contexts, a caring orientation is acquired through engaging in caring practices and reflecting and debating the values and virtues necessary for care in the context of interpersonal relationships. Applied to the public sphere, this implies that care as a democratic practice requires the potential for decision-making roles and positions to be open to different participants. Just as personal care cannot be imposed without discussion between care giver and care recipient, nor can care full decisions be reached without dialogue between those making policies and those subject to them. While not all citizens are equal, the achievement of equality is a political goal. This has implications for the nature of the democratic processes necessary to achieve socially just outcomes.

> In all, a society that took caring seriously would engage in a discussion of the issues of public life from a vision not of autonomous, equal, rational actors each pursuing separate ends, but from a vision of interdependent actors, each of whom needs and provides care in a variety of ways and each of whom has other interests and pursuits that exist outside the realm of care. (Tronto, 1993, p 168)

Thus from a rather different perspective we come back to the importance of participative policy making. But we now have some indication of what this should look like and we can develop this by applying Tronto's principles of care to the process of deliberation.

This starts with the necessity of attentiveness to care. Deliberative practices which enable dialogue about experiences deriving from the disadvantage and marginalisation resulting from disability, old age or mental distress, from experiences of giving and receiving care, of abuse, discrimination and marginalisation can encourage attentiveness to such experiences and give recognition to them. This implies a preparedness to listen and to hear what is being said, even if it is expressed in ways that fall outside communicative norms familiar to public officials. Bowden (1997) similarly considers the importance of dialogue and conversation, and identifies the ability to listen as an ethical resource. This also encourages a recognition of the particularity of those who are the subject of policies, which can act as a counter to the tendency to view people as members of categories – a single mother; a young person with learning disabilities; a person with cancer, for example – and to base policy decisions on categorical assumptions rather than attentiveness to the particularities of differences.

The process of attending to voices that may be expressed in ways other than is usual in official policy contexts, and which demand a response because of the substance of what is said, can encourage a preparedness to take responsibility to act to improve the situations being described. Emotional expressions emphasise the significance of the issues that are the substance of debate and the particularity of the situations that demand a response. Thus care full deliberation offers a way of understanding the difference between responsibility and obligation – rather than following a set of formal rules and procedures those involved in making and assessing policies need to think hard about precisely what should be done to produce positive outcomes in particular situations.

The focus on positive outcomes reflects the importance of the principle of competence. Tronto argues: 'Intending to provide care, even accepting responsibility for it, but then failing to provide good care, means that in the end the need for care is not met' (1993, p 133). We could say: 'Intending to enable people to take part in policy making, even taking responsibility to set up opportunities for this to happen, but then failing to conduct deliberation in a way that enables people to feel their contributions are recognised and valued, means that the purpose of participation is not fulfilled'. The difficulties officials can experience in engaging in face to face dialogue with people who may be angry or upset by the way in which they have been treated, or whose styles of communication are very different from what they are familiar with in official deliberations, force them to confront their own competence in relating to others who are different from them. We can also suggest that attentiveness to the consequences of policy implementation, via hearing from those directly affected by it, also highlights when a lack of competence is evident in the way policies are framed and/or implemented.

The principle of responsiveness refers to the need to understand how those receiving care respond to it – that is, it emphasises care receiving as a key part of the practice of care. But it also recognises that we do not start from positions of equality – that those who are very young, old and frail or ill are more vulnerable than many of those who make decisions about their care. There is a responsibility on officials engaging people in policy deliberation to be aware of the power differentials that exist, to use their power creatively and not to behave in ways that undermine or devalue their contributions to the process. But there are many examples of just this happening (Barnes et al, 2007). Fischer (2009) suggests it may be necessary to call in community psychologists to facilitate initial emotional exchanges to deal with this. Other models of participation that shift the power balance between officials and service users include separate organisation and then inviting officials to meet on users', rather than their own, terms (eg Barnes and Bennet, 1998).

But the evidence of direct testimony from older people, people with mental health problems and others often regarded as incompetent or lacking in capacity also makes it hard to continue to ignore their individual and collective agency. It should be possible to develop ethical sensitivities and skills to enable effective direct deliberation. In earlier chapters I have argued the need to develop the responsiveness principle to reflect the significance of care receiving as part of the relational process of care. I have also discussed Pettersen and Hem's (2011) work on 'mature care' that stresses the epistemological dimension of care recipients' contributions to the process of care. In the context of participative processes intended to enable service users to contribute to policy making, this takes on a collective significance. Care recipients are asked to care not only for what happens to them, but for what happens to others in a similar situation. They are asked to contribute their experiential knowledge in order that others may be better cared for, as well as themselves. In many cases this is precisely what they want to do and what collective organisation is designed to achieve (Barnes and Cotterell, 2012). This is yet another example of the way in which including 'reciprocity' within the principle of responsiveness can help expand understanding of the reciprocal nature of processes embodying care. David Prior and I argued some time ago that reciprocal trust between providers of welfare services and those who use them can be enhanced by collective action that enables users to develop capacity to engage with providers as co-producers of welfare (Barnes and Prior, 1996). Trust is both a condition for and outcome of care full deliberation.

Those who use welfare services, who are subject to social policy interventions of one kind or another, are likely to experience a range of emotions. These can include:

- the pain and fear associated with illness, disability and, in some cases, ageing;
- shame, fear and self-loathing resulting from physical or sexual abuse;
- grief and loss following giving birth to a disabled child, or an adult child developing mental illness;
- frustration and anger associated with receiving services that are disrespectful, unresponsive, which undermine people's sense of who they are and which do not recognise people as active agents capable of making their own decisions;
- frustration and anger resulting from experiences of discrimination, stigmatisation and injustice in their daily lives.

They may also experience satisfaction from seeing the care they provide improving the day to day lives of an elderly parent or spouse; pride in being able to contribute to the development of new forms of service;

or joy in being cared for or supported to overcome difficulties and develop new skills.

Normative criteria for deliberation based solely in cognitive competence and the importance of reasoned argument fail to recognise the significance of the emotional dimension of social policy. Thus as well as cognitive competence in relation to deliberation we also need to develop affective competence – the way in which we express our awareness of another's hurt, shame, and needs in the context of deliberations about policies that are intended to respond to such experiences. I suggest that an application of the principles of an ethic of care to the process of deliberation can help to develop such competences. Graham Martin (2008) has identified the way in which involvement is encouraged by appeals to 'ordinary people' who 'care' about health. Care is invoked as a motivator, but is usually absent from any consideration about what the practice of participation might look like. My aim here has been to suggest that we should bring care into the process of deliberation if we are to create the conditions which hold the potential for achieving social policies that can deliver justice and well-being.

I will offer one example to illustrate what this might look like in practice. Along with colleagues at the University of Birmingham I was commissioned to produce an 'expert paper' to inform the Department of Health in the process of developing policies for mental health services for women (Barnes, Davis et al, 2006). One thing we specified in our tender for this was that we understood the concept of 'expert' to include not only expertise deriving from research, but also from the experience of those delivering mental health services and of the women using them. One way in which we sought to access the latter form of expertise was by hosting a consultation day that we called Women's Voices, Women's Choices. This was designed to enable women service users to contribute in different ways:

- to drop in and out of themed discussion groups;
- to have one to one spontaneous exchanges with each other or members of our group;
- to talk to a video camera supported by a facilitator;
- to have their say for three minutes by standing on a soap box in the final session of the conference;
- to post a written record of their views on a graffiti wall and on a series of poster outline figures representing key professionals – including GPs, social workers, and nurses. Each of these figures was

divided vertically into two halves. One side was headed 'what they are like'; the other 'what I would like them to be'.

Two women graphic artists made attractive wall displays for the themed discussions, graffiti wall and professional posters. They also summarised the outcomes of the morning's work, pictorially and in word form on a large sheet to provide direction for the afternoon. In the closing session of the workshop they captured women's soap box contributions and audience responses in pictures and words.

This was a very different space in which women could contribute to policy making from those that are governed by official rules and norms. It was deliberately designed to enable emotional expression in a context in which that emotion was recognised as an important part of what women were saying about their experiences, rather than a somewhat embarrassing side issue, or inappropriate to an understanding of their views about mental health services. Reflecting Young's (2000) identification of the importance of 'greeting' to enabling dialogue in situations where people's voices have been marginalised or disrespected, literal 'greetings', the offering of food and opportunities to share social contact, and the spontaneous recognition of the validity of what women had to say, encouraged many women to speak out about things they rarely talked of. This event provided opportunities to tell stories in different ways and women responded to this in powerful ways. A discussion group on hopes and aspirations proved particularly important as a forum in which women could focus on their own needs, imagine more positive futures and demonstrate their creativity in working for change. The contribution of the artists enabled the creation of a collective story, built up from the different accounts offered during the course of the day. Women were able to literally see the way in which their stories contributed to an overall picture of what living with mental illness is like and how services may either help or make things worse.

This was an environment in which service users, academic researchers and some service providers, who all cared about mental health services for women, were able to share knowledge and expertise and demonstrate care for each other in the process of developing ideas and possible solutions. It is one example of how the principles of an ethic of care can inform the design of an environment that has the potential to generate care full policy.

Conclusion

My argument in this chapter is that the process of policy making needs to be carried out with care. Those involved in policy making need to care about the lives of those who will be affected by the decisions they reach; and in order to care about those lives, they need not only to know about, but also to understand them and what contributes to the injustices, oppressions and lack of care experienced in them. Policy making demands moral reasoning and such reasoning requires attentiveness to the particularity of the circumstances to which policy is addressed.

The spaces that have been created to enable policy makers and those whose lives are directly affected by policy to come together to share knowledge have the potential to promote ethical decision making informed by the principles of care. But it is not enough simply to set up opportunities for participation. If the potential of participative policy making is to be realised, such practices need to be capable both of including the emotional dimension of everyday lives and of learning from it, and of enabling diverse ways of exchanging knowledge and developing understanding that extend beyond the processes of rational argumentation promoted by deliberative democrats.

NINE

Care: ethics, policy and politics

> In everyday life we often find ourselves having to make ethical decisions in conditions which are so unethical and unfair as to compromise our efforts. Where there are structural sources of avoidable suffering, it generally takes collective political action to remove them: but without compassion and a sense of justice, why should we care? (Sayer, 2011, pp 248-9)

In this final chapter I want to reflect on what we have learnt from the discussion so far in which I have applied an ethic of care perspective to consideration of the place and significance of care in different contexts. These contexts have included kin and non-kin relationships; relationships with known and unknown others; how people experience and interact with the places in which they live and work and how this, in turn, impacts their social relationships; and finally, how public officials and those who use public services interact during the policy process. My overall argument is that adopting a care perspective can help develop an understanding of what is necessary to achieve individual nurturing and well-being, and that such a perspective is also necessary to ensure collective benefit and social justice. In this chapter I want to build on the critical and political work on care ethics to summarise the key aspects of 'care' that I have developed in this book, to consider the politics of care, and to reassert the necessity of care thinking to social policy. My position here reflects Sayer's (2011) challenge: if we don't care about other people's suffering and the injustices they experience, what likelihood is there that we will bother to do anything to improve their situation?

Revisiting care

In Chapter One I identified my approach to care in this book as encompassing a view of care as a way of considering different types of relationships; as a set of moral principles; and as a practice. In applying these ideas to different contexts it becomes clear that the practice of care can involve some very different types of activity. Caring about what happens to the children of migrant care workers who are left behind when their mothers travel to the West to look after older people may prompt policy analysis and campaigning to minimise harms, but it is unlikely to mean we rush to the Philippines to take care of them ourselves. Tronto's identification of the four phases of care – caring about, taking care of, care giving and care receiving – do not imply that in all cases all phases of care are practised by the same person. They do imply a collective responsibility for ensuring attention to all four phases, and for recognising that such responsibilities cannot be enacted solely within the boundaries of an individual nation state. Kittay's concept of 'nested dependencies' offers another way of thinking about this. The hands on care given to a parent or partner with dementia, a sibling who develops cancer, or a child born with severe learning difficulties, will not be undertaken by us all. But collective responsibility for enabling appropriate support to those who are ill, frail or otherwise in need means that those who provide direct, hands on care should also be cared for so that they are not disadvantaged. And, while it is important to understand the different relationships involved where the care giver is a paid worker rather than a close relative or friend, we also need to think about what is necessary to enable paid care workers to give good care. This implies attention not only to the level of resourcing dedicated to services designed to support those who are ill, frail, disabled, troubled or otherwise in need, but also to the values that underpin the design of policies and practices. It requires opportunities for care workers to reflect on their practices and the consequences of them for care receivers, as well as employment practices that reflect workers' needs for care. Care is an intensely political issue as well as central to our capacity to live well together in our private lives, and to our confidence that those who are paid to care for us will do this well. I return to the significance of this later.

But before I consider the practical policy implications of care thinking I want to develop some of these ideas about collective responsibility through an exploration of the principle of reciprocity. Reciprocity, like care itself, is subject to different meanings and interpretations. Tronto (1993) did not name reciprocity as one of the moral principles of care and Kittay (1999) warned against understanding reciprocity in care in terms of an equivalent exchange: if I give you this level of help or support now, I expect to receive something equivalent from you if and when I have need of it (see Chapter Three). Robinson (1999) warned against a similar contractarian notion of reciprocity in the context of international relations. A fundamental principle of care is that it is given in response to an awareness of current need, rather than in exchange for care given in the past, or anticipated in the future. But reciprocity does feature in lay discourse about help and care. Tronto drew an important distinction between responsibility and obligation.

> Often our responsibilities are conceived formally as the need to conform to obligations ... Compared to obligation, responsibility has both a different connotation and a different context ... Responsibility is a term that is embedded in a set of implicit cultural practices, rather than in a set of formal rules or series of promises. (1993, pp 131-2)

I suggest a similar distinction can be made in relation to the different meanings of reciprocity, and that a cultural take on the meaning of reciprocity is more in tune with lay normativity in this respect than is a contractarian view.

Engster (2007) gives an example of a walker coming across an injured stranger in a deserted landscape to argue that the walker has a responsibility to help the injured person because no-one else is in a position to meet that need. Another way of understanding this is to suggest that part of the culture of walking in the wild is that you help someone in difficulty. Collectively, such cultural expectations about help and care being available when they are needed have been enacted through the establishment of welfare states. So when older people like Daniel (Barnes, 2006, chapter 5) find themselves in need towards the end of their lives, they experience it as an unfairness that, having contributed to the development of health and social care services through their taxes while they were working, they find themselves uncared for. What they have understood, culturally, as a system based in a form of reciprocity over a lifetime turns out to require a specific monetary exchange before a service will be given. And even if this does generate the service needed, the message that Daniel, and others like him, receive is that they are a burden because they are unable to look after themselves.

Neither older people who have become physically frail, nor younger disabled people, nor those who are temporarily incapacitated by accident or illness, want to feel a burden on others. At the same time there are occasions in most people's lives when 'laying down their own burden' is a real relief. Whether it is knowing that someone else will sort out the practicalities of daily life while you, temporarily, feel too ill to cope, or accepting that permanently giving up the day to day responsibilities of looking after a house is worth it in old age because of the worries that go with those responsibilities, recognising and accepting a dependence on others can be a relief. But psychologically as well as philosophically accepting dependence can be assisted by being able to locate this within a culture of reciprocity and interdependence. And it is hard to create such a culture if care is not valued.

Considering the meaning of reciprocity through the relational perspective offered by feminist care ethics provides a better 'fit' with its significance in everyday life, not only in relation to the help given and received in old age (Breheny and Stephens, 2009), but also in relation to help with care for school-age children (Hansen, 2004). At various points in this book I have argued that we need to develop our understanding of the principle of responsiveness and the moral moment of 'care receiving' (Tronto, 1993). Others have also argued this and it is perhaps in this area that work on care ethics has taken some of the most important steps in recent years. I do not feel comfortable with conceptualising this in terms of the 'gratitude' that Mullin (2011) suggests should accompany the receipt of good care, but the perspective of Pettersen and Hem (2011) who consider the necessity of responsiveness to 'mature care' is perhaps more helpful. If care is given and received through relationships then how people respond and what contribution they make to care needs to be understood as part of the process or dynamics of care. The response of the care receiver may make it easier or harder to give care, as well as providing important information about how care is being given and how it is being received. Such responses may include gratitude, they may include respect for the skills and sensitivities of the care giver, or feelings of love where care is both given and received as part of loving relationships. But they may also include discomfort, resentment, anger or embarrassment. The type of emotion experienced and expressed becomes part of the care process. It shapes what is possible and what needs to be done. Care may also be rejected. One consequence of the negative connotations of 'burden' and 'dependence' is that those who may benefit from becoming recipients of care refuse help that is available and offered. In such cases care cannot be completed.

Conceptually linking responsiveness to the reciprocal contributions of care receivers opens up what I think is another aspect of care that also needs to be further developed. This is the epistemological dimension. Sevenhuijsen (1998) names epistemology as a characteristic of an ethic of care and refers to the 'knowing and thinking subject' put forward by feminist care ethics (p 89). But I think we need to both expand on and detail the implications of including knowledge within the morality and practice of care. The emotional response of the care receiver to the process of care is part of this as these emotions carry important information. But as we have seen, care receivers also contribute experiential knowledge about what works for them and care givers need to be alert to non-verbal as well as verbal articulations of this. They may also have learnt from others experiencing similar problems or living with similar conditions; they may have sought out research information, found out about new treatments or drawn from other aspects of their lives to suggest ways in which help might be provided. There are also likely to be others who are part of the social network of the care receiver who have knowledge to contribute. As well as family and close friends, this may include neighbours, teachers, voluntary workers or others who 'know about' the care receiver from different perspectives. And there is an expectation that all paid workers involved in caring relationships have particular knowledge on which to draw. This includes knowledge about different professional practices; about the origins and nature of the type of problem being experienced that may derive from research; the range of different services available that might be called on to provide help with different aspects of the lives of care receivers; and relevant policies that may affect entitlements. 'Competence' in care giving requires drawing on the range of different types of knowledge that will contribute to ensuring good care that is appropriate to the particular personal, social and cultural context of the care receiver.

As I discussed in Chapter Eight, this applies not only in relation to face to face care giving, but also to the process of making policies. It implies not only that policy makers need to care about the people and the issues that are the subject of policy, but that they need to adopt practices that enable a sharing and valuing of different types of knowledge in the policy process. That implies participative and deliberative practices designed and structured in ways that respect not only the different content and perspectives that service users, care givers, single mothers or others have to contribute, but also the diverse ways in which these may be communicated. And it is also relevant to, for example, the way in which responsibilities are exercised to ensure social justice at an international level, the way in which policies relating to the regeneration of disadvantaged neighbourhoods in Western cities are made and implemented, and the way in which policies focusing on young people and families are designed and implemented (White, 2000). As Robinson argues:

> This is not to suggest that we must gain an intimate understanding of the details of every person's life before we can begin to respond morally to their suffering; it does mean, however, that we should see it as a priority to gain

> as much knowledge as possible of the context of particular cases of poverty and suffering in order to respond to them usefully and effectively. (1999, p 156)

It is why development programmes based in simply offering aid, or in sending out Northern 'experts' to 'problem solve' in Sub-Saharan Africa, cannot be understood as care full responses to need. Such responses do not engage the recipients of care in the process of care; rather they encourage a dependency in which the powerful donor reinforces their power through an enforced reciprocity. But, nor can 'passing the buck' to disadvantaged communities to take responsibility for problems arising from structural inequalities and the power of global companies to impact the life chances of workers be understood as demonstrating care.

Emphasising this epistemological dimension of care also emphasises that care is not a soft option. The vocabulary of care can be seen to suggest a 'soft' concept and practice – words such as compassion, concern and love imply a naturally occurring emotional response – but the practice of care requires much more than this. Care is hard to do. It requires not only an emotional and ethical sensibility, but the capacity to understand different personal, economic, social and cultural contexts, to read particular responses to acts of care and to draw from diverse sources and types of knowledge to make good judgements with others about the right things to do in situations that may be messy, confused, and changing. And this has to be done in situations where there may be conflicts between care givers and receivers, and between different care givers; where paid care workers may feel unsupported or that they are operating in a policy context that does not reflect the values of care. Unlike a response based in procedural rights which emphasises universal principles and requires a specified form of practice in all situations, care requires an exploration of the particular and how that is perceived from different perspectives, as well as an anticipation of the likely responses and consequences of action (or inaction).

This is another way of demonstrating the point I have also argued throughout, that care cannot be divorced from justice. Both procedural and substantive rights are necessary but insufficient for delivering justice in conditions of inequality and vulnerability. If we add participatory parity to the need for both recognition and redistribution for social justice (Fraser, 2009), then we need to look at how participation is enabled as well as how redistributive rights are achieved, and whether recognition promotes group differentiation (affirmative recognition), or destabilises the processes that give rise to such categorical differences (transformative recognition).

Struggling over, for and against care

What then of the politics of care? Tronto's work has been hugely important in developing an analysis of care as a political as well as a personal virtue and much of the work on care ethics that has followed has sought to apply and develop this perspective. I have considered some aspects of this in earlier chapters: Fiona Robinson's (1999) work on care and international relations, for example. The focus of this book has been on the everyday significance of care and my aim is not to offer the type of comprehensive political and economic theory of care offered by Daniel Engster (2007). But it is important for my argument to give some consideration to the way in which care has been a site for different types of political struggle and contestation. This is because the everyday experience of and struggle over care are themselves a political struggle – 'the personal is the political' still offers a key insight into the ways in which we need to think about the relationship between how people are able to live their lives, the sorts of political values that dominate political decision making, and who are the decision makers.

One of the boundaries that Tronto seeks to dismantle is between morality and politics. Her work is an argument for 'care thinking' to be brought in to political thinking. The vocabulary of care is one that should also be a political vocabulary and the questions that politics should address are the moral as well as the practical questions that care confronts us with about how we can live well together and enable all to flourish. In Chapter Eight I argued that care thinking affects how we need to do politics in the context of political processes that are intended to enable people other than 'politicians' to take part. The deliberative spaces I discussed in that chapter can be considered to occupy a political space between the private spaces in which interpersonal care is given and received, and the formal political spaces in which policies affecting care are made. In Chapter Five I also considered the role of care in sustaining and modelling supportive relationships among service users and others involved in collective action for self-help and social change. My position on this has long been that an understanding of the politics of care cannot be restricted to formal or mainstream political spaces or processes and that a transformative politics necessitates including the contestation and creativity that takes place within user forums in service settings, in user groups and in participative research processes (Barnes and Cotterell, 2012). Thus in addressing the politics of care we cannot restrict ourselves to considering the way in which care is contested within formal politics. This is an area in which existing work on an ethic of care needs further development. For example,

Sander-Staudt (2008) makes a strong case for broadening our concept of the political sphere to include both direct care giving and direct democracy in the development of a 'care movement'. She argues the need for a redistribution of caring responsibilities to enable care givers to take part both in representational politics and in more direct forms of political action, and links the need for this with the valuable knowledge that can be accessed as a result: '... caregivers should be encouraged to participate as formal politicians, not only for the intrinsic value their participation might yield, but because they are in the best epistemic and motivational positions to offer strategic plans for moving toward a more institutionally caring society' (p 280).

She identifies the importance of both 'care-based' and 'oppositional-based' political agency, countering the notion that a politics of care can only be based on conciliatory responses in the struggle for more just and caring institutions. But she does not name the struggles of care receivers in her argument and this tends to reinforce a view that care receivers lack political as well as personal agency.

Fiona Mackay's (1998, 2001) interest in what difference women politicians can make to the politics of care reinforces Sander-Staudt's argument of the need for a redistribution of caring responsibilities to enable care givers' political participation. In her study of Scottish women politicians she identified care responsibilities both as barrier to political activity and as a resource for it. The women politicians she interviewed were acutely aware of the constraints they experienced as care givers, negotiating responsibilities for child care and taking part in meetings that lasted all day or started when they were due to pick up the children from school. They also recounted stories of the lack of sympathy they met with from male colleagues in relation to these dilemmas and the distaste encountered when embodied evidence of care giving entered formal political spaces – in particular the need to conceal evidence of breast feeding from the male gaze. At the same time, they regarded women's everyday experiences of the challenges of combining care with other activities as important to their understanding of social policy issues, and the skills developed in juggling competing demands and managing the complex relational issues associated with child care as providing a helpful resource in reflecting on and negotiating complex political issues. Mackay suggests:

> There are parallels between women politicians' concerns with care as a political idea and value and the ideas of care thinkers. The councillors discussed their desire to practise a politics in which context-sensitive and effective solutions

> would be negotiated. These ideas are strikingly similar to Tronto's 'integrity of practice' and Sevenhuijsen's 'judging with care', both of which feature key components of attentiveness, responsibility, competence and responsiveness. (2001, pp 175-6)

But in addressing the politics of care it is also necessary to reflect on the many different ways in which the word care has been defined and employed. This is vital because to look at care as a subject for political campaigning, contestation and negotiation soon makes it very evident that people are talking about and mean different things. Such differences derive from the different disciplinary perspectives from within which care has been addressed, as well as the different positioning of those actively involved in the politics of care. It makes a difference whether one is a woman politician seeking to get care taken seriously as a political issue and value; a disabled activist campaigning for disability to be recognised as a civil rights movement; a mother of a teenage son in difficulties because of drug use; or an elderly spouse seeking to ensure respectful support both for their partner with dementia and for themselves. Care is both relevant and important in each of these cases, but it may mean rather different things and affect the stance that is taken over, for or against care.

I noted some differences in the way in which care has been understood and approached in my introductory chapter. Daly and Lewis (2000), writing in a sociology journal but from a more mainstream, social policy perspective than I have taken here, offer a rather different view from the one that I have taken in approaching care. They make a strong case for the centrality of care to any analysis of welfare states, their ideologies, differences, and the changes that are taking place within them. The definition they offer of 'social care' is: 'the activities and relations involved in meeting the physical and emotional requirements of dependent adults and children, and the normative, economic and social frameworks within which these are assigned and carried out' (p 285). While encompassing care as labour, as obligation or responsibility, and as practice (what they call 'activity'), with costs extending across public and private boundaries, they offer little in terms of identifying care as a value, nor do they address the actual practices and experiences of care giving and receiving, or the challenges and resistances of those subject to social policies and practices. But their definition, which is intended to be multidimensional and to embrace both child care and adult care, crosses boundaries often separated in practical policy and in the academic study of social policy, and is an important one in understanding the way in which care has been a focus of academic analysis that has been linked to political struggle, particularly in the UK and in European welfare states.

Such struggles have focused on the public/private interface and where responsibilities for care should lie, as well as on the overall resourcing of care, and on the way in which dependency has come to be constructed as a 'problem'. And because of the gendered assumptions underpinning both official and populist discourse, such struggles have often focused on assumptions that mothers, daughters and other female relatives carry the prime responsibility for care when the state is unable or unwilling to accept this. Much of the European work in this area has focused on child care and women's struggle for equal employment rights. It is only comparatively recently that the situation of women as carers of older and disabled people has received a similar level of attention and it is in the UK that this work is perhaps most developed. The origin of the carer movement in the UK was explicitly based in a challenge to the assumptions that unmarried daughters would care, unpaid, for elderly parents and the first carers' organisation was called the National Council for the Single Woman and her Dependants (see Barnes, 1997a and 2011a). Early campaigns focused on securing financial benefits for women unable to work because of their caring responsibilities and financial support for carers continues to be a campaigning issue within the UK carer movement. Campaigning has also focused on the availability of services and supports for carers themselves as well as for those they care for. Respite services, to enable carers to have a break, have been and continue to be a particular focus for action and contention. The concept of respite recognises that caring is demanding and carries the danger of naming care receivers as 'burdens'. From the care givers' point of view, respite can be essential to their continuing capacity to care, a source of guilt at not being able to cope, and anxiety that the person they care for will not receive good quality care and will be distressed by the experience. Carers also seek recognition for the knowledge and expertise that they develop through active involvement in individual care planning, and in the development and governance of services. But they also want good information and advice from medical, social care and other professionals to support and improve the care that they give.

The history of the UK carer movement has been one in which the shared experience of caring in different contexts has been emphasised in order to strengthen the political argument for the recognition of care givers. But distinctions between the experiences of care giving in different contexts are also important and underpin the organisation of carers within support groups that may or may not also have political objectives. Thus, for example, for parents involved in groups based around issues such as drug dependency, behavioural difficulties and gay and lesbian parenting, an important aspect of collective action was to be able to address issues that could attract stigmatisation within a 'safe' environment (Williams, 2004c). A particular focus of such groups can be understood to concern the importance of care in situations in which it is hard to care – either because the care receiver may be difficult to care for, or because the social context creates difficulties.

The UK disability movement has adopted a similar strategy of collective action across lines of difference that relate not only to different types of disability (physical, sensory or learning disabilities), but also to experiences of mental health problems, alcohol misuse and long-term illness (Beresford and Branfield, 2012). As I have noted, this political strategy has led to significant success in relation to core movement objectives regarding disabled people's rights to choose what kind of help they receive, to control this via the use of personal budgets and, in some cases, direct employment of support workers. It has also been effective in securing anti-discrimination legislation that has become more encompassing in terms of the range of conditions covered, and thus the range of responsibilities of public authorities and others to ensure that people are not discriminated against either as workers or as citizens. Both represent significant advances in terms of social justice, but are insufficient in terms of developing the ethical sensibilities necessary to what Sevenhuijsen (1998, p 8) has described as a 'caring justice', capable of taking into account the situatedness of human needs and the relationality of the processes through which needs are met. Just decision making requires the capacity to engage in moral reasoning as well as to be responsive to the emotional and embodied experience of care receivers. But arguing for justice in this way does not mean arguing against the importance of human and civil rights.

As I noted earlier, resistances to the gendered assumptions about women's natural responsibility to care have focused as much on child care and care for older people as on care of disabled children (eg Lewis, 2001). But it was when feminist arguments turned to the consequences of community care policy in relation to long-term care for disabled adults that a confrontation between disabled activists and care givers emerged. Disabled people resisted being identified as 'burdens', constraining women's capacities and desires to choose paid work or other activity rather than unpaid care (eg Morris, 1993). One way of summing up such differences might be to say that the carer movement campaigns *for carers*, while the disability movement campaigns *against care*. But to conclude that such a distinction is a useful basis on which to proceed is too crude a political analysis. While it is possible to locate a cause for such disputes in the insufficiency of state financing of support services – both care givers and care receivers have an interest in ensuring adequate funding for good quality health and social care services, as well as financial benefits to meet the additional costs of living with a disability, for example – a more fundamental source of such conflict is the categorical separation of care receivers from care givers and the assumptions of a different moral weight attached to these two distinct identities. And it is this that a feminist ethic of care challenges. As I have demonstrated in different ways throughout this book, it is neither empirically accurate nor morally defensible to define people as only givers or receivers of care. Whether it is an adult child with learning disabilities caring for elderly parents; young people in residential care looking out for each other; a disabled mother giving birth to an able-bodied child; or a woman with dementia seeking to continue to play a role as a grandmother, there are too many cases in which people reciprocate care contemporaneously or over time for moral worth to be attached to someone on the basis of an assumed autonomy or dependence at a particular moment in time. And in those cases where people are for all or most of their lives dependent on others for most aspects of their everyday needs, this is a difference in the degree of dependence that is experienced, rather than an absolute distinction between dependence and an independence assumed to be the 'natural' state of most adults. To draw moral boundaries between human individuals on the basis of levels of cognitive capacity or dependence on others is a route to social Darwinism. The political argument needs to be about care and the necessity and value of care, rather than the comparative merits of protecting the rights and interests of those who are currently assessed as 'dependent' or 'independent'.

From this perspective the strategy of 'transformative recognition' developed by Fraser (1997) as one part of the strategy for social justice appears most useful as a basis for a politics of care. Fraser draws a distinction between 'affirmative' remedies to injustices and 'transformative' ones. Affirmation involves correcting the inequalities experienced by different social groups without doing anything to unsettle the underlying frameworks or conditions that produce those inequalities. In contrast, transformative remedies are designed to address the processes through which inequalities are generated. Thus strategies based in transformative recognition would, in the case of sexuality for example, seek to undermine the notion that homosexuality is a fixed identity constructed in a devalued opposition to heterosexuality.

Applied to the 'care giver/care receiver' binary, this approach has the potential to destabilise distinct categorisations that lead to competitive constructions of political objectives based in separate identities. Elsewhere I have considered how this might break down a competitive response to the needs of those who in UK social policy are named as carers or as service users (Barnes et al, 2010).

Similar points are made by McLaughlin (1997) who suggests that 'The political possibilities of an ethic of care can be achieved by recognising it as an element in the subjugated discourse of women' (p 21), and by Robinson (1999) who identifies the way in both the naming of difference and the processes of social exclusion are the products of relationships. Valentine (2008) adopts a similar position in highlighting the limitations of the 'contact hypothesis' in overcoming the prejudice of the white majority towards migrants: 'everyday encounters do not necessarily change people's general prejudices ... because they do not destabilize white majority-community based narratives of economic and/or cultural victimhood' (p 333).

Combined with insights from care ethics about the universal significance of care, transformative recognition also has the potential to break down the boundaries that define care as only of relevance in the context of specific aspects of everyday life. I have noted the way in which, for example, policies regarding the spatial arrangements of housing and public services contribute to the privatisation of the experience of caring for children (Chapter Seven). A care perspective on urban design thus offers the potential to generate the sort of 'joined up' solutions to policy problems that policy initiatives based around places, such as the neighbourhood renewal initiatives of the early 2000s in England, sought to achieve.

Such a transformative political analysis of care as a value across a range of social and public policies is important to politics as conducted within formal political spaces as well as the diverse political contestation prompted by social movements and within the invited spaces of participatory governance. Mackay (2001) suggests that Tronto's principles of care – attentiveness, responsibility, competence and responsiveness – which I applied to deliberative processes in Chapter Eight could be applied to a formal politics in which the complex and contextual nature of policy problems needs to be understood as a basis on which good decisions can be reached. She also highlights the value of naming the 'privileged irresponsibility' and 'care demanding' that lie behind much of the failure to recognise care as central to the capacity to do politics and virtually all other human activity. Her focus, as well as that of Sander-Staudt (2008), is on the political participation of women as care givers. But this type of argument is also relevant to the lives and experiences of other marginalised groups.

> The care debate exposes inequalities and could potentially empower and mobilize members of marginalized groups. The vocabulary of care would expose 'costs' of care and the inequalities which arise from the way in which politics (like much of the world of work) is premised upon others taking care of care. (Mackay, 2001, p 188)

Care full policy

An ethic of care has now been applied to the analysis of many different areas of policy – both within and beyond the terrain usually covered by the term social policy. It is not my intention here to review such work which is referenced throughout this book. Nor am I attempting to offer a comprehensive view of what social policies based in care ethics would look like. One of the fundamental insights of an ethic of care is the need to reflect and deliberate on the particular contexts and dynamics of a situation before concluding how to care. Care cannot be delivered by applying a standard template. But in concluding, I want to offer some general reflections about the necessity of an ethic of care to issues that are at the heart of mainstream social policy.

As I was working on this book news was breaking about yet another scandal in a residential home for people with learning disabilities in England (www.bbc.co.uk/news/uk-england-bristol-13712123). A TV programme exposed serious abuse of residents who were terrorised by staff. The case of a private provider of residential homes that was in the process of going bankrupt also hit the headlines. In this instance financial failure was leading to closure and a danger of the loss of home for residents. Both offer examples of the dangers of social policy that does not start from care. In the first case the complete absence of care in the practice of workers within the home is further evidence of the invisibility of ethics identified by Ash (2010) in her study of residential facilities for older people, and of the dangerous consequences of this also highlighted by abuses identified in the Health Service Ombudsman's (2011) report cited in Chapter Four. The second example illustrates the dangers of making 'care' dependent on the success of market forces. While financial exchange does not per se mean that care is lacking from the service that is provided, the dependence of services on the market puts at risk the long-term security necessary to enable trust that caring about can sustain care giving. In his discussion of care theory and economic justice Engster (2007) does not conclude that care necessitates socialist economics, but, drawing on Folbre's work, he does illustrate the dangers of market-based competition and low wages on care provision:'The for-profit systems of elder care and child care generally translate into under staffing, high burn-out rates among workers, and less personal contact between professional workers and their clients (Folbre, 2001: 57-64; see also Folbre and Nelson, 2000)' (p 131).

In the UK and elsewhere, the development of markets in social and health care means that accountability is increasingly exercised through regulatory systems. But is this an adequate way of implementing our collective responsibility to ensure proper care for those using services? One response to a further report on the inadequacy of, in this case, domiciliary care services, published in England late in 2011 (Equality and Human Rights Commission, 2011) was a call for increasing regulation. It was suggested that unannounced inspection of care workers doing their work in people's homes could address the problems caused by inadequate time, training and support for workers faced with deciding whether their priority should be to give an older person something to eat or to clean them after they had soiled themselves when they only had 15 minutes to spend before moving on to the next person. In a context in which financial pressures act to reduce the quality of care it is clearly inadequate to propose that the solution lies in more robust inspection. While personalisation is laudable in terms of emphasising the need for attentiveness to individual need, the fragmentation of services through an increasing use of personal budgets passes responsibility for ensuring quality of care to care receivers. There is a danger that conflicts between low paid care workers and care receivers could be exacerbated by the interests of care receivers in stretching their personal budgets as far as possible to enable support. The capacity of service users to exercise choice may be at the expense of a lack of choice for care workers (Shutes, 2012). Downplaying the relational character of care giving and receiving by emphasising this as a process controlled by the care receiver carries similar dangers to seeing this as a process controlled by the care giver.

These and other examples that I have considered throughout this book all point to the necessity of care as a core value in social and health care, both as a basis on which service systems are built and on which interpersonal practice is developed. It almost seems perverse to have to make this point (how can we talk about social care and health care without addressing care?), but from a perspective within contemporary UK social policy the 'abandonment' (Barnes, 2011b) of care from policy discourse renders it necessary. But the concept of care that we need to employ is one that understands care as integral to justice, as attentive to the conflicts and power relations that are part of both personal and social relationships, as well as the necessity of such relationships to flourishing and well-being.

In another key area for social policy, debates within the UK and elsewhere about raising the age at which workers can retire and access not only their state but also their occupational pensions are being conducted through a discourse of affordability, active citizenship and a work ethic in the context of an increase in population ageing (Hutton, 2011). There is little consideration of the implications of such a policy for care giving, either within personal relationships or through older people's work as volunteers. There is some evidence that socioeconomic inequalities and their relationship to participation increase into older age (Scherger et al, 2011) and a critical ethic of care suggests a need to consider the consequences of prioritising an extension of paid working life over alternative ways of pursuing positive relationships in old age that can contribute to both individual and collective well-being.

This links to the dominant perspective on well-being as a policy objective. Although the current profile of well-being as a policy discourse and objective indicates an awareness of a public responsibility to ensure personal flourishing, of older people as well as younger people, the way in which well-being is being constructed and the means by which it is to be achieved emphasise individual endeavour rather than the web of relationships which older people themselves identify as key to their subjective experience of being well (Taylor, 2011; Ward et al, 2012). Care is rarely named within policy discourse relating to well-being, but it is central to older people's understanding of what is necessary to ensure this and to a relational concept of what it means to be well within their social and material worlds. If there is a genuine wish to include well-being as well as welfare within the purposes to be achieved within welfare states and internationally (Gough and McGregor, 2007), then this requires care thinking with its emphasis on relational understandings of what it is to be human.

The concept of care I have sought to develop, building on the work of feminist ethic of care theorists, is also one that recognises its significance beyond those areas of policy that are designated by reference to the word 'care'. If we understand care as value and practice that are important to the way in which we design and maintain physical environments and work environments; to the way in which we engage people living in disadvantaged neighbourhoods in the process of making them better places to live; and to the way in which we in the North understand our responsibilities for reducing the many different injustices experienced by people living in the global South, then perhaps the resistance to care as a value may be reduced. Care is not separate from, or in competition with, justice as a core value for social policy. But it needs to be named as a distinct value and practice, rather than being ignored and undermined.

A key insight of feminist care ethics is the way in which it has been possible for predominantly male policy makers in the public sphere to devalue the predominantly female work of care in the private sphere. This separation of spheres has been underpinned by philosophical distinctions between the abstract values of liberal justice, and an understanding of moral reasoning as encompassing the particularities of different circumstances where just decisions need to be made. This, in turn, has produced evaluative distinctions between individuals on the basis of their assumed capacity as autonomous rational actors. An ethic of care aims to break down these unhelpful moral boundaries (Tronto, 1993). Far from essentialising care as a 'women's issue' care ethicists have named care 'as a normal aspect of human existence' (Sevenhuijsen, 1998, p 18) and have demonstrated the value of care ethics to both understanding and developing just responses to different forms of oppression and disadvantage wherever they occur.

Starting from an everyday lives perspective I have argued that it is not possible to abandon care if we are to both understand and support human flourishing. The expansion of the academic literature on this topic evidences a hunger to develop a robust alternative to the individualising and ultimately sterile dominance of the autonomous subject of neo-liberalism. The challenge is still to suffuse these ideas through the everyday practice of policy and politics.

Bibliography

Abrams, P., S. Abrams, et al (1989). *Neighbourhood Care and Social Policy*. London, Department of Health/HMSO.

Adam, B. D. (2004). 'Care, intimacy and same-sex partnership in the 21st century.' *Current Sociology* **52**(2): 265-79.

Aldred, R. (2011). 'Editorial introduction.' *Critical Social Policy* **31**(2): 171-3.

Anttonen, A. and L. Häikiö (2011). From social citizenship to active citizenship? Tensions between policies and practices in Finnish elderly care. *Participation, Responsibility and Choice: Summoning the active citizen in Western European welfare states*. J. Newman and E. Tonkens (eds). Amsterdam, University of Amsterdam Press: 67-86.

Ash, A. (2010). 'Ethics and the street-level bureaucrat: implementing policy to protect elders from abuse.' *Ethics and Social Welfare* **4**(2): 201-9.

Baldassar, L. (2007). 'Transnational families and aged care: the mobility of care and the migrancy of ageing.' *Journal of Ethnic and Migration Studies* **33**(2): 275-97.

Banks, S. (2010). 'Interprofessional ethics: a developing field? Notes from the *Ethics & Social Welfare* Conference, Sheffield, UK, May 2010.' *Ethics and Social Welfare* **4**(3): 280-94.

Banks, L. and M. Barnes (2011). *Evaluation of the East Sussex Carers' Breaks Demonstrator Site*. Brighton, Social Science Policy and Research Centre, University of Brighton.

Barnes, M. (1997a). *Care, Communities and Citizens*. Harlow, Addison Wesley Longman.

Barnes, M. (1997b). Families and empowerment. *Empowerment in Everyday Life: Learning disability*. P. Ramcharan, G. Roberts, G. Grant and J. Borland (eds). London, Jessica Kingsley: 70-87.

Barnes, M. (1999). 'Users as citizens: collective action and the local governance of welfare.' *Social Policy and Administration* **33**(1): 73-90.

Barnes, M. (2001). From private carer to public actor: the carer's movement in England. *Care Work: The quest for security*. M. Daly (ed). Geneva, International Labour Office: 195-210.

Barnes, M. (2006). *Caring and Social Justice*. Basingstoke, Palgrave.

Barnes, M. (2007). Participation, citizenship and a feminist ethic of care. *Care, Community and Citizenship: Research and practice in a changing policy context*. S. Balloch and M. Hill (eds). Bristol, The Policy Press: 59-74.

Barnes, M. (2008a). 'Passionate participation: emotional experiences and expressions in deliberative forums.' *Critical Social Policy* **28**(4): 461-81.

Barnes, M. (2008b). 'Is the personal no longer political?' *Soundings* **39**: 152-9.

Barnes, M. (2009). Alliances, contention and oppositional consciousness: can participation generate subversion? *Subversive Citizens: Power, agency and resistance in public services*. M. Barnes and D. Prior (eds). Bristol, The Policy Press: 33-48.

Barnes, M. (2011a). Caring responsibilities. The making of citizen carers. *Participation, Responsibility and Choice: Summoning the active citizen in Western European welfare states*. J. Newman and E. Tonkens (eds). Amsterdam, University of Amsterdam Press: 161-78.

Barnes, M. (2011b). 'Abandoning care? A critical perspective on personalisation from an ethic of care.' *Ethics and Social Welfare* **5**(2): 153-67.

Barnes, M. (2012) 'An ethic of care and sibling care in older age', *Families, Relationships and Societies* **1**(1):7-23.

Barnes, M. and G. Bennet (1998). 'Frail bodies, courageous voices: older people influencing community care.' *Health and Social Care in the Community* **6**(2): 102-11.

Barnes, M. and R. Bowl (2001). *Taking Over the Asylum: Empowerment and mental health*. Basingstoke, Palgrave.

Barnes, M. and P. M. Brannelly (2008). 'Achieving care and social justice for people with dementia.' *Nursing Ethics* **15**(3): 399-410.

Barnes, M. and P. Cotterell, (eds) (2012). *Critical Perspectives on User Involvement*. Bristol, The Policy Press.

Barnes, M. and C. Gell (2012). The Nottingham Advocacy Group: a short history. *Critical Perspectives on User Involvement*. M. Barnes and P. Cotterell (eds). Bristol, The Policy Press: 19-31.

Barnes, M. and D. Prior (1995). 'Spoilt for choice? How consumerism can disempower public service users.' *Public Money and Management* **15**(3): 53-8.

Barnes, M. and D. Prior (1996). 'From private choice to public trust: a new social basis for welfare.' *Public Money and Management* **16**(4): 51-8.

Barnes, M. and D. Prior (2000). *Private Lives as Public Policy*. Birmingham, Venture.

Barnes, M. and D. Prior (2007). 'Review article. Conceptualising connectedness: implications for policy and practice.' *Social Policy and Society* **6**(2): 199-208.

Barnes, M. and D. Prior, (eds) (2009). *Subversive Citizens: Power, agency and resistance in public services.* Bristol, The Policy Press.

Barnes, M., J. Newman, et al (2003). 'Constituting the public for public participation.' *Public Administration* **81**(2): 379-99.

Barnes, M., P. M. Brannelly, et al (2006). *Able Authorities? The Disability Discrimination Act, disabled people and local authorities in England.* London, Department for Communities and Local Government.

Barnes, M., A. Davis, et al (2006). 'Women's voices, women's choices: experiences and creativity in consulting women users of mental health services.' *Journal of Mental Health* **15**(3): 329-41.

Barnes, M., J. Newman, et al (2007). *Power, Participation and Political Renewal: Case studies in public participation.* Bristol, The Policy Press.

Barnes, M., C. Skelcher, et al (2008). *Designing Citizen Centred Governance.* York, Joseph Rowntree Foundation.

Barnes, M., C. Gell, et al (2010). Participation and social justice. *Social Policy Review_22.* I. Greener, C. Holden and M. Kilkey (eds). Bristol, The Policy Press: 253-74.

Barnes, M., E. Harrison, et al (2012). 'Ageing activists: who gets involved in older people's forums?' *Ageing & Society* 32: 261-80

Beel-Bates, C. A., B. Ingersoll-Dayton, et al (2007). 'Deference as a form of reciprocity among residents in assisted living.' *Research on Ageing* **29**(6): 626-43.

Bell, K. (2011). 'Environmental justice in Cuba.' *Critical Social Policy* **31**(2): 241-65.

Beresford, P. (2008). *What Future for Care?* York, Joseph Rowntree Foundation.

Beresford, P. and F. Branfield (2012). Building solidarity, ensuring diversity: lessons from service users' and disabled people's movements. *Critical Perspectives on User Involvement.* M. Barnes and P. Cotterell (eds). Bristol, The Policy Press: 33-45.

Blum, L. (1980). Compassion. *Explaining Emotions.* A. Rorty (ed). Berkeley and Los Angeles, University of California Press: 507-18.

Blunkett, D. (2003). *Civil Renewal: A new agenda. The CSV Edith Kahn Memorial Lecture, 11th June 2003.* London, Home Office Communication Directorate.

Bowden, P. (1997). *Caring: Gender sensitive ethics.* London and New York, Routledge.

Bowden, P. (2000). 'An "ethic of care" in clinical settings: encompassing "feminine" and "feminist" perspectives.' *Nursing Philosophy* **1**(1): 36-49.

Bowey, L. and A. McGlaughlin (2005). 'Adults with a learning disability living with elderly carers talk about planning for the future: aspirations and concerns.' *The British Journal of Social Work* **35**(8): 1377-92.

Brannelly, P. M. (2006). 'Negotiating ethics in dementia care. An analysis of an ethic of care in practice.' *Dementia* **5**(2): 197-212.

Brannelly, P. M. (2011). 'That others matter: the moral achievement – care ethics and citizenship in practice with people with dementia.' *Ethics and Social Welfare* **5**(2): 210-16.

Brannelly, P. M., A. Boulton, et al (2009). *Evaluation of Multisystemic Therapy Alcohol and Other Drug Services.* Palmerston North, NZ, Massey University, School of Health and Social Services for Hutt Valley District Health Board.

Brechin, A., R. Barton, et al (2003). Getting to grips with poor care. *Reconceptualising_Work with Carers: New directions for policy and practice*. K. Stalker (ed). London, Jessica Kingsley.

Breheny, M. and C. Stephens (2009). '"I sort of pay back in my own little way": managing independence and social connectedness through reciprocity.' *Ageing & Society* **29**(8): 1295-313.

Buchs, M., N. Bardsley, et al (2011). 'Who bears the brunt? Distributional effects of climate change mitigation policies.' *Critical Social Policy* **31**(2): 285-307.

Buonfino, A. and G. Mulgan (2009). *Civility Lost and Found.* London, The Young Foundation.

Cahill, M. (2003). The environment and green social policy. *Social Policy: Second edition.* J. Baldock, N. Manning and S. Vickerstaff (eds). Oxford, Oxford University Press: 121-26.

Cahill, M. (2010). *Transport, Environment and Society.* Maidenhead, Open University Press.

Campbell, J. and M. Oliver (1996). *Disability Politics: Understanding our past, changing our future.* London, Routledge.

Cangiano, A., I. Shutes, et al (2009). *Migrant Care Workers in Ageing Societies: Research findings in the United Kingdom.* Oxford, COMPAS.

Catney, P. and T. Doyle (2011). 'The welfare of now and the green (post) politics of the future.' *Critical Social Policy* **31**(2): 174-93.

Chatzitheocari, S. and S. Arber (2009). 'Lack of sleep, work and the long hours culture: evidence from the UK Time Use Survey.' *Work, Employment and Society* **23**(1): 30-48.

Clarke, J., J. Newman, et al (2007). 'The antagonisms of choice: New Labour and the reform of public services.' *Social Policy and Society* **7**(2): 245-53.

Coetzee, P. (2003). Particularity in morality and its relation to community. *The African Philosophy Reader.* P. Coetzee and A. Roux (eds). London, Routledge: 273-86.

Coltrane, S. and J. Galt (2000). The history of men's caring. *Care Work: Gender, labor and the welfare state.* M. Harrington Meyer (ed). New York, Routledge: 15-36.

Connors, C. and K. Stalker (2007). 'Children's experiences of disability: pointers to a social model of childhood disability.' *Disability and Society* **22**(1): 19-33.

Cooper, D. (2007). '"Well, you go there to get off". Visiting feminist ethics through a women's bathhouse.' *Feminist Theory* **8**(3): 243-62.

Dalley, G. (1988). *Ideologies of Caring*. Basingstoke, Macmillan.

Daly, M. (2001). Care policies in Western Europe. *Care Work: The quest for security.* M. Daly (ed). Geneva, International Labour Office: 33-56.

Daly, M. and J. Lewis (2000). 'The concept of social care and the analysis of contemporary welfare states.' *British Journal of Sociology* **51**(2): 281-98.

Davies, C., E. Barnett, et al (2006). *Citizens at the Centre: Deliberative participation in health care decisions*. Bristol, The Policy Press.

Day, K. (2000). 'The ethic of care and women's experiences of public space.' *Journal of Environmental Psychology* **20**: 103-24.

Dessein, J., (ed) (2008). *Farming for Health: Proceedings of the community of practice farming for health*. Merelbeke, ILVO.

DETR (1999). *New Deal for Communities: First year of the pathfinders*. London: The Stationery Office.

Dew, A., G. Llewellyn, et al (2004). 'Post-parental care: a new generation of sibling-carers.' *Journal of Intellectual and Developmental Disability* **29**(2): 176-9.

Di Iacovo, F. and D. O'Connor, (eds) (2009). *Supporting Policies for Social Farming in Europe*. Florence, Arsia.

Doyal, L. and I. Gough (1991). *A Theory of Human Need*. Basingstoke, Macmillan.

Dryzek, J. (2002). *Deliberative Democracy and Engagement: Liberals, critics, contestations*. Oxford, Oxford University Press.

Duffy, S., J. Waters, et al (2009). 'Personalisation and adult social care: future options for the reform of public services.' *Policy and Politics* **38**(4): 493-508.

DW (2007). White Paper for Social Welfare. Pretoria, Department of Welfare, Republic of South Africa.

DWP (2009). *Empowering Engagement: A stronger voice for older people*. London, Department for Work and Pensions.

Dwyer, P. (2000). *Welfare Rights and Responsibilities*. Bristol, The Policy Press.

ECLAC (2007). *Ageing and Development in a Society for All Ages*. New York, United Nations.

Ehrenreich, B. (2010). *Nickle and Dimed*. London, Granta Books.

Ehrenreich, B. and A. R. Hochschild, (eds) (2003). *Global Woman: Nannies, maids and sex workers in the new economy.* London, Granta Books.

Emond, R. (2003). 'Putting the care into residential care: the role of young people.' *Journal of Social Work* **3**(3): 321-37.

Engster, D. (2007). *The Heart of Justice: Care ethics and political theory.* Oxford, Oxford University Press.

Equality and Human Rights Commission (2011). *Close to Home. An enquiry into older people and human rights in home care.* Manchester, Equality and Human Rights Commission.

Ferguson, I. (2007). 'Increasing user choice or privatizing risk? The antimonies of personalization.' *The British Journal of Social Work* **37**(3): 387-403.

Finch, J. and J. Mason (1993). *Negotiating Family Responsibilities.* London, Tavistock/Routledge.

Fine, M. (2007). *A Caring Society? Care and the dilemmas of human service in the 21st century.* Basingstoke, Palgrave Macmillan.

Fine, M. and C. Glendinning (2005). 'Dependence, independence or inter-dependence? Revisiting the concepts of "care" and "dependency"'. *Ageing & Society* **25**(4): 601-21.

Fineman, M.A. (2004). *The Autonomy Myth: A theory of dependency.* New York, The New Press.

Fischer, F. (2009). 'Policy deliberation: confronting subjectivity and emotional expression.' *Critical Policy Studies* **3**(3-4): 407-20.

Flint, J. (2009). Subversive subjects and conditional, earned and denied citizenship. *Subversive Citizens: Power, agency and resistance in public services.* M. Barnes and D. Prior (eds). Bristol, The Policy Press: 83-98.

Forbat, L. (2005). *Talking About Care.* Bristol, The Policy Press.

Frank, A.W. (2004). *The Renewal of Generosity: Illness, medicine and how to live.* Chicago, University of Chicago Press.

Fraser, N. (1997). *Justice Interruptus: Critical reflections on the 'postsocialist' condition.* London and New York, Routledge.

Fraser, N. (2009). *Scales of Justice.* New York, Columbia University Press.

Fraser, N. and K. Bedford (2008). 'Social rights and gender justice in the neoliberal moment: a conversation about welfare and transnational politics.' *Feminist Theory* **9**(2): 225-45.

Fraser, N. and L. Gordon (2002). A genealogy of dependency: tracing a keyword of the US welfare state. *The Subject of Care. Feminist perspectives on dependency.* E. F. Kittay and E. K. Feder (eds). Lanham, MD, Rowman and Littlefield: 14-39.

Fraser, N. and A. Honneth (2003). *Redistribution or Recognition? A political–philosophical exchange.* London, Verso.

Friedman, M. (1993). *What Are Friends For?* Ithaca and London, Cornell University Press.

Ganyo, M., M. Dunn, et al (2011). "Ethical issues in the use of fall detectors." *Ageing & Society* **31**(8): 1350-67.

Gary, F. (2005). 'From the guest editor – research on the stigma of mental illness among ethnic minority populations in the United States.' *Issues in Mental Health Nursing* **26**(10): 971-7.

Gilligan, C. (1982). *In a Different Voice: Psychological theory and women's development*. Cambridge, MA, Harvard University Press.

Glendinning, C. and P. Kemp, (eds) (2006). *Cash and Care: Policy challenges in the welfare state*. Bristol, The Policy Press.

Glendinning, C., M. Powell, et al, (eds) (2002). *Partnerships, New Labour and the Governance of Welfare*. Bristol, The Policy Press.

Gosling, J. (1996). The business of 'community'. *The Politics of Attachment*. S. Kraemer and J. Roberts (eds). London, Free Association Books: 138-51.

Gough, I. and A. McGregor, (eds) (2007). *Wellbeing in Developing Countries: From theory to research*. Cambridge, Cambridge University Press.

Grant, L. (1999). *Remind Me Who I Am, Again*. London, Granta Books.

Groch, S. (2001). Free spaces: creating oppositional consciousness in the disability rights movement. *Oppositional Consciousness. The subjective roots of social protest*. J. Mansbridge and A. Morris (eds). Chicago, University of Chicago Press: 65-98.

Gutmann, A. and D. Thompson (1996). *Democracy and Disagreement*. Cambridge, MA, Belknap Press.

Habermas, J. (1984). *The Theory of Communicative Action, Volume 1: Reason and the rationalization of society*. Boston, Beacon Press.

Habermas, J. (1987). *The Theory of Communicative Action, Volume 2: Lifeworld and system: A critique of functionalist reason*. Boston, Beacon Press.

Hall, J. A. and F. Trentmann, (eds) (2005). *Civil Society. A reader in history, theory and global politics*. Basingstoke, Palgrave Macmillan.

Hankivsky, O. (2004). *Social Policy and the Ethic of Care*. Vancouver, UBC Press.

Hansen, K. (2004). 'The asking rules of reciprocity in networks of care for children.' *Qualitative Sociology* **27**(4): 421-37.

Harley, D. and G. Fitzpatrick (2009). 'Creating a conversational context through video blogging: a case study of Geriatric1927.' *Computers in Human Behaviour* **25**(3): 679-89.

Harvey, J. (2007). 'Moral solidarity and epathetic understanding: the moral value and scope of the relationship.' *Journal of Social Philosophy* **38**(1): 22-37.

Haugen, G. M. D. (2007). 'Caring children: exploring care in post-divorce families.' *The Sociological Review* **55**(4): 653-70.

Health Service Ombudsman (2011). *Care and Compassion? Report of the Health Service Ombudsman on ten investigations into NHS care of older people*. London, The Stationery Office.

Heath, S. (2004). 'Peer-shared households, quasi-communes and neo-tribes.' *Current Sociology* **52**(2): 161-79.

Held, V. (2006). *The Ethics of Care: Personal, political and global*. Oxford, Oxford University Press.

Held, V. (2010). 'Can the ethics of care handle violence?' *Ethics and Social Welfare* **4**(2): 115-29.

Hess, J. (2003). 'Gadow's relational narrative: an elaboration.' *Nursing Philosophy* **4**(2): 137-48.

Hillyer, B. (1993). *Feminism and Disability*. Norman OK and London, University of Oklahoma Press.

HM Government (2007). *Putting People First. A shared vision and commitment to the transformation of adult social care*. London, Department of Health.

HM Government (2008). *Carers at the Heart of 21st Century Families and Communities: A caring system on your side, a life of your own*. London, Department of Health.

Hollway, W. (2006). *The Capacity to Care: Gender and ethical subjectivity*. Hove, Routledge.

Honneth, A. (2005). *The Struggle for Recognition: The moral grammar of social conflicts*. Cambridge, Polity Press.

Hughes, N., P. Mason, et al (2007). The socialisation of crime policy? Evidence from the National Evaluation of the Children's Fund. *Social Justice and Criminal Justice*. R. Roberts and W. McMahon (eds). London, Centre for Crime and Justice Studies: 216-31.

Hutton, J. (2011). *Independent Public Service Pensions Commission: Final report*. London, Independent Public Service Pensions Commission.

James, S. (1993). Mothering: a possible Black feminist link to social transformation? *Theorizing Black Feminisms: The visionary pragmatism of Black women*. S. James and A. Busia (eds). London and New York, Routledge: 44-54.

Jordan, B. (2008). *Welfare and Well-being: Social value in public policy*. Bristol, The Policy Press.

Kabeer, N., (ed) (2005). *Inclusive Citizenship: Meanings and expressions*. London, Zed Books.

Kittay, E. F. (1999). *Love's Labor. Essays on women, equality and dependency.* London and New York, Routledge.

Kittay, E. F. (2001). 'A feminist public ethic of care meets the new communitarian family policy.' *Ethics* **111**(3): 523-47.

Kittay, E. F. (2010). The personal is philosophical is political: a philosopher and mother of a cognitively disabled person sends notes from the battlefield. *Cognitive Disability and its Challenge to Moral Philosophy*. E. F. Kittay and L. Carlson (eds). Chichester, Wiley-Blackwell: 393-413.

Kittay, E. F. and L. Carlson, (eds) (2010). *Cognitive Disability and its Challenge to Moral Philosophy.* Chichester, Wiley-Blackwell.

Koggel, C. and J. Orme (2010). 'Editorial. Care ethics: new theories and applications.' *Ethics and Social Welfare* **4**(2): 109-14.

Krenichyn, K. (2004). 'Women and physical activity in an urban park: enrichment and support through an ethic of care.' *Journal of Environmental Psychology* **24**: 117-30.

Lawson, V. (2007). 'Geographies of care and responsibility.' *Annals of the Association of American Geographers* **97**(1): 1-11.

Le Grand, J. (2007). *The Other invisible Hand: Delivering public services through choice and competition*. Princeton, Princeton University Press.

Lewis, J. (2001). Legitimizing care work and the issue of gender equality. *Care Work: The quest for security*. M. Daly (ed). Geneva, International Labour Office: 57-75.

Li, C. (2008). 'Does Confucian ethics integrate care ethics and justice ethics? The case of Mencius.' *Asian Philosophy* **18**(1): 69-82.

Lipsky, M. (1980). *Street Level Bureaucracy: Dilemmas of the individual in public services*. New York, Russell Sage Foundation.

Lister, R. (1997). *Citizenship: Feminist perspectives*. Basingstoke, Macmillan.

Lloyd, L. (2000). 'Caring about carers: only half the picture?' *Critical Social Policy* **20**(1): 36-57.

Lloyd, L. (2004). 'Mortality and morality: ageing and the ethics of care.' *Ageing & Society* **24**(2): 235-56.

Lloyd, L. (2010). 'The individual in social care: the ethics of care and the "personalisation" agenda in services for older people in England.' *Ethics and Social Welfare* **4**(2): 188-200.

Louw, D. (2010). Power sharing and the challenge of ubuntu ethics. *Power Sharing and African Democracy: Interdisciplinary perspectives*. C. W. Du Toit (ed). Pretoria, Research Institute for Theology and Religion, University of South Africa: 121-37.

Lymbery, M. (2010). 'A new vision for adult social care? Continuities and change in the care of older people.' *Critical Social Policy* **30**(1): 5-26.

Lynch, K., J. Baker, et al, (eds) (2009). *Affective Equality: Love, care and injustice.* Basingstoke, Palgrave Macmillan.

McDowell, L. (2004). 'Work, workfare, work/life balance and an ethic of care.' *Progress in Human Geography* **28**(2): 145-63.

MacIntyre, R. (1996). Nursing loved ones with AIDS: knowledge development for ethical practice. *Caregiving: Readings in Knowledge, Practice, Ethics and Politics.* S. Gordon, P. Benner and N. Noddings (eds). Philadelphia, University of Pennsylvania Press: 141-52.

Mackay, F. (1998). 'In a different voice? Scottish women politicians and the vocabulary of care.' *Contemporary Politics* **4**(3): 259-70.

Mackay, F. (2001). *Love and Politics: Women politicians and the ethics of care.* London and New York, Continuum.

Mackenzie, C. and N. Stoljar, (eds) (2000). *Relational Autonomy: Feminist perspectives on autonomy, agency and the social self.* Oxford, Oxford University Press.

McKie, L., S. Gregory, et al (2002). 'Shadow times: the temporal and spatial frameworks and experiences of caring and working.' *Sociology* **36**(4): 897-924.

McKie, L., J. Hearn, et al (2008). *Organisation Carescapes: Researching organisations, work and care.* Hanken School of Economics Working Papers. Helsingfors, Hanken School of Economics.

McLaughlin, J. (1997). 'An ethic of care: a valuable political tool?' *Politics* **17**(1): 17-23.

Manderson, D. (2002). 'The care of strangers.' *Australian Financial Review* **24 August**: http://francais.mcgill.ca/files/crclaw-discourse/manderson-carestrangers.pdf

Marsh, P. and G. Crow (1997). *Family Group Conferences in Child Welfare.* Oxford, Blackwell.

Martin, G. (2008). '"Ordinary people only": knowledge, representativeness and the publics of public participation in health care.' *Sociology of Health & Illness* **30**(1): 35-54.

Martinsen, E. (2011). 'Harm in the absence of care: towards a medical ethics that cares.' *Nursing Ethics* **18**(2): 174-83.

Mason, J. (2004). 'Managing kinship over long distance: the significance of "the visit"'. *Social Policy and Society* **3**(4): 421-9.

Massey, D. (1994). *Space, Place and Gender.* Cambridge, Polity Press.

Massey, D. (2005). *For Space.* London, Sage.

Means, R., H. Morbey, et al (2002). *From Community Care to Market Care? The development of welfare services for older people.* Bristol, The Policy Press.

Mencap (2007). *Death by Indifference.* London, Mencap.

Michel, S. (2000). Claiming the right to care. *Care Work: Gender, labor and the welfare state.* M. Harrington Meyer (ed). New York, Routledge: 37-44.

Miller, S. C. (2010). 'Cosmopolitan care.' *Ethics and Social Welfare* **4**(2): 145-57.

Millie, A., (ed) (2009). *Securing Respect: Behavioural expectations and anti-social behaviour in the UK.* Bristol, The Policy Press.

Misztal, B. (2000). *Informality: Social theory and contemporary practice.* London, Routledge.

Mol, A. (2008). *The Logic of Care: Health and the problem of patient choice.* Abingdon, Routledge.

Molyneaux, V., S. Butchard, et al (2011). 'Reconsidering the term "carer": a critique of the universal adoption of the term "carer"'. *Ageing & Society* **31(**3): 422-37.

Mooney, G. and A. Law, (eds) (2007). *New Labour/Hard Labour? Restructuring and resistance inside the welfare industry.* Bristol, The Policy Press.

Morris, J. (1991). *Pride Against Prejudice.* London, The Women's Press.

Morris, J. (1993). *Independent Lives: Community care and disabled people.* Basingstoke, Macmillan.

Morris, J. (1995). 'Creating a space for absent voices: disabled women's experience of receiving assistance with daily living activities.' *Feminist Review* **51**: 68-93.

Morris, J. (2001). 'Impairment and disability: constructing an ethics of care that promotes human rights.' *Hypatia* **16**(4): 1-16.

Morris, K. (2007). *Camden FGC Service: An evaluation of service use and outcomes.* Birmingham, University of Birmingham.

Morris, K. and G. Burford (2009). Family decision making: new spaces for participation and resistance. *Subversive Citizens: Power, agency and resistance in public services.* M. Barnes and D. Prior (eds). Bristol, The Policy Press: 119-136.

Morris, L. (2010). *Asylum, Welfare and the Cosmopolitan Ideal: A sociology of rights.* London, Routledge.

Mullin, A. (2011). 'Gratitude and caring labour.' *Ethics and Social Welfare* **5**(2): 110-22.

Murray, L. (2009). 'Making the journey to school: the gendered and generational aspects of risk in constructing everyday mobility.' *Health, Risk and Society* **11**(5): 471-86.

Murray, L. and M. Barnes (2010). 'Have families been rethought? Ethic of care, family and "whole" family approaches.' *Social Policy and Society* **9**(4): 533-44.

Needham, C. (2011a). 'Personalization: from story-line to practice.' *Social Policy and Administration* **45**(1): 54-68.

Needham, C. (2011b). *Personalising Public Services. Understanding the personalisation narrative.* Bristol, The Policy Press.

Newman, J. (2011). Mobilising the active citizen in the UK. Tensions, silences and erasures. *Participation, Responsibility and Choice: Summoning the active citizen in Western European welfare states.* J. Newman and E. Tonkens (eds). Amsterdam, University of Amsterdam Press: 106-20.

Newman, J. and E. Tonkens, (eds) (2011). *Participation, Responsibility and Choice: Summoning the active citizen in Western European welfare states.* Amsterdam, University of Amsterdam Press.

Noddings, N. (1984). *Caring: A feminine approach to ethics and moral education.* Berkeley, University of California Press.

Noddings, N. (1996). The cared-for. *Caregiving: Readings in knowledge, practice, ethics and politics.* S. Gordon, P. Benner and N. Noddings (eds). Philadelphia, University of Pennsylvania Press: 21-39.

Nussbaum, M. (2001). *Upheavals of Thought. The intelligence of the emotions.* Cambridge, Cambridge University Press.

Nussbaum, M. (2006). *Frontiers of Justice: Disability, nationality, species membership.* Cambridge, MA, Belknap Press.

O'Brien, R. (2005). *Bodies in Revolt: Gender, disability and a workplace ethic of care.* New York, Routledge.

Okely, J. (1999). Love, care and diagnosis. *Extending the Boundaries of Care: Medical ethics and caring practices.* T. Kohn and R. McKechnie (eds). Oxford NY, Berg: 19-48.

Pahl, R. and L. Spencer (2004). 'Personal communities: not simply families of "fate" or "choice"'. *Current Sociology* **52**(2): 199-221.

Parker, G. (1990). *With Due Care and Attention: A review of research on informal care.* London, Family Policy Studies Centre.

Parker, G. (1993). *With This Body. Caring and disability in marriage.* Buckingham, Open University Press.

Paszkiewicz, N. (2011). Care, Welfare and Enforcement: Responses to Asylum Seekers and Refugees. Brighton, University of Brighton. PhD.

Parkinson, J. (2006) *Deliberating in the Real World*, Oxford: Oxford University Press.

Peace, S. and C. Holland (2001). 'Homely residential care: a contradiction in terms?' *Journal of Social Policy* **30**(3): 393-410.

Peace, S., C. Holland, et al, (eds) (2006). *Environment and Identity in Later Life.* Maidenhead, Open University Press.

Peters, H., J.-A. Fiske, et al (2010). 'Interweaving caring and economics in the context of place: experiences of Northern and rural women caregivers.' *Ethics and Social Welfare* **4**(2): 172-87.

Pettersen, T. and M. H. Hem (2011). 'Mature care and reciprocity: two cases from acute psychiatry.' *Nursing Ethics* **18**(2): 217-31.

Pithouse, A. and A. Rees (2011). 'Care as regulated and care in the obdurate world of intimate relations: foster care divided?' *Ethics and Social Welfare* **5**(2): 196-209.

Porter, E. (2006). 'Can politics practice compassion?' *Hypatia* **21**(4): 97-122.

Power, A. (2007). *City Survivors. Bringing up children in disadvantaged neighbourhoods*. Bristol, The Policy Press.

Prior, D. (2009). 'The "problem" of anti-social behaviour and the policy knowledge base: analyzing the power/knowledge relationship.' *Critical Social Policy* **29**(1): 5-23.

Prior, D. and M. Barnes (2011). 'Subverting social policy on the front line: agencies of resistance in the delivery of services.' *Social Policy and Administration* **45**(3): 264-79.

Prior, D., K. Farrow, et al (2007). Anti-social behaviour and civil renewal. *Re-energising Citizenship: Strategies for civil renewal*. T. Brennan, P. John and G. Stoker. Basingstoke, Palgrave Macmillan: 91-111.

Purves, B. (2011). 'Exploring positioning in Alzheimer Disease through analyses of family talk.' *Dementia* **10**(1): 35-58.

Rabiee, P. and C. Glendinning (2010). 'Choice: what, when and why? Exploring the importance of choice to disabled people.' *Disability and Society* **25**(7): 827-39.

Ramose, M. (2003). The ethics of *ubuntu*. *The African Philosophy Reader*. P. Coetzee and A. Roux (eds). London, Routledge: 324-30.

Rawls, J. (1971). *A Theory of Justice*. Cambridge, MA, Harvard University Press.

Raymond, J. (1991). *A Passion for Friends: Towards a philosophy of female affection*. London, The Women's Press.

Reitz-Pustejovsky, M. (2002). 'Is the care we provide homeless people, just? The ethic of justice informing the ethic of care.' *Journal of Social Distress and the Homeless* **11**(3): 233-48.

Robinson, F. (1999). *Globalizing Care: Ethics, feminist theory and international relations*. Boulder, Westview Press.

Robinson, F. (2010). 'After liberalism in world politics? Towards an international political theory of care.' *Ethics and Social Welfare* **4**(2): 130-44.

Robinson, C., R. Reid, et al (2010). 'A home away from home: the meaning of home according to families of residents with dementia.' *Dementia* **9**(4): 490-508.

Roseneil, S. (2004). 'Why we should care about friends: an argument for queering the care imaginary in social policy.' *Social Policy and Society* **3**(4): 409-19.

Roseneil, S. and S. Budgeon (2004). 'Cultures of intimacy and care beyond "the family": personal life and social change in the early 21st century.' *Current Sociology* **52**(2): 135-59.

Rowe, D. (2007). *My Dearest Enemy, My Dangerous Friend: Making and breaking sibling bonds*. London, Routledge.

Rowles, G. (2000). 'Habituation and being in place.' *Occupational Therapy Journal of Research* **20** (Supplement): 52S-67S.

Rowles, G. and J. Watkin (2003). History, habit, heart and hearth: on making spaces into places. *Aging Independently: Living arrangements and mobility*. K. Schaie, H. Wahl, H. Mollenkopf and F. Oswald (eds). New York, Springer: 77-97.

Ruddick, S. (1989). *Maternal Thinking: Towards a politics of peace*. Boston, Beacon Press.

Rummery, K. (2011). 'A comparative analysis of personalisation: balancing an ethic of care with user empowerment.' *Ethics and Social Welfare* **5**(2): 138-52.

Ryan, S. and K. Runswick-Cole (2008). 'Repositioning mothers: mothers, disabled children and disability studies.' *Disability and Society* **23**(3): 199-210.

Ryan, J. and F. Thomas (1980). *The Politics of Mental Handicap*. Harmondsworth, Penguin.

Sabat, S. R. (2010). 'Flourishing of the self while caregiving for a person with dementia: a case study of education, counselling, and psychosocial support via email.' *Dementia* **10**(1): 81-97.

Sander-Staudt, M. (2008). 'Reassembling political assemblies: care ethics and political agency.' *Journal of Social Philosophy* **39**(2): 269-90.

Sayer, A. (2011). *Why Things Matter to People: Social science, values and ethical life*. Cambridge, Cambridge University Press.

Scharf, T. and B. Bartlam (2008). Ageing and social exclusion in rural communities. *Rural Ageing. A good place to grow old?* N. Keating (ed). Bristol, The Policy Press: 97-108.

Scherger, S., J. Nazroo, et al (2011). 'Leisure activities and retirement: do structures of inequality change in old age?' *Ageing & Society* **31**(1): 146-72.

Sennett, R. (2003). *Respect: The formation of character in an age of inequality*. London, Penguin.

SEU (2001) *A New Commitment to Neighbourhood Renewal: National strategy action plan*. London: The Stationery Office.

Sevenhuijsen, S. (1998). *Citizenship and the ethics of care: Feminist considerations of justice, morality and politics*. London and New York, Routledge.

Sevenhuijsen, S. (2000). 'Caring in the Third Way: the relation between obligation, responsibility and care in Third Way discourse.' *Critical Social Policy* **20**(1): 5-37.

Sevenhuijsen, S. (2003a). 'Trace: A method for normative policy analysis from an ethic of care'. Paper prepared for the seminar Care and Public Policy, University of Bergen, 19-21 November.

Sevenhuijsen, S. (2003b). 'The place of care: the relevance of the feminist ethic of care for social policy.' *Feminist Theory* **4**(2): 179-97.

Sevenhuijsen, S., V. Bozalak, et al (2003). 'South African social welfare policy: an analysis using the ethic of care.' *Critical Social Policy* **23**(3): 299-321.

Shakespeare, T. (2000). *Help*. Birmingham, Venture Press.

Shutes, I. (2012). 'The employment of migrant workers in long-term care: dynamics of choice and control.' *Journal of Social Policy* **41**(1): 43-59.

Silk, J. (1998). 'Caring at a distance.' *Ethics, Place and Environment* **1**(2): 165-82.

Smith, D. (1999). 'Geography, community and morality.' *Environment and Planning A* **31**: 19-35.

Smith, D. (2000). 'Moral progress in human geography: transcending the place of good fortune.' *Progress in Human Geography* **24**(1): 1-18.

Smith, G. (2009) *Democratic innovations: Designing institutions for citizen participation*, Cambridge: Cambridge University Press.

Smith, R. and M. Barnes (2011). *LifeLines: An evaluation of a prevention programme with older people*. Brighton, Social Science Policy and Research Centre, University of Brighton.

Smith, A. and L. McKie (2009). 'Researching "care" in and around the workplace.' *Sociological Research Online* **14**(4): 1-11.

Somerville, P. (2009). 'The feeling's mutual': respect as the basis for cooperative interaction. *Securing Respect: Behavioural expectations and anti-social behaviour in the UK*. A. Millie. (ed). Bristol, The Policy Press: 139-67.

Spandler, H. (2004). 'Friend or foe? Towards a critical assessment of direct payments.' *Critical Social Policy* **24**(2): 187-209.

Sparks, K., G. Cooper, et al (1997). 'The effects of hours of work on health: a meta-analytic review.' *Journal of Occupational and Organizational Psychology* **70**(4): 391-408.

Spencer, L. and R. Pahl (2006). *Rethinking Friendship: Hidden solidarities today*. Princeton, Princeton University Press.

Squires, P. (2008). Introduction: why anti-social behaviour? Debating ASBOs. *ASBO Nation: The criminalisation of nuisance*. P. Squires (ed). Bristol, The Policy Press: 1-35.

Star, D. (2002). 'Do Confucians really care? A defense of the distinctiveness of care ethics: a reply to Chenyang Li.' *Hypatia* **17**(1): 77-106.

Steckley, L. and M. Smith (2011). 'Care ethics in residential child care: a different voice.' *Ethics and Social Welfare* **5**(2): 182-95.

Stroud, J. (2008). 'A psychosocial analysis of child homicide.' *Critical Social Policy* **28**(4): 482-505.

Surr, C.A. (2006). 'Preservation of self in people with dementia living in residential care: a socio-biographical approach.' *Social Science and Medicine* **62**: 1720-30.

Swain, J., V. Finkelstein, et al, (eds) (1993). *Disabling Barriers, Enabling Environments*. London, Sage.

Taylor, D. (2011). 'Wellbeing and welfare: a psychosocial analysis of being well and doing well enough.' *Journal of Social Policy* **40**(4): 777-94.

Tester, K. (1992). *Civil Society*. London, Routledge.

Traustadottir, R. (2000). Disability reform and women's caring work. *Care Work: Gender, labor and the welfare state.* M. Harrington Meyer (ed). New York, Routledge**:** 249-69.

Tronto, J. (1993). *Moral Boundaries. A political argument for an ethic of care.* London and New York, Routledge.

Tronto, J. (2010). 'Creating caring institutions: politics, plurality and purpose.' *Ethics and Social Welfare* **4**(2): 158-71.

Twigg, J. (2000). *Bathing - the Body and Community Care*. London, Routledge.

Valentine, G. (2004). *Public Space and Culture of Childhood*. Aldershot, Ashgate.

Valentine, G. (2008). 'Living with difference: reflections on geographies of encounter.' *Progress in Human Geography* **32**(3): 323-37.

Vanderbeck, R. (2007). 'Intergenerational geographies: age relations, segregations and re-engagements.' *Geography Compass* **1**(2): 200-21.

Visvanathan, S. (2005). Knowledge, justice and democracy. *Science and Citizens: Globalization and the challenge of engagement*. M. Leach, I. Scoones and B. Wynne (eds). London, Zed Books: 83-96.

Wahl, O. (1999). 'Mental health consumers' experience of stigma.' *Schizophrenia Bulletin* **25**(3): 467-78.

Walker, A. (2009). 'The emergence and application of active ageing in Europe.' *Journal of Ageing and Social Policy* **21**(1): 75-93.

Walker, G. and K. Burningham (2011). 'Flood risk, vulnerability and environmental justice: evidence and evaluation of inequality in a UK context.' *Critical Social Policy* **31**(2): 216-40.

Waller, M. and S. Patterson (2002). 'Natural helping and resilience in a Diné (Navajo) community.' *Families in Society: The Journal of Contemporary Social Services* **83**(1): 73-84.

Walmsley, J. (1993). 'Contradictions in caring: reciprocity and interdependence.' *Disability, Handicap and Society* **8**(2): 129-41.

Ward, N. (2005). Social Exclusion and Mental Well-being: Lesbian Experiences. Birmingham, University of Birmingham. PhD.

Ward, N. (2011). 'Care ethics and carers with learning disabilities: a challenge to dependence and paternalism.' *Ethics and Social Welfare* **5**(2): 168-80.

Ward, L. and B. Gahagan (2010). 'Crossing the divide between theory and practice: research and an ethic of care.' *Ethics and Social Welfare* **4**(2): 210-16.

Ward, L., Barnes, M. and B. Gahagan (2012) *Well-being in Old Age: Findings from Participatory Research*, Brighton, University of Brighton and Age UK Brighton and Hove.

Ward, L., M. Barnes, et al (2011). 'Alcohol use in later life: older people's perspectives'. *Quality in Ageing and Older People* **12**(4): 239-47.

Warren, L. (1990). 'We're home helps because we care': the experience of home helps caring for elderly people. *New Directions in the Sociology of Health*. P. Abbott and G. Payne (eds). London, The Falmer Press: 70-86.

Watson, N., L. McKie, et al (2004). '(Inter)dependence, needs and care: the potential for disability and feminist theorists to develop an emancipatory model.' *Sociology* **38**(2): 331-50.

Webler, T. (1995) 'Right' discourse in citizen participation: an evaluative yardstick. *Fairness and Competence in Citizen Participation*. O. Renn, T. Webler and P. Wiedemann (eds). Dordecht: Kluwer Academic Publishers.

Weir, A. (2005). 'The global universal caregiver: imaging women's liberation in the new millennium.' *Constellations* **12**(3): 308-30.

Wenger, C (1993) 'The formation of social networks: self help, mutual aid, and old people in contemporary Britain.' *Journal of Aging Studies*, **7**(1): 25-40.

White, J. A. (2000). *Democracy, Justice and the Welfare State*. University Park, Pennsylvania State University Press.

Wilkinson, J. and M. Bittman (2003). *Relatives, Friends and Strangers: The links between voluntary activity, sociability and care*. Sydney, Social Policy Research Centre, University of New South Wales.

Wilks, T. (2005). 'Social work and narrative ethics.' *The British Journal of Social Work* **35**(8): 1249-64.

Williams, F. (2001). 'In and beyond New Labour: towards a new political ethic of care.' *Critical Social Policy* **21**(4): 467-93.

Williams, F. (2004a). *Rethinking Families*. London, Calouste Gulbenkian Foundation.

Williams, F. (2004b). 'What matters is who works: why every child matters to New Labour. Commentary on the DfES Green Paper Every Child Matters.' *Critical Social Policy* **24**(3): 406-27.

Williams, F. (2004c). 'Care, values and support in local self-help groups.' *Social Policy and Society* **3**(4): 431-8.

Williams, F. (2010). 'Review article. Migration and care: themes, concepts and challenges.' *Social Policy and Society* **9**(3): 385-96.

Wong, S. I. (2010). Duties of justice to citizens with cognitive disabilities. *Cognitive Disability and its Challenge to Moral Philosophy*. E. F. Kittay and L. Carlson (eds). Chichester, Wiley-Blackwell: 127-46.

Wood, R. (1991). Care of disabled people. *Disability and Social Policy*. G. Dalley (ed). London, Policy Studies Institute.

Wright, K. (2000). 'Computer-mediated social support, older adults and coping.' *Journal of Communication* **50**(3): 100-18.

Yanow, D. (2003). Accessing local knowledge. *Deliberative Policy Analysis: Understanding governance in the network society*. M. Hajer and H. Wagenaar (eds). Cambridge, Cambridge University Press: 228-46.

Young, I. (1990). *Justice and the Politics of Difference*. Princeton, Princeton University Press.

Young, I. (2000). *Inclusion and Democracy*. Oxford, Oxford University Press.

Ytterhus, B., C. Wendelborg, et al (2008). 'Managing turning points and transitions in childhood and parenthood – insights from families with disabled children in Norway.' *Disability and Society* **23**(6): 625-36.

Index

A

B

C

M

N

O

P

R

S

Y